ROUTLEDGE LIBRARY EDITIONS: BRITISH SOCIOLOGICAL ASSOCIATION

Volume 1

PRACTICE AND PROGRESS

PRACTICE AND PROGRESS
British Sociology 1950–1980

Edited by
PHILIP ABRAMS, ROSEMARY DEEM,
JANET FINCH AND PAUL ROCK

Routledge
Taylor & Francis Group

LONDON AND NEW YORK

First published in 1981 by George Allen and Unwin Ltd

This edition first published in 2018
by Routledge
2 Park Square, Milton Park, Abingdon, Oxon OX14 4RN

and by Routledge
711 Third Avenue, New York, NY 10017

Routledge is an imprint of the Taylor & Francis Group, an informa business

British Library Cataloguing in Publication Data
A catalogue record for this book is available from the British Library

ISBN: 978-1-138-49942-3 (Set)
ISBN: 978-1-351-01463-2 (Set) (ebk)
ISBN: 978-1-138-48370-5 (Volume 1) (hbk)
ISBN: 978-1-138-48371-2 (Volume 1) (pbk)
ISBN: 978-1-351-05416-4 (Volume 1) (ebk)

Publisher's Note
The publisher has gone to great lengths to ensure the quality of this reprint but points out that some imperfections in the original copies may be apparent.

Disclaimer
The publisher has made every effort to trace copyright holders and would welcome correspondence from those they have been unable to trace.

Practice and Progress: British Sociology 1950–1980

Edited by

PHILIP ABRAMS
ROSEMARY DEEM
JANET FINCH
PAUL ROCK

London
GEORGE ALLEN & UNWIN
Boston   Sydney

First published in 1981

GEORGE ALLEN & UNWIN LTD
40 Museum Street, London WC1A 1LU

British Library Cataloguing in Publication Data

Practice and progress: British sociology *1950–1980*.
1. Sociology
I. Abrams, P.
301'.0941   HM51

ISBN 0-04-301131-4
ISBN 0-04-301132-2 Pbk

Cover design by David Driver

Set in 10 on 11 point Times by Computacomp (UK) Ltd
and printed in Great Britain
by Billing and Sons Ltd., Guildford, London
and Worcester

Contents

Introduction

The papers collected in this volume are a selection from those given at the annual conference of the British Sociological Association in 1980, marking the Association's thirtieth anniversary. The *Transactions* of the conference as a whole may be obtained directly from the Association. The conference focused on developments in and reflections about British sociology in the period 1950–80. During that period many changes occurred, not only in the theories, methodologies and research practices of the discipline, but also in the institutional setting of sociology, with the rapid expansion of the subject in secondary and higher education. There were important changes, too, in the role of the BSA within the community of sociologists. All these changes have reflected shifting perspectives and concerns within the discipline but they have also been closely linked to the history of British society as a whole which has affected the kinds of sociological problems that are felt to require investigation as well as emphasising the power of certain modes of explanation and analysis at the expense of others. It is important to bear in mind, however, that the shifts in theories and methodologies and problems which have occurred and are discussed in this volume are indeed complex and subtle *shifts* of emphasis and attention rather than radical transformations. As Hall (1980, p. 57) has pointed out:

> In serious, critical intellectual work, there are no 'absolute beginnings' and few unbroken continuities . . . What we find, instead, is an untidy but characteristic unevenness of development. What are important are the significant *breaks* . . . Changes in a problematic do significantly transform the nature of the questions asked, the forms in which they are proposed, and the manner in which they can be adequately answered.

These forms of development are clearly visible in the history of British sociology during the decades 1950–80. The type of dramatic change of paradigm envisaged by Kuhn (1970) as marking the progress of the natural sciences is scarcely applicable to sociology since in social analysis substantial elements of previous approaches are always apparent in new perspectives, even if only in a negative form as springboards from which to launch new ideas. In the social sciences the past is a source and resource for the present in a quite distinct way.

Some of the significant breaks and changes which have taken place in British sociology since 1950 are summed up by Johnson (1979, p. 50) as a pattern of movement, 'from various functionalisms, through a focus on symbolic or cultural interactions to some kind of combination of the concern with culture or knowledge with a reworked Marxism'. Such shifts are found not only in the mainstreams of sociology but also in the various areas of specialisation. This, of course, does not mean that the older perspectives disappear altogether; indeed, most persist alongside newer ones. Not all developments in sociology can, of course, be contained in any one framework of change, but whatever relation is supposed, or preferred, to exist between theory and research, it cannot be doubted either that theoretical swings have had a significant impact on empirical research, whether explicitly or implicitly, or that theoretical shifts themselves have had a strong grounding in historical, political, economic and social events, whether at the macro or micro level. For example, the kinds of crises that Jessop refers to as having occurred in the British state since the Second World War have clearly influenced both the research it has been possible to do and the theories that have been used to explain events. Jessop (1980, p. 23) refers in particular to

> the chronic structural and cyclical crisis in Britain's economy, to its declining weight in an international economy which was itself entering a period of instability and prolonged crisis, to an emergent crisis of representation (centred on the political parties, trade unions and capitalists' associations) and to a growing crisis of hegemony in the political sphere.

The appearance of such crises has been particularly important in the gradual demise of structural functionalism which proved unable to account for either the appearance or the persistence of such economic, political and social crises (see Gouldner, 1971). But there have also, especially since the 1960s, been links between developments in sociology and many forms of popular politics, such as the early 'New Left', the women's and students' movements, black power and several counter-cultural movements.

The effects of these popular movements on the growth of particular areas of sociology – education, political sociology, women's studies – have been considerable, but there have also been more far-reaching consequences for sociology as a whole, pushing it more and more in the direction of at least examining the relation between knowledge and action and, for example, of attempting to remove the patriarchal and sexist shaping of much sociological work. As Barker and Allen note (1976, p. 2), 'For the most part sociology has included women completely within the term "men" (or as part of their husbands) rather than asking how and when the relationship between the sexes . . . is pertinent to the explanation of social structure and behaviour.'

The feminist intervention in sociology has been a particularly important one because it has been able to show how one-sided the theories and researches of many sociologists – both male and female – have been hitherto. Stacey, in this volume, demonstrates how limited are explanations which fail to take account of gender, gender relations and different sites of the division of labour.

It is also interesting to examine some of the sources of inspiration for recent British sociology. Much British empirical social research of the nineteenth and early twentieth centuries has been absorbed not into sociology itself but into the allied fields of social administration and social policy. Structural functionalism in Britain was largely influenced by American writings, particularly those of Talcott Parsons and Robert Merton. The shift away from structural functionalism towards phenomenology, ethnomethodology and symbolic interactionism was also largely American-inspired, through the works of writers such as Garfinkel, Douglas and Goffman. The influence of European thought, expecially the work of the Frankfurt school and critical theory, has been much less marked, and only in recent trends towards a 'reworked Marxism' has there been any significant European input, largely in the form of French structuralism. This, of course, is not to deny the influence of certain classical European theorists in the late nineteenth and early twentieth centuries – Comte, Simmel, Durkheim and Weber, as well as Marx – on our empirical and theoretical traditions, but with the exception of Marx, even the works of these writers have often been mediated to British sociologists through American work. An important point of consensus at the 1980 conference was the evident feeling of most participants that at least British sociology had now reached a point where it had little or nothing to gain from continued American tutelage.

Several sociologists have commented recently upon the existence and possible origins of an intellectual crisis in sociology, manifested in the theoretical and methodological disarray of the 1970s. Two writers in particular have analyses pertinent to the papers discussed here, because they address those theoretical and methodological issues with which this volume is concerned. Hawthorn, for example, argues that there has been a gradual shift, starting in the nineteenth century, from metaphysical speculation towards empirical inquiry. This is not, he hypothesises, because the metaphysical questions about the place of human beings in the world and the extent of the separation between society, individuals and nature have been answered, but rather because no adequate answers have yet been found (1976, p. 258): 'Thus as disillusion has piled upon disillusion virtually all have come to despair of providing any rational and certainly any comprehensive account of how the present may connect to the future.' Hawthorn suggests that because of this disillusion and despair the gap between what he terms 'abstract metaphysics' and 'limited empiricism' has widened, and indeed the problems posed by this gap are taken up by a number of contributors to this volume.

Giddens (1978), in an analysis of the prospects for contemporary social theory, is concerned not so much with disillusionment as with the dissolution of the orthodox consensus which is claimed to have held sway in the 1950s and 1960s. The orthodox consensus, Giddens suggests, had two main strands. First, it concerned itself with a theory of industrial society, contrasting this form with 'traditional' society and noting the gradual disappearance of class conflict and ideology. Secondly, it contained a more abstract appraisal of the form and possible achievements of the social sciences, focusing on both functionalism (concern with unfolding models of change and the progress of order) and naturalism (which sees a parallel between the logic of natural and social science). This consensus was not, of course, without its problems nor was it uncontested even in its period of supremacy, although it undoubtedly at that time defined the terrain upon which theoretical debates took place. The failure of the orthodox consensus to take as a central problem the point that every sociological generalisation is potentially an intervention in society because of the reflexive rationalisation of human agents, the reliance on an outmoded philosophy of language which holds that language merely describes the social world, the assumption that both social science and natural science are *always* revelation, the absence of a satisfactory theory of action in which power plays a central role, and the dependence on a positivistic model of natural science using logical-empiricist concepts and a hypothetico-deductive method have all, argues Giddens, contributed to the downfall of the orthodox consensus.

The responses to the decline of the consensus may be characterised, Giddens suggests, in three ways; first, by a shift away from the metaphysical concerns about social conduct towards practical social research; secondly, by a reversion to dogmatism, for instance, in the form of orthodox Marxism; and finally in a tendency to rejoice in intellectual disarray and to celebrate the diversity of theory, because these indicate the difficulty of encompassing sociological subject matter in precise laws. Not all of the contributors to this book would agree with Giddens's categorisation of the directions of development since the break-up of consensus, although Abell and Cain and Finch comment critically on the gap between theory and practical research, and Phillipson examines the problematic way in which sociologists see new philosophies of language in relation to their own practice. Sklair does not accept the proposition that the developing connections between Marxisms and sociology have been dogmatic or in any way unfruitful and Stacey points to a fourth reaction unmentioned by Giddens: the feminist intervention. Nevertheless, the image of sociology conjured up by Hawthorn and Giddens can be regarded as a context for several of the contributions to this volume.

One final point which should be made before looking at the various chapters in more detail is that sociology in the period 1950–80 has experienced both a very rapid growth, especially as a discipline in higher education and schools, but also in the area of applied social research, *and* a much more recent contraction both in development and in its public popularity. The decade since 1970 has seen marked shifts in educational policies and ideologies following the break-up of what Finn, Grant and Johnson (1979) refer to as the 'social democratic consensus' about education. It also saw dramatic but related shifts in political life towards a 'strong state' which have brought with them huge cuts in public expenditure, including spending on education and research, aggressive maintenance of official secrecy and increasing hostility towards critical social inquiry – all graphically traced by Edward Thompson (1980) among others. It may be the case as Abrams suggests in this volume that sociologists have overreacted to the institutional aspects of this 'domestic crisis'; nevertheless, its intellectual effects and impact cannot be ignored and have certainly flavoured more than one contribution to the volume.

The chapters themselves are divided into three sections. The four chapters – Barnes, Urry, Heath and Edmondson and Abrams – which comprise Part One are concerned, in the main, to attempt an evaluation of the discipline and the progress and problems of its practitioners and departments to date. Barnes, for example, discusses professionalism in British sociology and notes that questions about what kind of sociology is needed and how practitioners should be stratified are as important, though with different manifestations, in 1980 as they were in 1950. The difference, however, between those two periods is that whereas in 1950 the BSA was the main focus of professionalism, by 1980, Barnes suggests, although the BSA is still concerned about credentialism and professionalism, control over these matters has begun to pass to other bodies, such as the Council for National Academic Awards and the Social Science Research Council. Barnes argues that while professional control over sociology is still of importance, we have not come far along the road to it and there is a danger that there will be too strong an emphasis on professional credentials and not enough on ensuring that the insights of sociological research are available to both professional sociologists and laypersons.

Heath and Edmondson examine a particular aspect of professionalism in the development of sociology: the contribution of Oxbridge to sociology. Oxbridge showed strong initial reluctance to embrace sociology as an academic discipline, but despite this has come to be seen, by university teachers, for example, as possessing the 'top' departments of sociology. Edmondson's research on pieces of work considered good examples of competent sociology also gave prominence to writers and researchers from Oxbridge, the LSE, Manchester and the Tavistock Institute. Most of the conventional possible explanations for the dominance of Oxbridge and a small number of other institutions (for example, that centres of excellence predominate, or that large departments produce more research through economies of scale), are rejected, and it is claimed that academic achievements are unpredictable and random occurrences, not necessarily related to any particular department.

Urry concentrates not on theoretical development or institutions or even on professionalism, but rather on exposing what he describes as the 'fifth myth of sociology': the belief that the discipline has a distinct essence and coherent common tradition. He argues that sociologists often appropriate theory and empirical work from other disciplines, citing as examples recent BSA conferences on Power and the State, Culture, and Law and Society, and contemporary sociological analysis of the state. He demonstrates that sociology's development cannot be understood in terms of shifting paradigms; nor do sociologists constitute a scientific community, because of the parasitical dependence of sociology on other disciplines. Nevertheless, Urry contends, this parasitism should be seen as a strength and not as a weakness because it leaves the discipline open to ideas generated elsewhere and leaves it relatively free of the constraints of authority and control. Further, sociology can be seen as an important academic discourse just because it is able to take up questions of social relations occurring in the other social sciences which cannot be dealt with adequately by the originating disciplines themselves.

Finally in Part One Abrams takes up a question of topical relevance, the prospect of 'the collapse of British sociology', and argues that despite the effects of public expenditure cuts on the profession as well as on teaching and research in sociology, and notwithstanding the intellectual crisis which many feel sociology is facing, there is in fact little possibility that a major institutional dissolution of sociology will occur. He argues that sociologists must be careful not to give their attackers weapons with which to destroy the discipline, by eroding the market for their work, either by popularising sociology too much or by overemphasising the relation of political practice to sociological research. And he suggests that the growth of sociology in the 1960s and the intrusion of Marxism have been important contributory factors to a crisis in sociology around these two issues. Instead, he reasons, we should look at the failure to work out the relation between sociology and the domain of public action; sociology is polemical, but there is no one necessary relationship between knowledge and action, and sociologists must, he contends, try to be more effective in arguing for the cases and causes they wish to advance. He looks towards the reconciliation of professionalism with a kind of rational humanism so that sociologists can continue their task of demystifying the social world.

While the chapters in Part One concentrate mainly on an evaluation of British sociology during the period 1950–80, Part Two focuses on problems of methodology and the creation of sociological knowledge in British sociology, both in the present and past, and also in terms of some possible future directions. Jennifer Platt surveys journal articles, methods textbooks, teaching syllabuses and general books published in the discipline in the timespan 1950 to 1980, and suggests that although positivism, as defined by quantitative data, the employment of mathematical models and hypothesis-testing, did increase in influence during the 1960s there has been little noticeable decline in its influence subsequently. This is contrary to the account often given in sociology courses, that positivism is a phase in the past development of sociology. Instead, she points to the likelihood that, in one sense, most empirical research is likely to be positivistic because it must produce evidence which cannot be constructed independently of the externally observable world. Unlike some methodologies, positivism is apt to make its intellectual procedures explicit. Positivism, in any case, is not necessarily a useful way of categorising sociological schools, since the term is frequently used to include writers and researchers of very diverse interests and with very different approaches. Indeed it is often no more than a polemical term. If we are to construct a history of our discipline, Platt argues, we need a better and more systematic treatment and categorisation than has so far been devised.

Both Husbands and Cain and Finch move on to a rather different issue: that of the shortcomings and problems of 'knowledge creation' in British sociology. Husbands tackles the relative absence of a significant body of quantitative research and of knowledge of quantitative research methods, emphasising the importance of such research and methodology to the employment prospects of future sociologists in a contracting job market. He analyses the sources of hostility to quantitative methods under two headings: first, problems associated with measurement in large-scale survey research; and secondly, epistemological issues about the extent to which social processes are amenable to quantification. Husbands also diagnoses other sources of hostility to quantitative work in the amateur empirical tradition of early British sociologists, the low status of empirical research during and after the 1960s, the quantitative ignorance of many sociologists and the influence of French structuralist Marxism. He presents a strongly argued case for the greater use of quantitative techniques in appropriate areas of sociological endeavour.

Cain and Finch are less concerned with what methods should be used than with stressing the importance of restoring empirical data to prominence in British sociology, a place which they argue they have steadily lost. Cain and Finch emphasise the importance of linking empirical research and theorising and discuss the relationship of the two in different kinds of sociological work. They claim that the validation of sociological knowledge cannot be carried out by subjects, things, scientists, or theoretical practices but rather that the appropriateness of both the inert objects and of the theory used in data constitution is given by their purpose. In other words, they claim that useful knowledge *must be valid*; and they suggest possible criteria for the validity of sociological data, stressing constantly that the creation of data and theory are simultaneous and that data are 'value-full' and so cannot 'stand alone'. Cain and Finch do not see the use of data in sociology as meaning any necessary neglect of subjectivity, a claim which has often been made in this context. They suggest that by rehabilitating data, sociological knowledge can be made both accountable and responsible to those from whom the knowledge was constructed and to those who use it.

Abell's major interest lies in the claims of different sociological methodologies to provide ways of gaining social scientific knowledge, in the future of methodology and in the concern about whether methodology has gained prominence at the expense of theory in British sociology. He takes issue with the prevalent belief that somewhere the 'right' method exists which is resistant to conceptual criticism. Such a method, Abell holds, cannot exist. He argues for the closer integration of theory and methodology in the analysis of empirical problems, and also defends the need for generalisation in sociology. Generalisation is necessary, Abell points out, to explain 'structural regularities' in social action, although clearly voluntaristic phenomena are not thus explicable. Abell argues for a sociological methodology which tackles both structural and voluntaristic phenomena but which is both comprehensible and non-positivistic, combining inductive and deductive methods.

Phillipson points to a further deficiency of most British sociology. Although sociologists have begun to analyse language in a variety of ways from conversational analysis to cultural studies, Phillipson suggests that the analytical philosophy of language has not so far influenced the practices of British sociologists, despite their strong commitment to empirical work which projects the world as constituted in and through language. Phillipson comments on the subservience of theorising to empiricism and argues that the split between the two provides contradictory views of the relation between sociological speech and its referents; theorising has an indirect relationship but observation a direct one. Elaborating this argument, he suggests that in empiricism phenomena are first 'seen' and then transformed into sociological speech; that speech is seen as a neutral medium for channelling information about non-linguistic phenomena. Sociological practice is seen as technically superior to other discourses and is often perceived as a metatheoretical or metaphorical practice which fails to recognise the practical and moral character of the transformation which sociology itself brings about by pre-interpreting the world. Empirical sociology, then, has failed in this view to take note of the theoretical and philosophical analysis of language, and to recognise the reflexivity of sociological language.

In Part Three, Sklair and Stacey examine two developments which have exerted a considerable influence on the direction and interests of British sociology, namely, Marxism and feminism. Whilst Sklair examines the various connections and separations between Marxisms and sociologies, Stacey's purpose is to show that feminism can contribute much to expanding and improving our understanding of the division of labour and how it works. Sklair looks at the rejection of formal links between Marxisms and sociologies prior to the 1960s, and at some of the reasons for the gradual acceptance of those links from the 1960s onwards, including the economic and political as well as the ideological contradictions of that decade. Two works – Marcuse's *One Dimensional Man* and Bottomore and Rubel's *Karl Marx: Selected Writings* – are seen as critical for the growing links between sociology and Marxism in the 1960s, in providing easily accessible Marxist writing and a powerful Marxist critique of contemporary society. In the 1970s Sklair identifies new aspects of the relationship of sociology to Marxism in the emergence of the British New Left, the impact of Althusserian Marxism, and the Gould Report which attacked the so-called Marxist subversion of sociology. Sklair argues that far from subverting sociology, the influences of Marxisms have been beneficial in developing new creative energies, opening up fresh lines of inquiry and encouraging a sharper epistemological awareness.

For her part Stacey presents an analysis of how a feminist-informed sociology would re-examine two taken-for-granted accounts of the division of labour; one provided by Adam Smith in terms of the production and social control of workers; the other the conventional account, embedded in the story of Adam and Eve, of domestic gender relations and the reproduction and social control of women. These two aspects of the division of labour need reconciliation, argues Stacey, but it is only as a result of the feminist challenge to received habits of thought that the problematic nature of social reproduction as a basic feature of the social order has been realised. Prior to this, most theories of the division of labour had been worked out in relation to industrialisation, production and the public sphere of life, from which women were largely excluded. The private sphere of life, especially the family, had largely been ignored. Stacey gives us an impressive review of work and theories on the division of labour and points out that much of the work in this field, as well as concentrating on the market place, has also seen the gender order as 'natural'. She suggests that there are two important factors in analysing the division of labour sociologically: first, the way gender order in the family is transferred to the public sphere and reinforced by that public sphere's division of labour; and secondly, the crucial importance of understanding the nature of 'people work', in both the public and the private spheres. Whereas the division of labour in the public sphere is tied to wages, fees and profits, the division of labour in the private sphere is related to production, reproduction and sexuality. Stacey also raises as an important issue the centrality of children in the division of labour. This contribution emphasises the capacity of a sociology informed by feminist thought to broaden the range of sociological concerns and problems and to make women sociologically 'visible'.

The contributions to this volume then, manifest their own high degree of diversity. Many developments have been left out – the growth of social policy and social administration, the increasing application of sociology to government, a thorough analysis of the phenomenological and ethnomethodological moment in sociology, the contributions of semiotics and discourse theory, the importance of cultural studies – and the concentration here has been largely on more general institutional, theoretical and methodological developments. However, these developments together point to an important relationship between changes in sociological perspective and the conditions of sociology's existence, a relationship which has had a profound influence on the development of British sociology in the period under scrutiny. As Hall says (1980, p. 57),

> shifts in perspective reflect not only the results of an internal intellectual labour, but the manner in which real historical developments and transformations are appropriated in thought and provide thought, not with its guarantee of 'correctness' but with its fundamental orientations, its conditions of existence.

Part One

Intellectual Debates and Institutional Contexts

1

Professionalism in British Sociology

J. A. BARNES

Ever since the British Sociological Association was founded its members have argued about whether sociology, or sociologists, should become professional. With few exceptions members of the Association have not seriously questioned the value of sociology; their arguments have been about what kind of sociology is needed and how its practitioners should be identified and stratified. Recently, market forces conducive to professionalism have increased significantly. The debate has quickened accordingly but we should remember that professionalism has remained a perennial topic of controversy among British sociologists during the last thirty years, despite wide fluctuations in the market for sociologists. Similar controversies have occurred within the ranks of cognate disciplines during the same period and in other countries as well as in Britain (see Tapper, 1980).

Within the Association this debate has manifested itself mainly in arguments about who could join, how its membership should be stratified, what activities it should undertake and what relation it should have with government departments and agencies. The debate began before the Association started and continues both inside and outside its ambit. Despite the variety of arguments and proposals that have been advanced, the term 'professional' has, however, remained virtually unexamined and uncontested, both by those who champion professionalism and by those who oppose it. The corpus of writings on the sociology of the professions has grown prodigiously during the thirty years under review but has had little impact on how sociologists perceive their own backyard. Yet if sociology is to be taken as a significant enterprise, the entailments of professionalism in sociology must be examined in sociological terms, rather than by reference to native common sense and gut feelings.

Sociology in Britain does not start with the Association (see Abrams, 1968). Many of the standard American histories of sociology are quite contemptuous about the slow progress made in Britain during the formative period at the turn of the century when sociology was being established in the United States and on the mainland of Europe. For example, Barnes and Becker (1938, p. 794) write that 'It is disconcerting to begin a survey of sociology in Great Britain with the necessary statement that it is almost as rare as gold in sea-water'. Nevertheless a Sociological Society was founded in 1903 by a group of academics and other professional men and women, most of them inspired by the writings of Frédéric Le Play. This group transformed itself into the Institute of Sociology and its journal, the *Sociological Review*, was still being published in 1939. It had however lost touch with the only academic centre of sociology in Britain, at the London School of Economics, and, partly because it concentrated its message on the evils of industrial civilisation, it was ignored when sociological teaching began to expand after 1945 (Farquharson, 1955). With more persons being trained in sociology and with the general public more conscious of both the need for and the possibility of social intervention, some new organisation for the mobilisation of common interest was clearly needed.

Discussions about the formation of a British sociological association began in 1950. Right from the start the issue of professionalism was on the agenda (Marshall, 1953; Tropp, 1956; Banks, 1967 and 1975). The promoters of the new association were generally agreed that there should be a two-tier membership distinguishing those potential supporters who had technical qualifications – academic, practical, or publications – though not necessarily in sociology, from those who lacked qualifications and simply had an interest in sociology. Applications for membership were soon received from persons who appeared to lie on the borderline between the categories and at least one associate member appealed successfully for reclassification as a full member. The two-tier system was abandoned after only two years because of the difficulties experienced in distinguishing between the two categories. It was to be replaced by a three-category scheme: students, who were to pay a lower subscription; the main body of ordinary members; and a third category, a select body of fellows who were to add lustre to the Association and at the same time be specially represented on the executive committee. At the annual general meeting in March 1952 several of those present made clear their doubts about the creation of a class of fellows. In December, at a meeting called to change the basis of membership, the general secretary made explicit the rationale behind the proposal for the creation of this elevated class. The Association, he said, had a dual function. On the one hand it was to be an organisation for all persons who, irrespective of qualifications, had an interest in sociology. But at the same time it was intended to be a learned society, engaged in advancing knowledge and raising standards of scholarship. This second function might be vested in a category of fellows. The executive committee, seeing itself as an administrative body, was however not able to specify the qualifications and functions of fellows and hence had no option but to leave the matter in abeyance for the time being. Accordingly the new constitution made no provision for fellows, though the executive committee did retain its right to refuse an application for membership. With this modification the new scheme was accepted.

Almost all the former associates accepted the invitation to become full members. Although the idea of an honorific class of fellows was never taken up again, a vestige of the idea survived in the creation in 1956 of the office of president, which was seen as a way in which the Association could honour eminent sociologists.

The proposal for a class of fellows, supported mainly by those senior members of the Association who sought to establish an orthodox professional structure for sociology, had been foiled by outspoken younger sociologists. In 1956 they counter-attacked with a conference on 'The present state and development of professional sociology' (Banks, 1967, p. 4) in which the initiative was taken by younger university teachers. In 1958 there was another proposal for the creation of a separate category of membership for professional sociologists, and a couple of years later an attempt to limit attendance at a conference on the teaching of sociology to teachers of sociology met with criticism. The two functions of the Association, as identified in 1952, were already working in opposite directions.

A group of members who wanted what Parkin (1979) calls an exclusionary strategy to provide them with a professional basis took a decisive step in 1961 by holding a closed conference for professional discussions relating to university teaching and research in sociology. The exclusionary flavour of this strategy was manifested not only in the impressively complicated set of criteria for membership of the Sociology Teachers' Section which was established following the conference but also in the exclusion of professors from the conference itself. Those of the postwar generation who had been trained in sociology wished to mark themselves off from their elders who had moved into sociology from other disciplines, though in fact several leaders of this young group soon achieved professorial rank. The exclusiveness of the new section did not go unchallenged, particularly its exclusion of lecturers in sociology at teacher training colleges. On the other hand an independent suggestion was made at about this time that the membership list of the Association should indicate who was a professional sociologist and who was not.

At the end of the 1960s the Association, like many other groupings in the social sciences, felt the effect of the swing towards what we might call epistemological populism. The notion that some members knew more and knew better than others came under attack and in the minds of many the whole idea of professionalism began to be equated with repression. The vision of the Association as a learned society began to fade, and with it the goal of maintaining standards and advancing knowledge that had been one of the objectives of the Association's founders. The Teachers' Section, the only segment of the Association where exclusiveness was openly practised, was disbanded. The policy of the Association came to be more concerned with maintaining and increasing its membership, and with ensuring that within its own ranks all members had an equal opportunity to participate and decide.

The first twenty years of the Association's existence were characterised by a sustained expansion in academic activity generally and in particular in social science teaching and research (see Fincham, 1975). The reversal of this trend, which by about 1976 had become unmistakable, had its effects on attitudes towards professionalism. Emphasis on consumer-sponsored research, increasing competition for academic posts and pressure on teachers and researchers alike to demonstrate the 'relevance' of their activities all pointed towards a greater emphasis on professional standards and to some form of supervision of credentials, if not yet to undisguised restrictions on recruitment and other features of credentialism. The initiative towards greater professionalism has come principally from outside the Association, though the summer schools and other training schemes sponsored by the Association do constitute a mild step in the professional direction. The main pressure, as I see it, has come from the Social Science Research Council (SSRC) which is itself subject to pressure from the government and other research councils. For the first decade or so of its existence the SSRC took the same attitude towards the social science disciplines as the executive committee of the Association had taken, ten or more years earlier, toward the nomination of fellows. The Council avoided, as far as possible, making judgements about the relative merits of university departments and abstained completely from telling them what they should teach their graduate students. With the growth in the number of potential outlets the Council considered itself forced to discriminate and thus, however reluctantly, to develop standards for recognition which, to be politically acceptable, must be couched in universalistic terms. It therefore seems likely that the task of maintaining standards or, to speak more bluntly, of imposing intellectual criteria, may be pre-empted by the SSRC, and perhaps by other major sponsors, rather than remaining latent in the hands of a democratic Association.

If the Association has, so far, failed to function as a learned body, as an Academy of Fellows of Sociology, what about other aspects of its corporate life? Because my concern in this chapter is with professional sociology I need comment only briefly on the success or failure of the Association as a body open to all with an interest in sociology, irrespective of qualifications, as this is reflected in the size and distribution of its membership. The experience of other associations in the past might seem to suggest that there is no inherent incompatibility between the activities of an open, or nearly open, association and the pursuit of professional objectives. In certain contexts a large body of passive affluent lay members may continue happily to subsidise the activities of a small core of active but impoverished professionals who speak at meetings, edit journals and dominate committees. For better or worse the Association has never experienced this state of affairs. Now that the learned lecture, illustrated with magic lantern slides, has been superseded by television as the relaxation of the upper middle class, this option is probably no longer available to the Association. Two other aspects of the Association's activities have a more direct bearing on the phenomenon of professionalism. In a well-established profession, medicine being a good example, there is a division of labour between the learned body and the professional association, narrowly defined. A learned body exists to seek truth and promote scholarship, unsullied by material and ephemeral considerations; the Royal Society of Medicine seems to fill this niche. The professional association, in this case the British Medical Association, is then left free to concentrate its energies on the defence and furtherance of the mundane interests of the professionals, their remuneration, legal protection, and the like. The two activities cannot be carried on entirely independently but they are sufficiently distinct to make good sense of an organisational disjunction. What, then, of sociology, a discipline less well entrenched and much smaller than medicine? If the Association functions with only limited success as a learned body, does it do better as an organisation protecting the collective interests of sociologists?

Just as opinion within the membership of the Association has been divided about the merits of professionalism as an intellectual stance, so there have been divided counsels about the defence of mundane collective interests. The proposal to introduce a category of fellows, and later the restrictions on the rights of student members, may both be seen as moves to protect the interests of segments of the membership against those of the rest. These were internal conflicts. When the Association was first established there seems to have been no discussion of how or whether it might represent the interests of sociologists to other bodies. As early as 1952, however, the Association appointed a committee to study the recruitment, training and employment of sociologists (Banks, 1967, p. 3). This step was taken at a time when the SSRC did not exist and when grants for research and postgraduate training in sociology were much harder to obtain than was the case some fifteen years later. The committee was concerned to discover what positions would be available for sociologists outside the confines of academia. It discovered that very few sociology graduates were unemployed. For our present purpose what is of interest is the perception held by this committee about the aims of the Association. The compatibility of the committee's inquiries with the newly acquired charitable status of the Association was queried. A suggestion that the Association should carry out a study of the employment possibilities open to those who graduated in 1953 was rejected on the grounds that the Association was not a research organisation and that 'an enquiry of this kind would inevitably have the character, not of disinterested scientific research, but of a preoccupation with the material interests of its members which would be inconsistent with the aims of the Association' (British Sociological Association, 1953). Despite these objections, surveys of the employment of sociology graduates were carried out under the aegis of the Association from time to time (Banks, 1954; Banks and Banks, 1956; Banks, 1958; Abbott, 1969; and see Smith, 1975).

A different view of the Association's role was expressed forcefully by a speaker at the AGM of March 1957, when the charitable status of the Association appeared to some members as an unwelcome constraint on their freedom of action. Following a proposal that the Association should be regarded first and foremost as a professional body and secondarily as a charitable organisation, the meeting agreed that the Association should proceed experimentally with any activity it thought appropriate until such time as this might in law be ruled as incompatible with its charitable status, whereupon the matter should be reconsidered. After this shaky start the Association has continued to take an interest in the position of sociology graduates in the workforce. The propriety of the Association concerning itself with the material interests of its members seems never again to have been queried.

Nevertheless a broad interest in the welfare of its members is a very weak substitute for collective bargaining over pay and conditions of service, as practised by some professional associations. The Association has never come near to doing this, partly because this activity has been pre-empted, for much of its membership, by bodies such as the Association of University Teachers and partly, I think, because the Association has never resigned itself to being an association of sociologists in one form of employment only, namely, of academic sociologists and sociologists elsewhere in higher and further education. Even if the interested lay public has become a relatively insignificant residual category in its membership, the Association certainly hopes to attract teachers of sociology in schools and, probably the largest category of all, those working on social surveys and other empirical inquiries within government departments, and commercial enterprises, including market research and opinion polling. With such diversity in the conditions of employment of its members, potential or actual, it is not surprising that the Association has never tried to negotiate with employers on their behalf.

Maybe this diversity provides part of the explanation for the absence of any moves, or rather of any successful moves, towards credentialism and its negative aspect, professional censure (Parkin, 1979, pp. 54–60). For example, no discussion of a professional code of ethics seems to have taken place in the Association until 1966. A few years later a fairly simple set of guidelines was adopted (Stacey, 1968; British Sociological Association, 1970). As with the ethical codes of almost all professional associations, there are no effective sanctions to enforce its injunctions. The Association does not issue certificates of good standing and has nothing to withdraw from those of its members who ignore its ethical norms. Expulsion from the Association carries no dire consequences; indeed, there are many active sociologists, including some who are academically eminent, who do not belong to the Association (see Hawthorn, 1975). The Association's committee on professional ethics serves a useful purpose but, like the few other ethics committees I know about, is concerned with the rights and wrongs of members as academics rather than as sociologists (see Anonymous, 1975).

The other aspect of the Association's activities which bears on professionalism, and where the distinctive characteristics of sociology have most impact, is the relation between the Association and public bodies. Here also there is a profound division of opinion (see Banks, 1967, pp. 7–8). At a recent AGM the secretary, in his report, described his efforts to achieve a better hearing for sociologically informed opinions in the corridors of Whitehall and put forward, apologetically, possible reasons for his lack of success. His failure was applauded vigorously by a member who insisted that the Association should continue to keep itself uncontaminated by contact with the corrupting Establishment. This sharp division has persisted throughout the life of the Association. Shortly after the Association was founded an initiative came, somewhat unexpectedly, from a government department seeking advice from the Association. More often the initiative was taken by members of the Association wishing to influence the findings of Royal Commissions and similar bodies. At the AGM in 1957 two members proposed that the executive committee should consider how the Association could be more effective in presenting sociological evidence to public bodies. The proposal gained support from some but was opposed by others, who argued that the Association was a learned body and did not exist for propaganda purposes. Members who felt strongly on some public issue should communicate directly with Whitehall without involving the Association. The same issue came up two years later in connection with the Registrar General's proposals for the 1961 census when, although there was no intention that the Association should negotiate with the Registrar General on behalf of members, it was agreed that he should be persuaded to consult the Association about any major changes proposed for the census. It seems that in most cases the executive committee preferred to pass on to public bodies submissions prepared by members, though occasionally it made direct representations.

This reluctance to present an authoritative view representing the professional opinion of the Association on a matter falling within the shared area of competence of its members stems sometimes from the existence of a major disagreement about a professional matter. For example, the work of the Public Schools Commission, set up by the Wilson administration to determine how the public schools could best be integrated with the state sector of education, was regarded by members of the Association with a variety of opinions and the Association presented no evidence to it. But even on those matters where there might have been a consensus view about what professional advice should be given, there was still a lack of agreement about whether it was appropriate for the Association to give the advice. There were two objections, one roughly from the right and the other from the left. The objection from the right was that the Association was a learned body and hence committed to the impartial and disinterested search for truth; it was not the business of the Association to try to change the world, for better or for worse. From the left came the objection that public bodies, Royal Commissions, government departments, and the like were all part of the apparatus of repression and that the practical consequence of advice tendered to these bodies could only be more efficient repression; at the same time the critical stance of the Association would be compromised and corrupted.

The Association's hesitant, and sometimes reluctant, presentation of the professional views of its members, convergent and divergent alike, contrasts sharply with the clear and unequivocal manner in which it has articulated the consensus in their value-judgements on certain matters of public policy that cannot be treated as merely technical questions. This articulation is seen in the Association's support for the censure of certain university departments for actions contrary to accepted academic practice and, even more clearly, in its stand on the equality of women and men, where a firm agreement in members' attitudes is reflected in unhesitatingly positive resolutions about the Association's own policy.

If my analysis has any validity, it seems that we may conclude that whether or not professional sociology is necessary, we have not got very far along the road toward it; we are at least spared the job of dismantling a professional sociology constructed in error. Or rather, that if professional sociology does exist in Britain, its institutional embodiment is not the British Sociological Association. One feature of professionalism, certification, or the authentication of certificates, may already be emerging through the activities of the SSRC and other financially powerful sponsors. Already only certain master's courses are recognised for the award of postgraduate studentships. The constraints on recognition are partly demographic and logistic, but they are partly intellectual. Just as the National Council on Academic Awards recognises only those undergraduate courses which conform to intellectual criteria it has laid down, so at least one subject committee of the SSRC withholds recognition of taught master's courses on intellectual grounds; the policy followed by the Sociology and Social Administration Committee seems currently to be in a state of flux. Whatever may happen in this respect to sociology, it is unlikely to resemble the fate of psychology, where professional certification has long been dominated by the professional association, the British Psychological Society. Among sociologists this society has a reputation for demonstrating clearly the hazards of following a determinedly credentialist strategy in achieving professional closure; I am not competent to say to what extent this reputation is deserved. What is certain is that although an association committed to the advancement of knowledge may encounter hazards in adopting exclusionary strategies to protect the livelihood of its members, there are serious hazards in allowing certification to develop under the aegis of a body as arbitrarily constituted as the SSRC or of entirely unrepresentative sponsors of research.

If some amount of certification, existing alongside informal sanctions derived from public reputation, is likely to come anyway, is the British Sociological Association the right body to ensure that certification does not entail ossification? With the experience of several other countries in mind, it is easy to paint a dreary scenario of a reassertion of a pragmatic positivism, of classical statistics and of an increasingly technically sophisticated and intellectually sterile applied sociology, effectively drained of theoretical innovation, imaginative insight and social criticism. With a glance at recent developments in the United States in the institutionalisation of so-called ethical controls, we should also include increasingly standardised and ineffective modes of empirical inquiry (Duster *et al.*, 1979; American Anthropological Association, 1980; Reinhold, 1980). If this path is to be avoided, will it be the Association which must take a lead in negotiating a more lively prospect?

It is not obvious that the answer must be yes; there are other candidates to consider. The catchment area of the Association is now partly colonised by other bodies with more narrowly restricted memberships, which are concerned with promoting sociology as a mode of discourse and inquiry and with furthering the interests of its practitioners and which as yet are not saddled with so conflicting a set of aims-as the Association was at its formation thirty years ago. Maybe these newer bodies contain within themselves the same inhibiting contradictions as have plagued and enlivened the history of the Association; time will tell. Alternatively it may be from their ranks that a recognisable professional sociology will emerge.

With hindsight it is easy to pontificate about what an older generation of colleagues ought to have foreseen, but in the eyes of history we doubtless shall appear equally naive. Let me risk making two observations. I think that during the last thirty years not enough attention has been given to what Klaw (1970) calls the Faustian bargain, whereby seekers after truth accept resources from a sponsor to enable them to sustain their quest but in the end have to pay a price in which their purity of purpose becomes contaminated. If sociologists want to study society, and particularly if they want to change it, they have to accept obligations and commitments they might not otherwise choose. In general, sociologists and most other social scientists as well have been too prone to reject contamination completely and thereby usually to find themselves completely ineffective, or else to accept the resources without taking precautions to protect their autonomy and intellectual integrity. The only way forward is an uneasy compromise.

This dilemma applies in any social science; my second observation applies particularly to sociology. Collectively sociologists have paid too little attention to the local consequences of what Giddens (1976, p. 79) calls the double hermeneutic, the process whereby the sociologist does not stand in an epistemologically privileged position in relation to the phenomena he or she studies. He or she and the actors, or members, or, as I prefer to call them, the citizens constitute an interacting system in which the analysis offered by the sociologists, whether or not it is first negotiated with the citizens, at once becomes inadequate, for the citizens begin to modify their acts in the light of the analysis previously made of them. I take this to be an adequate model for most sociological enterprises, apart from those colonial situations where the natural science paradigm still lingers on (Barnes, 1979, pp. 44–51). The hermeneutic model, or something like it, has been extensively discussed with reference to general epistemological issues but its practical implications have been ignored or merely subsumed under a wider stance of epistemological and political populism. Yet if the model is adequate, it follows that in sociology there cannot be the clear-cut division between professionals and lay camp-followers that may validly be drawn in most other scientific disciplines and intellectual specialisms. Sociological insights and counter-intuitive discoveries, within a generation, become commonplace truisms. If they do not, there must be something wrong with the insights. In this respect sociology is like experimental social psychology, whose task, Gergen (1978, p. 523) argues, 'is not so much to reflect the character of contemporary behavior, as to *create* it'. Building an edifice of professional sociological achievement is like building on quicksand; the scientific achievements of one moment are buried as common sense in the next. Thus while in the process itself of sociological inquiry there is a strong call for enduring levels of skill, the results of an inquiry are, in principle, only ephemerally esoteric and professional (see Gergen, 1973, pp. 312–13). Once the results are published, the contra-process of popular absorption and distortion begins. They become weapons of the intellect, as Luxemburg (1970, p. 784) aptly called them, but are used by both sides in the battle (see Nettl, 1966, pp. 230–4). Hence while there is every need to ensure that the specification of sociological professionalism is handled as imaginatively and democratically as possible, there is an equally strong need to recognise that the results of sociological research and their integration into social theory are, both in principle and often in practice, accessible and intelligible to others who lack these professional qualifications. The informed laity will not hesitate to criticise the professional practitioners and there is no reason why many of their criticisms should not strike home. The continual denigration of sociology in the popular media, in literary journals and by colleagues in other disciplines is not, as many sociologists seem to think, evidence for the immaturity of their discipline, something it will grow out of. On the contrary this denigration is, in my view, a permanent feature of sociology and is evidence for the maturity of the society in which sociology has been institutionalised. It is a rational defence developed by the laity against the claims of sociologists to know best. I therefore infer that it is a forlorn task to attempt to establish a comprehensive professional monopoly of sociological discussion and debate. A better strategy would be to try and learn as much as possible from lay supporters and critics as well as from colleagues.

Although the *results* of sociological inquiry are accessible to the public, empirical inquiry itself, along with other modes of sociological research, does indeed call for the exercise of difficult skills that are not, and are never likely to become, mere common sense. It is here that there is a real basis for a professional identity. But would this be adequate for defining a professional identity for sociologists? I hope not. This follows from the distinctive social task of sociology. For if the pursuit of sociology consisted entirely in carrying out surveys, experiments, field observations, and the like, and in the analysis of data collected in sophisticated and validated ways, then the case for professionalism would be strong. In as much as sociologists do engage in these activities, the arguments in favour of professional sociology must be conceded. A professional identity defined only by reference to competence in empirical inquiry is however quite inadequate. If much of the merit of sociology lies in its ability to provide a sophisticated, sustained and constructive critique of accepted social forms and ideologies, then we must ensure that this aspect of the discipline is recognised as such, even though sociologists cannot and should not claim a professional monopoly as social critics (see Dawe, 1973). There is a real danger in failing to execute competent and imaginative empirical research, and a greater danger in being confined to a narrowly perceived range of research techniques. To avoid these dangers some amount of autonomously generated and controlled professionalism is probably necessary. But there is a greater danger to society, particularly at a time when widespread change unceasingly undermines the value of traditional wisdom, if empirical research is seen as the beginning and end of sociology. If sociologists are to demonstrate their ability to provide informed criticism and comment, sociologists need to engage in an arena where they argue with fellow citizens. Here they will be listened to only because their arguments are understood and accepted, not because they can wave certificates of professional respectability. Evidence from other countries shows clearly, in my view, how vulnerable is the link between research competence and effective social comment and how important it is to retain the link.

Since the results of our labours as sociologists will, of necessity, be continually derided by our critics and paymasters as preposterous nonsense or mere overblown common sense, we need more acutely than do most of our colleagues in other disciplines and professions the protection of a collective organisation. This need is easily demonstrated by examining the annual reports of the Association and the pages of *Network*. The Association represents the views of its members, however hesitantly, to the SSRC, the University Grants Committee, the Department of Health and Social Security, the International Sociological Association, and the like, and exchanges observers with associations similar to itself. It hopes one day to meet the Association of University Teachers. It provides, even if only on a limited scale, some machinery for the settlement of disputes. These activities are an appropriate concomitant of the educational work of the Association seen in its conferences, study groups and summer schools and in its diverse programme of publication. The work of the Association may be characterised as that of a specialised corporate body, based more on the common pursuit of sociology as a corpus of knowledge and understanding than on the collective interests of full-time practitioners. It functions best as an association of persons interested in the study of society, irrespective of qualifications, even if most of its members do happen to have qualifications. There is a need for an organisation of this kind and there are no competitors in sight. Its progress through the last thirty years shows its comparative success and value as an open forum, and its comparative failure as a certifying body or as a learned institution.

Thus on balance we probably do need some kind of professional sociology, if only because if we do not evolve our own professional structure we may have the wrong kind forced upon us. Whether this structure should develop under the aegis of the Association is a matter for debate. There is a need for a forum where sociology can be discussed and the Association supplies it. But I doubt if there is any place in sociology, as we know and enjoy it in this country, for a learned society to define orthodoxy and generate professional respectability. I am quite sure that the Association should not try to become one. Its initial aspirations to do so have never been realised and should now be firmly abandoned. Farewell, fellows that never were!

Note: Chapter 1

I am much indebted to Anne Dix for her help in consulting the archives of the Association, to members of a seminar held in the Department of Social Studies, Queen's University, Belfast, for their constructive criticisms, and to Cathie Marsh, Frances Barnes and Rory Barnes for comments on an early draft of this chapter.

2

Sociology as a Parasite: Some Vices and Virtues

JOHN URRY

Introduction

I think that Giddens is wrong in suggesting that there are only four myths in the history of sociology – there is a further myth, namely, that there is an essence to sociology, that it has some essential characteristics that give it and its practitioners a unity, coherence and common tradition (Giddens, 1977). Giddens of course is well aware of the ambiguous nature of sociology as a subject – but he leaves its character merely as uncertain through the employment of terms like 'social thought' rather than 'sociology'. In this chapter I want to consider the status of the subject in more detail: just what kind of academic discourse is it? It is only by carrying out such an investigation that we can see exactly what we are defending when, for example, we argue against cuts in sociological teaching and research. In particular, I want to make sense of an interesting contradiction which first led me to this problem. On the one hand, it is commonly argued in public debate that there is no such subject as sociology, that you can make it up since there is not a rigorous structure of learning, research and content, that since everyone knows about society there is no need for a specific subject to study it. On the other hand, sociologists generally perceive that their subject is both important and difficult, that most people are sociologically ignorant, that a long period of training is involved and that it is more complex and worthwhile than most of the other social sciences. Sociologists generally get round this contradiction by rejecting or even ridiculing the first view, that of public opinion, and by adopting the latter. However, I think there is something mistaken about this – there is more to the public opinion view than we are normally willing to acknowledge. What exactly this is I shall try to indicate below.

In particular, I want to consider one aspect, namely, that sociology is a parasitic subject since it has no essence, no essential unity. In a sense it feeds off developments in neighbouring disciplines to an extraordinary degree. To illustrate this, consider the past three BSA conferences, on the State, Culture and Ideology, and Law (see Littlejohn *et al.*, 1978, and Barrett *et al.*, 1979, on the 1977 and 1978 conferences). How much of the content of these conferences could be described as 'sociology' – indeed, how many 'sociologists' attended, how many gave papers or made substantial oral contributions, how much sociological material was referred to in these papers? In each case the answer is 'relatively few' or 'relatively little'. The developments in these three topics have been appropriated *within* sociology, but sociology *per se* has not contributed much to such developments, except in a rather special sense as we shall see. In the first part of this chapter I shall consider one such area in particular, namely, the state, and I shall show that most recent developments in its analysis have occurred outside mainstream sociological discourse. I shall then consider in the following section some important implications of this for the social and intellectual organisation of sociology. In particular, it will be seen, first, that sociology develops in part through *appropriating* theoretical and empirical work conducted in neighbouring disciplines, and related social movements; secondly, that it can never be understood in terms of the idea of a paradigm, or even of a scientific community, or communities (Kuhn, 1962); and thirdly, that its intellectual strength predominantly lies in its parasitism, its openness and relative lack of authority and control. It is perhaps the only scientific community to resemble Popper's ideal precisely because it is not organised like other natural or social scientific subjects (see Popper, 1970). This might suggest of course that it does contain some essence which produces these distinctive characteristics. But this is only so in one sense, that it has a particular organisation *as an academic discourse* and this is because its central concepts neither generate a discursive unity nor demarcate it in a strong sense from neighbouring subjects which may well employ similar concepts (but not necessarily the same terms). I shall conclude the paper with some more general comments on the virtues of sociology's parasitic character.[1]

Three provisos should be made before I proceed. First, although some of my argument rests on implicit comparisons with other social sciences, I am not claiming that sociology is unique among such sciences. It may well be that certain social sciences are also in part parasitic – 'politics' is the most obvious example. However, I would still want to argue for the greater parasitism of sociology, and hence, as we shall see, for its greater virtue. Secondly, most of my discussion is related to recent developments in British sociology. Yet there is little doubt that in Britain sociology has generally enjoyed a more marginal academic status than in the United States or Western Europe, and this has increased its tendency here to feed off and incorporate the more established (and 'respectable') social sciences. This is, however, only a question of degree. Indeed, for reasons that I shall discuss, this parasitism is particularly important in periods of advance within sociology, and British sociology since the mid-1960s has been so advancing. It is thus worth exploring for this particular reason. Thirdly, the term 'sociological discourse' refers to the set of social practices characteristic of the members of such a discourse – such practices being structured in terms of common concepts, beliefs, theories, traditions, institutions, methods, techniques, exemplars, and so on. In most cases those individuals who happen to bear the official label 'sociologist' are agents who are part of, and contributors to, this ongoing set of reproducible social practices known as 'sociological discourse'. However, this is not always the case, in part precisely because of sociology's parasitic and hence rapidly changing nature. There is thus an important disjuncture 'sociological discourse'/ practitioners of 'sociology' – the latter may not be agents of the former.

Sociology and the State

At the beginning of the collection of papers from the BSA conference on Power and the State (Littlejohn *et al.*, 1978) it is said to be a good thing that sociologists have at last begun exploration of the nature of the state. However, what is not pointed out is that most of the interesting parts of this collection related to the state as such were produced as a result of developments outside sociology, most noticeably because of debates within Marxism and within feminism (see chapters by David, Hindess, Jessop and Zubaida on the former, and by Leonard, Barker and Hanmer on the latter). It is agreed that many contributors recognised the value of alternative disciplines and paradigms (Littlejohn *et al.*, 1978, p. 3), but no indication is given as to what their value actually was. It is further implied that there is an authentic sociological tradition to which these alternative paradigms (ignoring the typically slipshod use of that much-maligned term) happened to give added value. By contrast in this section I shall suggest that there is no authentic, essential contribution made by sociology to our understanding of contemporary capitalist states. The important contributions have been produced outside the mainstream of sociological discourse and by non-practitioners of 'sociology'; those notions have then been taken up and discussed within that discourse.

Before showing this in a little detail I will initially deal with an obvious objection that might be made to these claims. It could be said that the case of the state is a rather special one and that what may be true of the state is not necessarily true of any other area of sociological inquiry. After all, sociology only really developed after the conceptual separation between the state and the civil society had been effected. So while politics studies the former, sociology and the other social sciences study the latter. Hence, it could be claimed, there is no particular reason to expect that sociology would study the state. However, this is a weak argument in fact since the distinction between these spheres of influence has never been consistently maintained. All those authors typically treated as part of the classical tradition in sociology addressed themselves to the political, and in more recent years the growth of 'political sociology' indicates how the area designated by the term 'state' has been part of sociological discourse. However, my claim is that sociological writing on the state failed to produce any distinctive insights, and that much of the important work on the capitalist state developed in neighbouring disciplines. Such claims will obviously be contentious; indeed some may argue that such judgements cannot in fact be made at all. I shall simply assume here that we have to make such judgements about the relative worth of different pieces of academic work.

In short, then, the major contributions to the recent analysis of the capitalist state are the texts related to first, the Miliband/Poulantzas debate; secondly, the critical theory tradition in the FRG; thirdly, the *Staatsableiting* debate also in the FRG; fourthly, American controversy over the suggested fiscal crisis of the state; and fifthly, writings within political science on the corporatist state.[2]

The first set of texts are those best known in Britain – to some degree the controversy on the state has been a debate about the respective merits of Miliband/Poulantzas, with Laclau as a kind of arbitrator.[3] This debate within Marxist discourse (of a neo-Gramscian variety) has revolved around whether the capitalist state is to be viewed as the instrument of the economically dominant class, or whether it is to be seen as the general factor of social cohesion in capitalist social formations and hence is relatively autonomous of the economy as such. These texts have all been criticised for ignoring the form of the state and for having related the state only to classes in struggle and not to the nature of capital and the requirements of accumulation (see, amongst others, Holloway and Picciotto, 1978).

The second main set of texts derive from the critical theory tradition, the best known being Habermas (1976) and Offe (1972 and 1975). Here there is a more systematic attempt to relate the state to the economy, and to establish the changing political conditions under which the state can effectively intervene. In Habermas (1976) there is discussion of the nature of legitimation crisis, while Offe analyses contradictions encountered in the employment of different political mechanisms necessary to sustain capital accumulation. These texts are in part sociological, but are also heavily influenced by debates within both systems theory and Marxism.

The third set of texts have been in part developed through a critique of some of the earlier work of Offe and Habermas; see Müller and Neusüss (1970). Much work has revolved around exactly how the nature of the capitalist state can be derived from capital. There have been four main approaches to the derivation of the state form: first, from the sphere of circulation (Flatow and Huisken, 1973); secondly, from the crisis character of late capitalism (Boccara, 1971); thirdly, from the nature of capital as individual capital units (Altvater 1973a and 1973b); and fourthly, from the capital relation as one of class domination (Hirsch, 1978; Holloway and Picciotto, 1978). These texts have been produced from within a fairly fundamentalist Marxist discourse; while the fourth set of texts derives more from a neo-Ricardian perspective. The main text here is O'Connor's *The Fiscal Crisis of the State* (O'Connor, 1973) which is an attempt, albeit ultimately unsuccessful, to explain the persistent tendency for the expenditures of contemporary states (divided into social capital, social consumption and social expenses) to outrun revenues. Particular emphasis is placed upon the interaction between monopoly capital and the state. The importance of class struggle, although still problematic, has begun to be extensively confronted within this and other Marxist works.

Finally, there are many texts now written on the theme of corporatism, some written from within Marxist discourse (Jessop, 1978), others which treat corporatism as a new economic system (Winckler, 1977). But the main discourse here has been that of political science, and the counterposing of corporatism to that of pluralism, with the tendency to reproduce some of the errors of the latter within the former (see Panitch, 1978, for discussion and criticism of these different formulations). Corporatism, on this view, is seen as a system of interest intermediation in which the different units are

organised into a limited number of singular, compulsory, non-competitive, hierarchically ordered, and functionally differentiated categories, recognised or licensed (if not created) by the state and granted a deliberate representational monopoly within their respective categories in exchange for observing certain controls on their selection of leaders and articulation of demands and supports. (Schmitter, 1974, p. 9)[4]

Thus far I have suggested that there are five main sets of texts which, since the mid-1960s, have advanced discussion, debate and understanding of the capitalist state. Indeed there seems to have been considerable theoretical advance. Sociology's contribution to these five has been very limited and discussions in sociology have seen the taking-up and then the elaboration of notions already advanced within these other discursive formations. So sociology has been parasitic. Its discussions have fed off, and made relatively little initial contribution to, the original theoretical ideas. This is clear, for example, from considering the material produced for the 1977 BSA conference, or for the BSA State and Economy Group. Generally speaking, then, sociology has been parasitic upon certain neighbouring discourses, particularly that of Marxism, and political science.

However, there is one sense in which sociology has been important and that is in providing a site in which these different texts have been placed in critical confrontation with each other. They have been taken up within sociological discourse and some of the respective merits and deficiencies have become clarified. Of course this has also happened within Marxism, in political science and economics – but it would seem that the debates have been very widespread and productive in sociology. Issues discussed have included: the nature of, and relationship between, competing 'problematics'; the relevance of empirical evidence to theoretical claims regarding the economy and the state; the relevance of the concept 'elite' to a 'ruling class' analysis; the importance of class 'fractions' in the analysis of class relations between capital and labour; the degree to which the analysis of a 'power bloc' is relevant; and the extent to which capitalist societies are broadly similar or are to be analysed in their diversity.

This discussion has supported my claim that there is something distinctive about the organisation of sociology as a discourse. In the following section I shall consider this in more detail. In conclusion here I will mention one or two of the differences between the discursive organisation of sociology and of Marxism. First of all, the latter is a relatively unified discourse, or as some would argue, pair of related discourses. This unity is based upon the central concepts, of capitalism, alienation, class, surplus-value, exploitation, politics, the state, ideology, the dictatorship of the proletariat, and so on. Sociology is not unified – we shall see below that the central term, 'society', may denote a number of quite different and opposed concepts. This means that when Poulantzas, in his famous debate with Miliband, talks of contrasting 'problematics', this conveys a misleading impression (Poulantzas, 1969). The organisation of the two problematics is not isomorphic, they are not equally unified. It is very doubtful if sociology can be seen as a 'problematic' at all. But furthermore, it is equally incorrect to treat Marx and Marxists as simply one element *of sociology*. For Marxist texts to be treated as sociological requires appropriation – which stems from sociology's parasitic character. But this only in a sense occurs after the theoretical work has taken place *within* Marxist discourse.[5]

The Organisation of Sociological Discourse

The parasitic character of sociology can be seen not only in the analysis of the state. Consider, for example, how the sociology of the family has recently been transformed, not because of the debate between sociologists on the relationship between industrialisation and the extended family, but because of the incorporation of arguments, insights and research material produced within both the anti-psychiatry and the women's movements (see Morgan, 1975, for very helpful discussion). Likewise, the sociology of development was greatly changed through the incorporation of work produced outside sociology, namely, certain texts of Frank on the manner in which development produces underdevelopment (see Frank, 1969, for example). Similarly, if we consider recent BSA conferences, the debates on Culture and Ideology in 1978 very largely reflected the theoretical and empirical insights of semiology, psychoanalysis and neo-Gramscian

Marxism (Barrett *et al.*, 1979). And the sociology of law, as in the 1979 conference, has been transformed through critical confrontation with Pashukanis's by now historic attempt to relate the legal subject to the commodity form (Pashukanis, 1978; and see, for example, Fine *et al.*, 1979). Even if we consider Bottomore and Nisbet's massive and authoritative *A History of Sociological Analysis*, many of the texts which are referred to were produced within philosophy, economics, politics, and so on (Bottomore and Nisbet, 1979). What is the explanation of sociology's parasitic character? I will try to answer this by considering Bottomore and Nisbet's 'Introduction' to this collection, which I will take as an authoritative statement about the history of sociology.

They argue that there is 'now a single discipline, a realm of scientific discourse outside of which sociological analysis cannot properly be pursued at all'; and this 'constitutes a relatively autonomous sphere' (Bottomore and Nisbet, 1979, pp. xiv–xv). What, though, provides the basis of this unity, around what central concepts or principles is this discourse organised? They say that this is provided by the 'more precise conception of society as an object of study', this being a concept separate from both the state and politics, and from vaguer notions of civilisation or mankind (Bottomore and Nisbet, 1979, p. viii). The concept of 'society' has constituted sociology as a scientific discipline. This has then developed in a fairly normal manner, first, through the continued elaboration of alternative paradigms and theoretical controversy among their adherents, secondly, through the accumulation of an ordered body of knowledge 'directed' by one or other paradigm, and thirdly, through the 'specialisation of research' (Bottomore and Nisbet, 1979, pp. viii–ix). However, they also say that there have been three unsatisfactory features of sociological development: that there has been a multiplicity of paradigms such that no particular theory ever dies and no new theory ever becomes dominant, that sociological knowledge is too close to everyday commonsense knowledge, and that there has been a failure to progress in important areas.

What are the deficiencies of Bottomore and Nisbet's interpretation? First, they imply that sociology is like any other science in being characterised by alternative paradigms and theoretical controversy. Since they quote Kuhn they must be employing the term 'paradigm' in his sense (Kuhn, 1962; Masterman, 1970). Yet for Kuhn it is the crucial fact of science that there are *not* alternative paradigms except in the limited periods of scientific revolution. If a particular discourse is, during normal periods, characterised by inter-paradigmatic competition, then it is not, as yet, a fully fledged science. So Bottomore and Nisbet's claim that sociology is more or less like other sciences is not substantiated. Further, they state that the concept 'society' has provided the basis for sociological progress, albeit of a limited kind. But what Bottomore and Nisbet have done is to construct a spurious teleology, to view all kinds of earlier social thought as somehow contributing to the end-state – the present organisation of sociology oriented around particularly the concept of 'society'. Yet it is clear that this structuring of history is largely a fiction – the history has no such unity, purpose, or direction. This is really implied by them when they refer to the three unsatisfactory characteristics of sociology – but they cannot have it both ways. If these three characteristics are important then sociology is not a conventional science comprehensible through even a minimally accumulationist model of its development. I will now try to show that these features are both correct and so important that they undermine Bottomore and Nisbet's attempt to suggest that we have already achieved a systematic, unified, sociological discourse. In particular, I shall argue that the term society does not provide the sought-for unity, that sociology cannot be demarcated adequately from the commonsense, and that there is little in the way of sociological progress, except in a highly paradoxical sense.[6]

First, then, let me consider the concept 'society' in relationship to the main perspectives incorporated within sociology. There are eight such perspectives, not necessarily similar in organisation, structure, or intellectual coherence. They are: critical theory, ethnomethodology, functionalism, interactionism, Marxism, positivism, structuralism and Weberianism (see Urry, 1980b, for more detail). There is no common external object 'society' which brings together these disparate perspectives into a unified discourse. This can be seen from the following where I set out the central notion of society specific to each of these various perspectives:

critical theory: society as a form of alienated consciousness judged by the criterion of reason

ethnomethodology: society as the fragile order displayed by the commonsense methods members use in practical reasoning

functionalism: society as the social system in which all the parts are functionally integrated with each other

interactionism: society as social order negotiated and renegotiated between actors

Marxism: society as the structure of relations between the economic base and the political and ideological superstructures

positivism: society as the structure of relations between observable (generally measurable) social phenomena

structuralism: society as the system of signs generated from fundamental structures in the human mind

Weberianism: society as the relations between different social orders and of the social groupings present within each order.

Obviously particular writers may disagree with these formulations – but in general this list indicates the diverse concepts of 'society' which are employed within perspectives generally taken to be part of sociological discourse.

Secondly, it has been plausibly argued by Bachelard that the objective of science is to create something which is in a radical discontinuity with the world of common sense (see the discussion in Lecourt, 1975). There has to be a discontinuity between the two and this provides one of the guarantees of scientific progress. Even if this is broadly true of natural science, it is clear that sociology is organised differently. Sociology is thoroughly contaminated with commonsense terms, concepts and understandings and most of the attempts to create and sustain a separate, purely academic, discourse have been unsuccessful. One reason for this has been the manner in which contemporary political and social movements affect sociology more than most of the other social sciences, let alone the natural sciences. In recent years, the students', black, and women's movements have all become, in a sense, part of sociological discourse, juxtaposed and assessed within that discourse. I have already mentioned how the previously dormant sociology of the family has been revitalised through incorporating the commonsense understandings and theoretical reflections of women seeking to develop alternative forms of social relations between the sexes.

Thirdly, there is little that can be described as sociological progress in the sense understood by that notion within science. Bottomore and Nisbet point out that specific theories are rarely worked through sufficiently to establish whether a particular research programme is progressive (see Lakatos, 1970, on this notion in science). There is considerable emphasis placed upon novelty – on making sociological reputations through developing and employing a new theory. Progress is thus generally achieved and indicated not primarily by working through existing theory, not by the puzzle-solving practices of normal science – it rather follows from the generation of new theories and of the critical discussions engendered through these. This is not, incidentally, to be arguing for that well-worn cliché in sociology, for theory rather than empirical research. It is rather that in sociology 'progress' seems to take the form of theoretical innovations – and these may derive from many sources which include empirical research, philosophical speculation, or the incorporation of, or juxtaposition between, contributions made from outside sociological discourse. This emphasis upon the making of theoretical innovations means that there is a tendency for the cyclical repetition of theories, rather than for one wholly to replace that already in existence. This is not entirely the case – Parkin suggests, for example, that Lloyd Warner is unlikely ever to make a comeback (1979, p. 603). But there is nevertheless a tendency for new theories to bear strong similarities with those once discarded. He also points out that most of what counts as important and interesting today in the field of class and stratification analysis is almost entirely derived from the competing theoretical perspectives of Marx/Engels, Weber and Pareto/Mosca (Parkin, 1979, p. 599).

I will conclude this section by relating the discussion of sociology to Kuhn's account of how a scientific discourse is organised (Kuhn, 1962; Lakatos and Musgrave, 1970). Kuhn presumes at least during normal science that there is a unity of the discourse which results from the role of the paradigm as exemplar. Sociology is obviously not organised in this manner, since sociological change and development does not result from the working through of the paradigm until anomalies arise. I am not presuming that Kuhn's account of change and revolution is philosophically correct – in particular he requires sociological categories to do too much epistemological work. But sociologically there are great differences between his account of the discourse of a natural scientific community, and my account of the discursive organisation of sociology. This means that attempts to employ Kuhn as providing philosophical protocols for developments in sociology are unjustified – whether these involve the non-radical advocacy of positivism as sociology's normal science, or the radical advocacy of sociological revolutions and the founding of a plethora of new paradigms (see my discussion of this in Urry, 1973).

The Virtues of Being a Parasite

I have so far argued that sociological discourse is organised as follows:

1   there is a multiplicity of perspectives with no common concept of 'society' which unifies them;
2   sociological concepts and propositions cannot be clearly demarcated from commonsense concepts and propositions;
3   it is difficult to establish that there is sociological progress – it mainly follows *theoretical* innovations;
4   one major form of such innovation results from the parasitic nature of sociology, from the fact that innovations originate in discourses outside sociology itself.

I shall now consider certain aspects of point 4 in more detail. What, we might ask, are the circumstances that permit this parasitism to occur? Within sociology's neighbouring disciplines there is a simultaneous process of both presupposing and rejecting what I will loosely call the 'social', by which I mean the general social relations which link together individuals and groups. In these disciplines, which include economics, geography, history, Marxism, psychology and politics, these social relations are presumed to be of importance, and yet are in part ignored.[7] The social is thus both present and absent simultaneously. Instead, in these disciplines some particular dimension or aspect of social life is abstracted for study, such as people's behaviour as agents in the market, or their distribution within space, or their behaviour in the past. But this means that each of these disciplines is discursively unstable. On occasions, certain texts will break through the limitations implied by that discourse. New understandings emerge which will involve more systematic comprehension of the general form of these social relations which will not obscure or neglect the realm of the social. How, though, does such a development in a neighbouring discipline relate to sociology? First, these other disciplines are to varying degrees discursively unified – which will mean that blocks will be placed upon the new, more 'social', interpretation. Yet, secondly, because there is no essence to sociological discourse, apart from a broad commitment to this idea of the interdependence of individuals and social groups, sociology may attract this new 'social' interpretation. So simultaneously we encounter two likely developments: first, a process of at least partial repulsion from the originating discourse, and secondly, attraction to sociological discourse. There are a number of examples of where both developments have occurred. I will mention one for each of the social sciences listed above: in economics, Frank and the development of the underdevelopment thesis; in geography, analysis of the growth of multinational corporations and changes in the spatial division of labour; in history, the nature of class relations in nineteenth-century Britain; in Marxism, the theorisation of the state and ideology; in psychology, the critique of the family in the anti-psychiatry movement; and in politics, the class structuring of local power structures.

Thus far I have claimed that in many social sciences there is a simultaneous presupposing and rejecting of the social. Where social relations in a sense break through, the innovation may get elaborated in part outside the originating discourse within sociology instead. So the latter is important in permitting analysis and elaboration of aspects of the social world which are generally neglected by the other social sciences. It can thus be defined negatively – as a discourse with minimal organisation, structure, or unity into which many contending developments from other social sciences get incorporated. So although it is parasitic it enjoys two crucially important features: first, to provide a site within which further elaboration of the original innovation may occur; and secondly, to provide the context in which a wide variety of contending social theories can be placed in juxtaposition with each other. This has the function of promoting inter-discursive debate and confrontation. I am not claiming that this is sufficient to permit a necessarily rational evaluation of such social theories – but there are nevertheless some very important positive effects of these processes which may then react back on the originating discourse.[8]

(1) *Positive overlap.* In some cases it becomes clear through the juxtaposition of perspectives that there are certain shared concepts and related propositions. There can be very positive effects which follow from this juxtaposing of related perspectives in terms of producing new bases of empirical work or novel theoretical insights. A good recent example is the collective work which resulted in the book

Capitalism and the Rule of Law (Fine *et al.*, 1979) – a book which developed from the positive overlap between the 'left interactionism and conflict theory' of the National Deviancy Conference and the fairly fundamentalist Marxism of the CSE Law and State Group.

(2) *Improved vigour and precision.* Because of the critical confrontation between two or more perspectives the original theory is made more specific, its referents are clarified and the logical consistency of the propositional structure is improved. This is what has happened in development studies where the original Frankian thesis that 'development produces underdevelopment' has been taken up and greatly clarified within sociological discourse, first in Laclau's critique, and then in many other texts, including some of those in the Oxaal collection (Laclau, 1979; Oxaal, 1975).

(3) *Mutual weaknesses exposed.* Through the critical confrontation of perspectives the relative deficiencies of each are brought more clearly into view. An example would be the recent debate as to the relationship between Marxism and psychoanalysis. The effort by Coward and Ellis (1977) to synthesise Althusserian Marxism with Lacanian psychoanalysis has demonstrated both that this cannot be satisfactorily achieved and that each perspective is theoretically problematic partly in ways highlighted by the other.

(4) *Further empirical research.* The challenge of perspectives produces increased specification of the research implications of one or both theories which then get taken up and elaborated. The theoretical debates between Marxist and neo-Weberian theories of class and stratification have produced more detailed empirical support for both: good examples, if very different, would be Nichols and Beynon (1977) and Goldthorpe (1980).

(5) *Synthesis.* In rare circumstances different perspectives can get incorporated into a single work and elements fused. A very good example of this is Newby (1979) in which there is an effective synthesis of a number of different theoretical traditions, in particular of political economy, political sociology, labour history and industrial sociology.

These points 1–5 are not intended to be exhaustive, only illustrative of the kinds of benefits that follow from sociology's parasitic character and of how a variety of perspectives may be brought into beneficial critical confrontation. One interesting effect takes us back to the Introduction, namely, that sociology is one of the most difficult social sciences because competent practitioners have to acquire familiarity with this successive range of incorporated perspectives. Recent examples of this would include the way in which Lacan, Foucault and Derrida have become part of contemporary sociological discourse. In recent years in Britain Giddens has been particularly important in providing a means by which this parasitism has been achieved (see Giddens, 1976, 1977 and 1979). He has interpreted the latest foreign import for sensitive Anglo-American readers and has located it within a sociological context. Sociology in such a Golden Age changes very rapidly and it may be difficult for the old guard to police effectively. Indeed, although Kuhn showed that generational differences are important in natural science, this is even more marked in sociology where new tendencies have been taken up and incorporated every four or five years. It is interesting to see how this produces difficulties for established sociologists who have to run hard just to keep up with the latest fashionable foreign import.

Finally, it might be wondered what the political implications are of my position. It is obviously the case that sociology involves a large degree of political struggle over exactly which aspects of which disciplines can be incorporated within it. And this struggle is likely to be more complicated and involve more diverse interests than in the neighbouring social sciences. In the latter the lines of struggle are more clearly drawn; in economics, for example, between the orthodoxy, once Keynesian, now part-Keynesian/part-monetarist, and the Marxists, as represented in the Conference of Socialist Economists. In the site of sociology many new developments enter, and the radicals of one generation may, five years later, be the conservatives of the new generation. Thus, it is not the case that sociological discourse needs to be dominated by the left – indeed my argument would suggest that domination is difficult for any perspective. And indeed, given the present move to the right, nationally and internationally, it would be possible, if horrifying, to expect that the next discourse on which sociology will be parasitic will be the conservative New Philosophy of the failed Parisian left. However, an even worse prospect would be that what has been a relatively Golden Age for sociology, especially in Britain, is just coming to a close. And one very important reason for that is the current rapid decline in the number of graduate students. It is an implication of any argument that graduates have been particularly important in effecting this parasitism. Yet with the current decline in the number of students this will not occur to anything like the same degree, and of course this would be even more the case if the Illsley plan for most graduates to be deskilled research trainees becomes implemented. So, my final claim would be that if the parasitic nature of sociology is in fact correct, and if the current main social grouping which has effected this is being decimated, then we have to consider very carefully just what kind of alternative social/intellectual structures can be devised. What are the means by which we can defend a space for sociology?[9] What are the social preconditions for sustaining this particular discursive structure? In general, I am pessimistic about the prospects.

Incidentally, it may be wondered whether to view sociology as a virtuous parasite is the same as seeing it as the Queen of Sciences. I think that depends on whether one regards monarchs not only as parasitic but also as virtuous. For me sociology, unlike a monarch, is both parasitic and virtuous. Whether this will continue to be the case is another and equally controversial question.

Notes: Chapter 2

I am grateful to Nick Abercrombie, Sue Scott and Sylvia Walby from the Lancaster Sociology Department, and Tony Garrett from Durham, for their comments on this chapter.

1   I shall use the term 'discourse' at various points in the following discussion. This is meant to imply a rejection of accounts of intellectual development which are either author-centric, or which uncritically employ the notion of a paradigm. See Tribe (1978), and, of course, Foucault (1972). I also employ the term 'perspective' on occasions to denote a theory relatively ungrounded in some systematic set of ongoing, reproducible social practices. It should be noted that although I do not consider the social conditions which generate particular discursive organisations I do not intend to preclude such analysis.

2   It will be noted by some readers that I make no reference to the Stamocap thesis of an increasing fusion of the state and the large monopolies, and hence of the viability of an anti-monopoly popular front; see Boccara *et al.* (1977), and Wirth (1971) for a readily available critique. See Urry (1980a) for further discussion of recent developments in the theory of the capitalist state.

3   The main texts in this debate are: Poulantzas (1969), Miliband (1970 and 1973), Laclau (1975, repr. 1979), Poulantzas (1976).

4   On corporatism see especially *Comparative Political Studies*, vol. 10, no. 1 (April 1977), which is devoted to this topic.

5   This is brought out by in the chapter by Sklair (1980) in this volume. Although we differ somewhat in our identification of the different forms of Marxism and sociology, I am generally sympathetic to his overall analysis.

6   I do not have the time here to consider the organisation of natural science, except to register a commitment to a modified Kuhnianism. See the brief discussion below.

7   Philosophy could also be included but its organisation clearly has some discursive instabilities similar to that of sociology; so I will omit that here.

8   In a conference held in the 1930s Mannheim conveyed a similar notion of sociology as a site – he said: 'Sociology, therefore is – as you see – on the one hand a clearing-house for the results arrived at by the specialised social sciences and on the other hand, a new elaboration of the materials on which they are based' (Mannheim, 1936, p. 188). I am indebted to Tony Garrett for bringing this to my attention.

9   This issue of 'space for sociology' was interestingly raised in John Eldridge's presidential address to the BSA, Lancaster, 1980.

3

Oxbridge Sociology: the Development of Centres of Excellence?

ANTHONY HEATH AND RICCA EDMONDSON

This chapter discusses the contribution, or lack of it, which Oxford and Cambridge have made to the development of sociology. Thus we started from the question have Oxford and Cambridge, when compared with other universities, made that contribution to British sociology which their relative resources and privilege might have led us to expect? To consider this question fairly we found ourselves led into a broader survey of sociology departments, their reputations and the work they have produced. We shall therefore be drawing on A. H. Halsey's recent survey of university teachers and their judgements of departmental reputations (Halsey, 1979), and we shall also be presenting some new material on what might loosely be termed 'top books and top places' in postwar British sociology. This material also allows us to make some incidental contributions to the debate among sociologists about the tasks of their discipline as they see it.

Uneasy suspicion has always characterised the Oxbridge attitude to sociology, and it would not be absurd to argue that sociology has been starved of resources as a result. For better or worse Oxbridge attracts very highly qualified students and staff (judged in terms of their formal educational credentials) (Halsey and Trow, 1971). They are two of the largest universities in the country with the greatest financial resources. They are privileged institutions, but have these privileges been shared *pro rata* by sociology?

Of the two, Cambridge was the first to be in any way welcoming to sociology, although this was not a competition either had been eager to win. Its first taste of sociology came in 1949 when T. H. Marshall was invited by the Faculty of Economics at Cambridge to give the lecture in honour of his namesake, Alfred Marshall. He treated them to a first draft of *Citizenship and Social Class* – a generous dowry for the new subject. But marriage did not follow immediately. Throughout the 1950s Cambridge continued to flirt with sociology, sampling the attractions of visiting professors from Harvard and Chicago such as Parsons, Warner, Shils and Homans. Parsons's presence in Cambridge is reputed to have put acceptance of the subject back by a decade, and in their suspicion of that famous figure the Cambridge economists, to give them their due, were rather ahead of the sociological fraternity.

In 1961 Cambridge finally took the plunge and with an inspired choice appointed David Lockwood to a university lectureship. At the same time W. G. Runciman held a fellowship at his old college, Trinity, while Kings advertised a research fellowship in sociology. As Halsey, then at Birmingham, remarked: 'These gentlemen initially proposed to elect a research fellow in the subject from among the graduates of Oxford and Cambridge; i.e. a first degree in sociology automatically disqualifies its holder from consideration' (Halsey, 1959). But they subsequently relented and the man who eventually got the fellowship, and shortly afterwards a university appointment, was John Goldthorpe. So began one of the best-known partnerships in British sociology, and while Cambridge failed to retain Lockwood and Goldthorpe for more than a decade, it did acquire a professor of sociology, a social and political sciences tripos, and some new university lectureships. If we arrange sociology departments in a league table according to size, Cambridge has now climbed up to join the large pack in the middle of the table with scores between ten and twenty.

In Oxford developments took a slightly different course. Sociology got off the ground earlier, but has remained in some ways more marginal to the university. The first full university lectureship came in 1955 with the appointment of John Mogey, who wrote his minor classic *Family and Neighbourhood* about two working-class areas in Oxford, St Ebbes and Barton. Peter Collison was also at Oxford in the 1950s at Barnett House,[1] writing about the notorious Cutteslowe Walls (remains of which are still to be seen in north Oxford and which ought to be on every visiting sociologist's itinerary). Margaret Stacey, too, began her classic work on Banbury while on the staff of the Delegacy for Extra-Mural Studies at Oxford, while Norman Birnbaum held a research fellowship at Nuffield. None the less, sociology was not admitted to the undergraduate curriculum until 1962, when it was given a place in the form of optional papers in PPE. And there it languishes still. Sociology has no honours school of its own at Oxford, nor is there a chair of sociology.[2] Progress at undergraduate level has been restricted to the addition of more optional papers in PPE and the inclusion of sociology as a compulsory, but small, part of human sciences.

Whereas Oxford sociologists have had little success in frontal assaults on the strongholds of the university, they have had more success with infiltration. As at Cambridge, there were two major appointments in the early 1960s, with Bryan Wilson and A. H. Halsey being appointed to cope, *inter alia*, with the new undergraduate teaching needs, but the total number of Oxford sociologists has now well outstripped that at Cambridge. This growth has come about partly through the 'conversion' of politics tutors such as Steven Lukes, partly through the 'infiltration' of sociologists such as Frank Parkin into politics fellowships, and partly through the accretion of new posts for teaching graduates. And then there is Nuffield. Founded in 1939 with endowments from Lord Nuffield's estate, its wealth has provided studentships, research fellowships, and two official fellowships now held by John Goldthorpe and Clyde Mitchell. So while sociology is still a marginal institution in Oxford in terms of its formal place in the undergraduate curriculum, in practical terms it has acquired substantial manpower and has been the beneficiary of considerable resources.

True, one response to the struggles of sociology to obtain a more central position at Oxford and Cambridge might be that its peripheral position is no bad thing. Establishment universities might well be expected to produce establishment sociology, and we might prefer to see sociology develop in less conservative institutions than those which cater for the social elite. It is perhaps not accidental, it might be argued, that Oxbridge sociology 'is now best known for philosophically inclined theory on the one hand and quantitative positivism on the other – to be adept at the computer console or the language games of philosophers enables even the sociologist to gain some intellectual respectability. But this, we hope, may be too cynical a view.

From speculation about intellectual milieux we shall now turn to some empirical material to help answer the question whether Oxbridge sociologists have made that contribution to their subject which the size and strength of their universities might lead one to anticipate. One way of dealing with the question is to compare Oxford's and Cambridge's reputations in sociology with their reputations in other, more favoured disciplines, such as economics and (at Oxford) politics. Halsey's evidence enables us to do this.

In his 1976 survey of university teachers, Halsey asked his respondents to rate the best three departments in their own subjects. The distribution of first choices in economics, politics and sociology is given in Table 3.1. Compared with economics and politics, Oxbridge sociology does not come off too badly. It gets fewer votes, but the differences are not so great as to substantiate a claim that it has been seriously penalised by its marginal status at the two ancient universities. If we combine the two universities together, they get 17·7 per cent of the votes in sociology, 25·2 per cent in politics and 27·3 per cent in economics. The differences are there, but they are much less striking than the fact that in none of the three subjects do the two ancient universities, even when combined, poll as many votes as the LSE. The similarity in the three rankings, with the LSE heading the list and followed by either Oxford or Cambridge, is the dominant feature of Table 3.1, not the differences. As far as the differences go, perhaps the most interesting is the dissensus among the sociologists compared with the much higher level of consensus among economists (and even among politics lecturers) about the top departments. In economics the top two departments pick up more than 70 per cent of the votes. Even in politics, a subject not noted for its intellectual unity, they pick up more than 50 per cent, but the top two in sociology cannot even reach 40 per cent. Why? Is there no agreement in sociology on the criteria for judging a good department? Is there simply no really outstanding department in sociology? Is there a sharing of mediocrity – or even perhaps of excellence?

Table 3.1   *Where Is the Best Department for Your Subject?*

% of vote given to each department, by subject

Economics		Politics		Sociology	
LSE	49·8	LSE	26·6	LSE	27·1
Cambridge	20·3	Oxford	25·2	Oxford	11·2
Oxford	7·0	Manchester	12·9	Essex	9·8
Edinburgh	3·0	Essex	7·2	Manchester and	
Warwick	2·2	Birmingham	5·8	Cambridge	6·5
(N = 136)		(N = 70)		(N = 107)	

We cannot fully answer these questions from the available evidence, but we might begin by asking if there is any simple hypothesis to account for the distribution of votes, both within and between subjects, in Table 3.1. The simplest hypothesis we can try is that of size: the bigger the department, the more votes it gets – perhaps because it is likely to have more well-known names or even, perhaps, because it has more members to feature in Halsey's poll. Does victory go in academic competition, as elsewhere, to the big battalions?

It is in fact quite difficult to determine how big social science departments are. Quite apart from the obscurity in which Oxford and Cambridge veil their proceedings,[3] there are plenty of other universities in which it is almost impossible to disentangle sociology from social work, social administration, or social anthropology. The relative ease with which one can isolate lecturers in economics and politics compared with the difficulties in sociology may in itself tell us something about the professional identity and organisation of sociology in Britain. The principle we followed was to include all professors, readers and lecturers, as listed in the *Commonwealth Universities Yearbook 1980*, but to exclude research officers. Local knowledge was used to distinguish sociology from economics and politics in the case of Oxford and Cambridge, but elsewhere the titles used in the *Commonwealth Universities Yearbook* have been followed. Sociology has been defined to exclude social work, social administration and social anthropology. Economics has been taken to exclude industrial relations, economic history, business studies and accountancy. But politics is taken to be the same as political science or government. The top five departments, ranked by size, in each subject are given in Table 3.2[4]

Table 3.2   *Where Are the Biggest Departments?*
Number of teaching staff (professors, readers and lecturers)

Economics		Politics		Sociology	
LSE	50	Oxford	41	Essex	31
Oxford	42	Manchester	30	Leicester	25
Cambridge	32	Essex	28	LSE	24
Warwick and		LSE	27	Warwick	20
Southampton	27	Lancaster	22	Manchester	19

There is considerable similarity between the list of the top five departments by size and the list of the top five by reputation. In both economics and politics four out of the five are the same; in sociology, three out of five. It may not be essential to be big to get a high reputation, but it certainly seems to help. True, there are exceptions. The LSE does noticeably better in politics and sociology votes for best departments than its size would predict, and the presence of Oxford and Cambridge in the sociology list is anomalous too. These three departments could, on this score, put forward a case to be recognised as 'centres of excellence'; but more of this later.

In general, then, size does a good but not perfect job in predicting whether a department will get a high reputation in its subject. Can it also explain the differences between subjects? The answer is not clear, but the hypothesis cannot be rejected out of hand. Of the departments under consideration, LSE economics is pre-eminent in reputation – and also in size with its thirteen professors, seven readers and thirty lecturers. The best that politics can offer is Oxford with two professors, three readers and thirty-six lecturers. And the best that sociology can offer is the thirty-one staff at Essex, which is very short of senior posts by LSE standards. More generally, we find that sociology departments are on average considerably smaller than those in economics (averaging 14·5 staff per department compared with 14·1 in politics and 19·9 in economics), and that their variation around this mean is smaller too (the standard deviation is 5·1 for sociology departments and 7·7 for both economics and politics). There seems to be some evidence that sociology departments are much of a muchness, at least on the criterion of size.

When Halsey's respondents were reporting their views on the best departments in their subjects, they may have had a number of criteria in mind. They may have been judging them as teaching institutions at undergraduate level, as nurseries for future academics, as producers of research and innovation, or more probably in varying mixtures of all three.

All are no doubt important for the development of a discipline, but it may be interesting to concentrate more specifically on the third. It is by our production of research and new ideas that we and our subject will probably be judged by later generations.

A source which we can utilise on this is a survey of British sociologists carried out by Ricca Edmondson, who wished to discover what sociologists actually regarded as competent explanations and to study the characteristics of those texts. In 1973 she wrote to a random sample of half the British Sociological Association, asking respondents to name 'at least three sociological works containing explanations which you regard highly'.[5] It was her view that this type of question might lead sociologists to *demonstrate* what tasks they took to be explanatory. Although the term 'explanation' is controversial in sociology, it is reasonable to assume that there are some sort of guiding interests behind sociological activities over and above the collection of descriptions. This negative content was, provisionally, the chief one that Edmondson gave to the term 'explanatory'. She also took it that it is sometimes productive to investigate sociologists' conceptions of these guiding interests by indirect rather than direct questioning.[6] We cannot expect people always to reflect fully when producing accounts of their interests and activities, but we might hope to reach some conclusions by considering *examples* of the works that they themselves regard highly.

According to this notion of example, concrete texts can be seen as models for dealing with specific areas and can be taken to represent diverse professional habits and attitudes of mind. They may function as embodiments of opinion and practice in the area in question, and an initial interpretation of 'explaining' within a given area might be based on whatever practices the leading examples in that area deploy.[7]

The response to Edmondson's survey was interesting and mixed.[8] Some respondents expressed bafflement, or objected to the question; others replied with enthusiasm and in detail, taking great trouble to say why they had chosen particular works. A total of 170 respondents between them provided titles of 340 sociological works, of which only 88 were mentioned more than once. Some gave quite long lists of titles, but we shall in this analysis restrict each respondent to the first three on his or her list. This reduces the total number of titles to 280, of which 76 were mentioned more than once. Table 3.3 gives the distribution of the most frequently cited works.

Immediately striking here is that while the classics head the list, their total number of citations is relatively small. (Incidentally, Marx received a total of 13 mentions, although no single work of his gets into the top group.) Even if we count all prewar writing as 'classical', thus including early Parsons and Evans-Pritchard as well as Mead, W. I. Thomas, Mauss and Michels, their total citations come to only 85 out of a total of 486. Among contemporary (that is, postwar) books the American just have the lead over

Table 3.3   *Works Containing Highly Regarded Explanations (the 1973 survey)*

	times mentioned
E. Durkheim, *Suicide*	21
M. Weber, *The Protestant Ethic and the Spirit of Capitalism*	18
J. H. Goldthorpe et al., *The Affluent Worker* series	9
D. Lockwood, *The Blackcoated Worker*	9
T. Burns and G. M. Stalker, *The Management of Innovation*	9
E. Bott, *Family and Social Network*	9
Barrington Moore, *Social Origins of Dictatorship and Democracy*	8
W. G. Runciman, *Relative Deprivation and Social Justice*	8
P. Berger and T. Luckmann, *The Social Construction of Reality*	8
J. Woodward, *Industrial Organization: Theory and Practice*	6
J. Banks, *Prosperity and Parenthood*	6
H. Becker, *Outsiders*	6
J. Rex and R. Moore, *Race, Community and Conflict*	6
E. Goffman, *Asylums*	5
C. Lacey, *Hightown Grammar*	5
M. F. D. Young, *Knowledge and Control*	5

the British by 191 to 188, but trans-Atlantic influence on British sociology is shown much more clearly by the way in which the American contribution dwarfs the continental European one – contemporary continental works elicited a meagre 17 citations.

Among the British works one feature stands out above all others. When the British sociologist thinks of an indigenous work containing an explanation which he regards highly, he thinks of a monograph, empirical but not in a stereotypically positivist sense. *The Blackcoated Worker, The Affluent Worker, Family and Social Network, The Management of Innovation, Relative Deprivation and Social Justice* – these are the British classics from the 1950s and 1960s. No doubt this tells us something about what sociologists mean by an explanation. Partly, too, it reflects the kind of work that was actually being carried out in Britain over this period. The British books provide an interesting contrast with the top works from the American list – *The Social Construction of Reality, Outsiders* and *Asylums* – works of predominantly interpretive cast, again no doubt reflecting the fact that in the 1950s and 1960s one had to turn to America to find good examples of this genre. But this also contrasts with the frequently asserted identification of an American with a positivistic influence on British sociology.

Another feature of the British list is the dominance of the research team. *The Affluent Worker, The Management of Innovation, Family and Social Network, Industrial Organization, Race, Community and Conflict* were all the products of collaborative research. It would perhaps be an exaggeration to say that this is another victory for the big battalions, but it seems a fair point that the kind of empirical work which the British sociologist typically respects requires greater resources than those available to the lone scholar.

Let us now move on to allocate these British works and authors to departments – to the departments, in so far as we can discover them, where the authors were working at the time their books were written. In many cases, but not all, prefaces and introductions indicate where the major part of the research and writing was done. Difficulties arise for us if an author moved in mid-project, as Woodward moved from South East Essex to Imperial College and Rex from Birmingham to Durham. Also, doctoral theses are often written at one university but turned into books at another. In these cases we attributed the work to the former university on the grounds that it had generated the basic research.

The results of this analysis are striking. Only five institutions are allocated more than five cited works each. They are the LSE with 18 works, Oxford with 14 works, Cambridge and Manchester both with 8 works and the Tavistock Institute of Human Relations with 5.[9] The similarity between this rank-ordering and that in Table 3.1 is uncanny, the only missing department being Essex – and this omission may merely reflect the fact that it has not been in existence so long as the others.

There are, however, some surprising aspects of the list. The presence of the Tavistock Institute is certainly one. But apart from Bott's famous study, Murray Parkes's classic on bereavement, Rice on the Glacier project, Trist on organisational choice and even some of R. D. Laing's work must be credited to the Tavi. The record of the LSE also has its surprises. An extraordinary proportion of its cited authors did their cited work there as graduate students; Joe and Olive Banks, Bernstein, Downes, Lockwood, MacDonald, Nelson and Bryan Wilson all did major work there as graduates. This may help us understand the discrepancies between Tables 3.1 and 3.2. The size of a department's graduate school may be as important for its reputation as its number of lecturers.

We may also legitimately wonder how Oxford and Cambridge managed to amass so many cited authors despite their relatively brief existence and small numbers. The names of Bryan Wilson and Alan Fox, John Goldthorpe and Tony Giddens are familiar enough as Oxbridge residents, but where do the others come from? The answer tells us something about the nature and the contribution which the ancient universities have made. At Oxford, for example, there were major figures such as the anthropologist Evans-Pritchard and the historian Keith Thomas, author of *Religion and the Decline of Magic*, whose work is, justifiably in our view, quoted as containing sociological explanations; Nuffield College gave a home to George Bain and Robin Blackburn as research fellows while they were doing their cited work; marginal institutions like the Delegacies for Extra Mural Studies and for Education provided employment for Margaret Stacey and D. F. Swift. In this way a large, diffuse and well-endowed university can provide resources for sociological work despite the absence of any formal, institutional blessing for the subject. It is again not the number of official lecturers in sociology but the total number of staff, research students, research fellows and non-sociologists engaged in sociological writing that matters.

Where does this leave our discussion of university departments and the development of sociology? We have seen a clear association between the size of a department and its reputation, and an even clearer association between reputation and the number of cited works produced. There are a variety of possible theories which might account for these findings. We might postulate that academic achievement, like many other kinds, is largely unpredictable and can as well arise in a small and isolated institution as in a large and vigorous one. This would still suggest that big departments will produce more 'great works' simply because they contain more people, but any given individual in a big department is no more likely to produce such a work than is any one individual in a small department. It is a quite different hypothesis from that of economies of scale, which suggests that large departments may give more scope for specialisation, fruitful collaboration, or aggressive competition, and thus stimulate their members to produce more and better work than they might elsewhere. Finally, to account for deviations from the size hypotheses, we might argue that there are centres of excellence which, because of the privileges or the intellectual milieux which they offer, are unusually good at attracting or producing distinguished workers.

The first of these hypotheses would predict a linear relationship between departmental size and reputation. The second would predict an exponential, or at least a non-linear relationship. And the third would predict no relationship or at least significant deviations from it.

At first glance there would seem to be some evidence for the third hypothesis: as we have already seen the LSE, Oxford and Cambridge all have higher reputations than their number of sociology teachers alone would predict and might wish to count themselves centres of excellence. And the second seems to have more support than the first: the proportions of the total votes cast in Halsey's ballot going to the large departments was much greater than the proportion of the total number of sociologists with posts in these departments. But the actual plausibility of the three hypotheses is, we would maintain, almost the exact opposite of this.

Consider the following points. If, as seems to be the case, when sociologists judge a department's reputation their main criterion is the research it has produced, we must take into account not only its current size but also its history. The older universities have clearly had more chance than the new to produce large quantities of sociological writing. In the case of Oxford and Cambridge, moreover, with their well-endowed colleges and other institutions, we cannot restrict ourselves to formal university appointments in sociology in our roll-call. The research fellows, research students, anthropologists and historians have also contributed to their universities' achievements.

Nor is the relationship between votes and size to be taken too seriously as support for the second hypothesis. True, the LSE gets 27 per cent of the votes whereas it certainly does not have 27 per cent of British sociology staff, even if we include past as well as present ones, but remember that Halsey's tables deal only with the distribution of 'first preference votes'. Suppose, for example, that all sociologists agreed that the LSE was *slightly* better than anywhere else. It would then collect 100 per cent of the votes, although by definition its standing would be only slightly higher than that of the second ranking university. The *difference* in the number of votes cast, therefore, cannot be taken as an index of the extent of its pre-eminence. In short, we have only an ordinal scale, not an interval one. A better index would be the number of cited works which a department can lay claim to, and this shows a distinctly less skewed distribution than does the number of votes.

So much for the negative points. On the positive side there is one more piece of evidence which we can bring forward. We find that departments like the LSE which have produced a large number of cited authors have by no means had a monopoly of the most-quoted works. Thus the top five departments in the 1973 survey (taken to be the LSE, Oxford, Cambridge, Manchester and the Tavistock) produced between them a total of 48 cited authors (out of a grand total of 88 cited British authors) and amassed a total of 103 citations (out of a total of 188 citations of British work in the survey). There were thus 2·15 citations per author from the top five departments and 2·12 per author from other departments – hardly a significant difference. This is certainly consistent with the theory of random achievement; it does not square so well with the other two.

We can now make a little more progress than this. In 1980 Dr Edmondson carried out a replication of her earlier survey, and the new results should provide some illumination.[10] If there really are centres of excellence, then they should dominate the new list as much as they did the old. The economies of scale argument should leave the largest departments clearly in command. And the random achievement hypothesis should lead to a greater diffusion of highly regarded books as the many newer departments in universities and polytechnics begin to produce such work.

Let us begin, however, with the most-cited works in the 1980 survey as listed in Table 3.4. It might have been anticipated that the kinds of works taken as authoritative or interesting by British sociologists would have changed fairly radically in the course of the last decade – a revival of interest in the classics, in Marxism and in continental European work might have been expected. But in fact, apart from a decline for the classics, the general character of the new list is surprisingly similar to the old. True, there are only six works common to the two lists, but the empirical monograph produced by the research team is again well represented. The style of

Table 3.4   *Works Containing Highly Regarded Explanations (the 1980 survey)*

	times mentioned
P. Willis, *Learning to Labour*	13
E. Durkheim, *Suicide*	8
J. H. Goldthorpe *et al.*, *The Affluent Worker* series	8
E. Goffman, *Asylums*	8
K. Marx, *Capital*	6
M. Weber, *The Protestant Ethic and the Spirit of Capitalism*	6
M. Weber, *Economy and Society*	5
H. Braverman, *Labour and Monopoly Capital*	5
G. Brown and T. Harris, *The Social Origins of Depression*	5
J. H. Goldthorpe, *Social Mobility and Class Structure*	5
J. Rex and R. Moore, *Race, Community and Conflict*	5
R. Dore, *British Factory – Japanese Factory*	5
Barrington Moore, *Social Origins of Dictatorship and Democracy*	4
D. Gallie, *In Search of the New Working Class*	4
A. H. Halsey *et al.*, *Origins and Destinations*	4
T. Johnson, *Professions and Power*	4
R. Sharp and H. Green, *Education and Social Control*	4
P. Townsend, *Poverty in the United Kingdom*	4

empirical research has not changed greatly either. *The Social Origins of Depression* is perhaps the most quantitative and positivist on the list (and is more 'scientific' in this sense than anything on the 1973 list), but it is balanced by new additions of a more radical or interpretive countenance than before. Diversity has perhaps increased, but classic British empiricism as exemplified by *British Factory – Japanese Factory* still predominates. Continuity rather than change prevails.

Of the main changes, perhaps the most interesting are the decline of the classics, now receiving only 43 citations out of a total of 431,[11] and of American sociology, now clearly lagging behind the British (by 136 citations to 215). Nor has continental Europe taken the place of either. It still receives only a meagre 24 citations. This might be taken to indicate that British sociology has at last reached maturity: its practitioners can now look to their own community for exemplars of the different styles of work and no longer need to look overseas. The most spectacular rise, for example, that of *Learning to Labour*, is of a work of interpretive methodology which had American but no British counterparts in the 1950s and 1960s.

When we turn to examine the departments which have generated the work cited in the 1980 survey, continuity again prevails over change. There are eight institutions which have produced more than five such works each: Oxford with fifteen, the LSE with eleven, Cambridge with ten, Manchester with nine, Essex with six and Warwick, Leicester and the

Tavistock Institute with five. The similarity to Tables 3.1 and 3.2 is again extraordinary; the biggest five are all on this list of 'top producers' as are all the top five by reputation.

The continued presence of Oxford and Cambridge at the head of the list gives some credence to the 'centre of excellence' hypothesis, but as before we must check how the two ancient universities have amassed their cited work. In the case of Cambridge writers like Maurice Dobb and Meyer Fortes have swollen the total, and at Oxford the psychologists Michael Argyle and Peter Marsh, Marxist literary critic Terry Eagleton and social historian Lawrence Stone (now at Princeton) do likewise.[12] Indeed, it is something of a paradox that the two universities which have perhaps been the most hostile to sociology have produced the largest number of non-sociologists whose works were cited in the two surveys. We do not venture an explanation for this, but it should remind us that sociology, perhaps more than most disciplines, is open to influence from others and that contributions to its development need not always be endogenous.

The economies of scale hypothesis does not receive great support either. True, the largest departments tend to head the list, but they are followed by a list of middle-sized departments with three or four cited works to their credit. It is not at all evident that the big departments produce more cited works per staff member than do the middle-sized ones. Indeed, the major change between the two surveys is the way in which the cited works have been diffused more evenly across the whole spectrum of departments (including those of the polytechnics which make a definite showing in the 1980 survey). Whereas in the 1973 survey the top five departments were credited 48 out of the total of 88 cited British authors, in the 1980 survey they only managed 39 out of the much larger total of 127 British authors. This is precisely what we would expect from our 'random achievement' hypothesis. We cannot deny that there may be some truth in the others, but their practical effects are likely to be small.

The weight of our evidence supports the hypothesis that academic achievement is unpredictable and can occur anywhere. This suggests, first, that the notion of 'centres of excellence' may have more to do with subjective preferences than with tangible achievements out of the ordinary. Secondly, our conclusion stands that in flat contradiction to much current planning in higher education which too uncritically attributes specifically academic virtues to tradition and size.

Notes: Chapter 3

We are very grateful to Professor Halsey for his help with this chapter and for his permission to use the results of the 1976 survey of university teachers, and also to all the members of the BSA who replied to Dr Edmondson's questionnaires.

1   Barnett House (now the Department of Social and Administrative Studies) dated from

1913 as a centre for discussion of the 'social question' out of which the honour school of PPE developed as well as an unbroken tradition of social work training.

2 The directorship of the Department of Social and Administrative Studies is a professorial appointment, now held by Professor A. H. Halsey. There is also a chair of social and political theory, once held by G. D. H. Cole, whose work contained important sociological components.

3 A number of sociologists at Cambridge, for example, are listed as lecturers in economics since they were originally appointed to teach sociology papers within the economics faculty.

4 A number of universities (Aston, Bath, City, East Anglia) had to be excluded from the analysis since they have combined departments which do not, at least in the *Commonwealth Universities Yearbook*, distinguish sociologists from economists or politics lecturers. The omission of research officers from the calculations was also because universities do not include them as a standard practice in the *Yearbook*.

5 Dr Edmondson wrote as follows:

> I am a sociologist working on problems of explanation in sociology, and since I do not want this work to be solely a piece of prescriptive philosophy, I need to know what sorts of explanation are highly regarded within the community of practising sociologists. For this reason, I should be grateful if you would help me compile a list of studies in which particular social phenomena can be regarded as explained, or in which there has been a contribution to an explanation. I am here using broad definitions both of 'sociology' and of 'explanation', and by 'studies' I mean anything in recorded form – books, articles, or whatever you may think apposite.

It should be made clear that our present use of the results of Dr Edmondson's survey is quite incidental to the original purpose of her study. A full treatment of the questions about sociologists' perceptions of explanation which the 1973 survey (and her 1980 re-study) raised will be given in her forthcoming book. See also her D.Phil. thesis 'Rhetoric and sociological explanation', Oxford University, 1979.

6 Direct questioning, even in terms of subtle and detailed questionnaires, seems to us liable to invite responses in terms of a conventional professional repertoire, not much more enlightening than the methodological writing already available elsewhere on this subject.

7 More complex methods would be needed to establish whether examples collected here are *authoritative* examples (an expression we prefer to the confused and mystifying 'paradigm'). Note, for example, that although we should expect to find several authoritative examples dealing with different aspects of a single discipline, it is not clear that in sociology we should interpret works from a given field as authoritative only for that field. As some responses showed, people may cite works in, say, the sociology of religion or tourism for their force (or potential force) in, say, the sociology of deviance or of the health services. This may be partly explicable by the fact that given social phenomena can appear in relatively diverse circumstances.

8 Questionnaires were originally sent to 390 people, of whom 23 had gone away, and a further 23 declined to be seen as competent experts in the field, leaving in effect 354 possible respondents. Of these 170 did furnish the titles of one or more sociological works. The low response rate was probably due, along with the usual problems of mailed questionnaires, to the fact that the BSA registers of members are revised only intermittently and the one available to Dr Edmondson at the time was somewhat out of date.

9 In assigning authors to departments, multi-authored works are given a score of 1 which is then divided equally between the collaborators if they belong to different universities or institutions. Rex and Moore, for example, bring half a point each to their respective departments for *Race, Community and Conflict*. Nor can Cambridge's high score be attributed to the fact that *The Affluent Worker* had four authors; for the purpose of the departmental analysis it counts only as a single 'author'.

10   In the 1980 re-study questionnaires were sent to a random sample of 420 members of the BSA, of whom 82 had gone away or declined to be seen as current practitioners in the field of sociology. A further 9 were unwilling to provide titles, but a total of 153 did respond and provide titles, giving a similar response rate to the 1973 survey. In view of the problems with the BSA register as a sampling frame, we did consider using an alternative such as the list of sociology lecturers contained in the *Commonwealth Universities Yearbook*. This has its problems too, but in any event we felt that, whatever the other costs involved, it was more important to maintain comparability between the two studies and use the same basis for sampling.

11   Given the terms of the question asked in the survey, it might still be the case that continental writers are highly regarded among British sociologists, but *ex hypothesi* for reasons unconnected with explanation in any sense of the term – for reasons, then, which in this chapter we have no evidence for describing.

12   Even if we exclude their historians, psychologists, and so on, Oxford and Cambridge still do somewhat better than their number of sociologists alone would predict, but the differences are much smaller – Oxford being reduced to nine cited works and Cambridge to six. The LSE also has markedly more cited works than its size alone would predict, but four of its ten cited works are pre-1960.

4

The Collapse of British Sociology?

PHILIP ABRAMS

If there were no difference between reality and appearance there would be no need for science. (K. Marx)

The evil that men do lives after them,
The good is oft interred with their bones. (W. Shakespeare)

The two quotations embody two distinct and equally plausible views (I shall call them 'the Marx theory' and 'the Shakespeare theory') as to why we might not unreasonably expect to see a withering away of sociology before too long. I shall come back to them. But they are far from exhausting the grounds on which it has become common of late to anticipate drastic erosions, if not the actual disintegration, of sociology as a distinct intellectual practice. Various scraps of hard evidence and a mass of rumour and gossip have been stirred together to produce a monstrous pudding of impending disaster. The problem for the sociologist interested in this particular collective phenomenon – 'the crisis for sociologists' as *New Society* has called it – is not so much to disentangle the evidence from the gossip as, having done that, to decide how much weight the gossip deserves.[1] And that is especially difficult because the gossip is of two quite distinct kinds. There are more or less sensational stories of institutional attrition (such as the Gould Report, and almost everyone else's tales of woe about what 'they' are doing to 'us'). And there is a prevailing mode of discourse devoted to the celebration of intellectual crisis – and the casual or reasoned identification of most other sociologists' work as part of the crisis. There is a supposed institutional crisis – whether induced from above or from below. And there is a supposed intellectual crisis – an occasion for best- selling books and the accepted frame for a great deal of talk about the condition of the discipline. The conflation of the two suppositions is the essence of the 'current demoralisation' to which Cohen and others have recently pointed.[2] In this chapter I shall try both to distinguish rumour from evidence and to distinguish the supposition of intellectual doom from the supposition of institutional doom. Making those separations seems to me to permit a certain optimism on some fronts as well as to justify considerable pessimism on others.

Certainly when, for example, the director of a polytechnic identifies an academic discipline as 'alchemy' and denies its 'suitability . . . as a vehicle for rigorous and disinterested intellectual training', when a High Court judge lambasts that same discipline as a 'nonsense' which has done 'much harm' to children, and when a minister for education has spoken of it as a 'mindless' enterprise providing no guidance, no standards, no discipline, practitioners of the discipline in question could be forgiven for feeling some qualms (whatever the facts about the intellectual condition of the director, the judge and the minister) about the security of their craft – not to mention their posts.[3] As they could when professors of sociology lend their authority to the view that the ranks of the profession are filled with public enemies and enemies of truth (Gould, 1977). And everyone seems to know (although it is never quite clear how) that the denunciations that surface in public are but the tip of an iceberg of mistrust and antipathy. The equation of sociology and subversion, or at best of sociology and uselessness, is rumoured to be a commonplace of the corridors of power. Strange tales reach the newspapers about high-level plans to confine the process of rationalising, and cutting, higher education to 'certain subjects' – two are named, and of course sociology is one.[4] Cuts are indeed imposed and although the process of decision-making is clouded in all its habitual evasions and strategic silences it is impossible not to notice that they have fallen disproportionately on sociology. For a subject to lose over 50 per cent of its opportunities for postgraduate research in the course of seven years is quite out of line with any normal conception of academic planning.[5] Then we observe the executive committee of the British Sociological Association sombrely debating what to do in response to 'the attack on sociology' – and finding it remarkably difficult to do anything except protest. Every colleague one meets seems to have some new horror story of the victimisation of sociology through frozen posts, rejected research, or devious backstage malignancy in this or that institution. Student numbers (undergraduates) fall or (postgraduates) are made to fall. The standards required of entering undergraduates are discreetly or immodestly lowered. Conferences of headteachers discover that sociology is not a subject. Employers in both government and industry speak of sociologists as unemployable; 'it is not clear that sociology graduates are the sort of people industry most needs' is one of the blander statements of an emerging orthodoxy (Abrams, forthcoming).

Meanwhile the intellectual life of the discipline, far from providing a secure and peaceful haven from such troubles, revolves in chaos. Factions flourish, enthusiastically proclaiming one another's sterility. Marxism, the most powerful single intellectual tendency of social analysis, appears to be both at the heart of sociology and implacably hostile to it – as well as being itself in alarming disarray.[6] The works that are hailed as important seem to be devoted to identifying actual or prospective intellectual bankruptcy. 'I've made Bernstein compulsory reading', one colleague assured me recently, 'he exposes the impossibility of sociology'. The commonest theme of book reviews in our professional journals, which in the 1950s used to be the lamentation of methodological incompetence (a curable disease of an essentially healthy body), now harps on the 'un-sociological' one-sidedness of work after work (this study has overlooked women; that piece of research is distorted by Marxist, or phenomenonological, bias; another is merely philosophy in disguise; above all theory and practice seem to dwell in 'separate realms' − a wholesale dismemberment of the body is proclaimed).[7] And eminent sociologists announce that their reflections have led them to a point at which sociology, as a distinct intellectual category, has no meaning for them − or at best, as Giddens somewhat opaquely puts it, only meanings which are 'not innocent' (Giddens, 1979, p. 8; and cf. Dawe, 1979). After two hundred years of false starts and flounderings at dead ends a thorough-going intellectual re-tooling is proposed. Of course, some people do go on quietly doing empirical social research but they, as Brecht might have put it, 'have simply not heard the terrible news'. That is not where sociologists say sociology is.

The question is, should we be worried by all this? In particular, do the small army of us who between 1956 and 1971 rushed or stumbled into (posts and careers in) sociology have any cause for concern in the face of the prevailing bad news of 1980? The 'school of '63' (as I shall call it for want of a better term) was given a virtually unique opportunity to help construct an academic discipline. Did it waste it as drastically as the virtually unique opprobrium that discipline enjoys today would suggest? If so, how? Or to put it another way: how much of the current 'crisis' is indicative of authentic institutional insecurity or intellectual inadequacy and how much is melodrama − froth whipped up perhaps from a few minor frustrations and a curious (but among academics not surprising) mixture of self-importance and self-doubt? Of course, the paranoid may really have enemies, but at least in this instance it seems desirable to know as far as possible just how the highly coloured tales told of and by the patient relate to the patient's actual condition. How far are we witnessing a drowning; how far is it only a wallowing? And if it is a drowning is it accident, suicide, or murder?

Two vexing difficulties face the would-be detective at the outset of the inquiry. On the institutional side most of the evidence is hopelessly circumstantial. On the intellectual side most of the witnesses are extraordinarily unreliable. In both respects the facts of the case prove highly elusive. And in both cases the elusiveness of relevant hard evidence seems to be rooted in a refusal of debate − a refusal forced on sociologists institutionally but apparently (and culpably) chosen by them intellectually.

The case of the proposal to close the Department of Sociology at North

East London Polytechnic is a good example of the institutional version of the problem. At first sight this venture looked as though it was going to provide one of the most clear-cut instances of the victimisation of sociology yet on record. Cuts, it was argued by those who urged the closure, were to be justified on 'educational grounds'. But no educational grounds relevant to, let alone justifying, the closure of the Department of Sociology were adduced when the proposal was made and the department itself was able to put up a strong case for the educational excellence of its work. The terms of debate were quickly redefined. It turned out that educational grounds did not mean educational standards and certainly not educational content, but some abstruse calculus of cost-effectiveness, staff/student ratios and projected market forces. The threat to the department was rapidly re-constituted as a matter of economic and administrative logic, innocent and value-free so far as any direct reference to the nature and content of any particular disciplines was concerned. That sort of discussion was simply taken off the agenda. The only people who were possibly making judgements about the contents of disciplines, it was argued, were the prospective students who were choosing not to study certain subjects – and since sociologists had created themselves academically on the back of student demand they could hardly now complain about suffering the consequences of a collapse of demand. At this sort of point the debate becomes very much more complicated and slippery precisely because substantive educational considerations have been eliminated. The sharpest and most legitimate grievances of the proposed victims turn out to be irrelevant; the alternatives available to them prove invidious (inflict the cuts on someone else) or fatuous (there should be no cuts). The staff and unions concerned have themselves to become engaged in refined, detailed and complex arguments about the economic management and administration of the institution as a whole; the discussion falls into the terms of reference chosen by, and most persuasive from the point of view of, those whose task and purpose it is to propose and implement cuts. The NELP case, as a matter of public record (hard evidence, that is), turns out not to be a case of 'the attack on sociology' at all. For whatever unfortunate reasons (probably of its own making), sociology has simply fallen foul of an ethically neutral administrative machine which is simply doing its proper work.[8] The general version of the position was very clearly put by Dr Rhodes Boyson to the delegation from the BSA that visited him early in 1980 in the hope of discussing the cutting of sociology: government as such neither has nor should have a policy towards specific disciplines in higher education (concretely, 'there's no secret file on sociology'); but it does have a duty, above all in difficult times, to impose financial restraints on the institutions of higher education; what institutions choose to do about particular disciplines within the limits of those restraints is of course entirely up to them.[9] It seemed that the BSA had taken its worries to the wrong place. Alternatively, the smoke-screen thickens, the wheel of responsible evasion turns, everyone is Pontius Pilate. There is a body on the floor, but no one has bloody fingers.

Even when relevant terms of argument are conceded, when an issue directly bearing on the standing, nature, achievements and prospects of the discipline is agreed to exist, it seems extraordinarily difficult actually to conduct the relevant argument with the relevant people. The recent dealings of the British Sociological Association with the Social Science Research Council provide an apt and important illustration of this second stage of elusiveness on institutional lines. Of course, the Association deals only with the Subject Committee not with the Council; it has in fact had progressively less and less contact with sociologists on the Council in recent years – indeed, there have been fewer and fewer such sociologists to have contact with. Up to the summer of 1979 the BSA executive committee appears to have taken the view that it would not help the Sociology and Social Administration Committee of the SSRC to administer the cuts the Council had charged it to inflict.[10] The task of the Association was seen, rather, as one of opposing the cuts root and branch and of trying to force a debate on the issue of the grounds on which sociology as a whole should or should not suffer cuts; of meticulously *not* becoming involved in any sort of collaboration with the SSRC in a hunt for suitable victims within the profession. By the spring of 1980, however, it seemed to have become clear both that the executive committee had been drawn into quite detailed discussions of where and how the cuts should fall among departments of sociology, and that in two major respects it had failed to obtain a debate on the appropriateness of the profession as a whole being a target for cuts.[11] The studentship cuts of 1979 were explained to the world by the chairman of the SSRC in terms of imbalances between postgraduate research and project research in the SSRC budget as compared with the budgets of other research councils; as the most imbalanced SSRC discipline sociology was logically a prime candidate for rationalisation.[12] In so far as this argument is not entirely formalistic and is meant to have some substance in terms of an idea of the proper organisation of research it obviously invites a debate centred on close comparison of the nature, needs, costs and uses of knowledge as between, say, sociology and physics, and involving detailed contrasts of both intellectual and organisational matters. It is obvious, too, that a very strong case could be made for the funding of social science research needing to take a form deliberately unlike that of natural science research on such grounds. It is no less obvious that attempts to draw those responsible for the cuts into a debate on such grounds (both by the BSA and by many individual sociologists and other social scientists) have been met by nothing better than icy silence or mere reiteration of the original formula.[13]

In much the same way the cuts of 1980 have been accounted for in terms of the general desirability of shifting resources within the social sciences away from relatively pure fields of inquiry towards relatively applied ones, from disciplines to vocations.[14] Since such a move cannot possibly be defended on grounds of standards or intrinsic intellectual content it is justified in terms of a presumption of the greater practical social value of applied research. Once again, the claim invites debate – especially as there is ample evidence from the natural sciences to suggest that pure or discipline research is in the medium term actually a good deal more productive (even in the sense of producing useful consumer durables) than vocation- or user-oriented research. Once again sociologists would have had a good case for preferential research funding as against, say, students of management or education. And once again the debate has simply not happened in the relevant quarters. The awkward questions are met with silence or discussion of other matters. And a peculiarly baffling further difficulty for the BSA executive committee in all this has been that as its links with SSRC are restricted to the Subject Committee it finds itself talking only to representatives of the policies it deplores who readily agree with it that those policies are deplorable. The contact it has been allowed to have with the SSRC has had the, no doubt unintended, effect of actually blanketing articulation of the issues it would most want to discuss.

All that this really amounts to is the observation that the institutional destiny of sociology is a political matter embedded in a field of power and that the structuring of debate and the art of silence are two of the essential resources of political power. The observation would be trite and unnecessary were it not for the fact that a number of people who are involved in administering the institutional erosion of sociology have indicated that they would resign the task at once if it ever became clear that what they were doing was political rather than administrative or academic. The whole point is that that is just what will never become clear – and that its failure to become clear simply cannot be treated as reliable evidence of the non-political nature of what is going on. A few zealots will write to newspapers urging the suppression of sociology because they dislike socialism, criticism, or independent thought. Many more will let it be known in private conversation that they 'know' that 'sociologists are all reds' or that 'all this research from the criminals' point of view' ought to be stopped. But political practice, including the practice of silence, is far too sophisticated nowadays for any of this ever to get attached to the sort of policy proposals and decisions which, as it were, just happen to have the effect of progressively undermining the institutional basis of sociology as an autonomous discipline.

Meanwhile the refusal of debate on institutional matters is matched by a possibly even more worrying reticence on certain intellectual questions. What I have in mind here is the tendency for sociologists to treat the difficulties that afflict them, and indeed the difficulties of higher education, research and intellectual life in general, as essentially domestic issues; as indicating the private troubles of sociologists rather than the public issues of a society. The propensity is to turn inwards towards the (epistemological, theoretical, conceptual, or whatever) forms and sources of the crisis *in* sociology, rather than outwards to the substantive relationships between sociology and a larger world and the crisis *for* sociology generated there. Stan Cohen raised the issue sharply when in a discussion of the cuts and their consequences he noted the 'depressing . . . absence, among what are supposed to be the most self-reflective groups in our culture, of genuine theory or even informed debate about the wider implications of all this'.[15] But perhaps it is just that we are *too* self-reflective? Perhaps the new subjectivist sociologies have made us too quick to see ourselves in the social, blinding us a little to society. Whatever the reason it is plainly odd and unprofessional of us as sociologists to behave so much in the manner of laypersons in privatising public matters, in avidly debating the troubles of sociology ('the theory-mongers now rule', and so forth) and so largely declining to debate, or even to explore, the sociological connections between those troubles and the non-sociological world in which they exist. Our own introspection echoes the silence of the politicians.

Notwithstanding the difficulties of obtaining firm evidence on the context and bases of institutional erosion, and notwithstanding the cuts that have already been made or that may occur in the next few years, my own feeling is that there is little reason to fear a major institutional dissolution of sociology. It is not just that academic institutions have a certain toughness. Rather, the refusal of debate actually works two ways; if it inhibits relevant protest from victims it also inhibits a good deal of direct onslaught on the part of those who might like to be persecutors. The attack, if one is to be made at all, has to work through general criteria of academic planning – such as the fetishism of staff/student ratios – and while such criteria will probably not leave us as well fed as we were in 1970 it is hardly likely that they will lead us to starvation either. Although the SSRC massacre of postgraduate studentships was both vicious and misguided, there is in fact still plenty of research money around – the SSRC now provides only 11 per cent of the funding for social science research after all – and sponsors who are willing to grant researchers ample autonomy. And there are plenty of prospective undergraduates of reasonable calibre coming forward – enough probably to mean that the adverse staff/student ratios sociologists have lived with for years will settle down a good deal closer to UGC norms but hardly below them. Our very success in getting sociology established in schools is bound to mean some falling-off in the number of those seeking to discover sociology in higher education – already by 1976, 100,000 people had A levels in sociology. And although it is a slow business surrounded by a great deal of noisy scepticism sociologists *are* steadily finding employment in the research establishments of national and local government; even our worst graduates do not seem to be more of a drag on the market than the worst graduates of other disciplines; and on the whole we seem to have fewer really bad graduates than many disciplines. From all this I conclude that if serious institutional attrition occurs it will be because actively or passively we have contrived to give the enemies of sociology weapons they do not at the moment possess. In other words the intellectual condition of sociology and our response to it seem to me to hold the key to the institutional future of sociology. The crucial issue is whether we choose to cultivate the crisis in sociology or to direct sociology, as authoritatively as possible, to the crises of society. I want to suggest that it is time to move away from the morose inner dialogue of sociology that has occupied so much energy and attention in recent years and try to engage in a somewhat aggressive public dialogue instead. The recipe is easy enough but unfortunately it does involve knowing the answers to some rather awkward questions about who and what we think sociology is for.

The main thing to understand, and perhaps understanding it is the main advance sociology has made in the last hundred years, is that we cannot expect many friends in high places. The principal reason sociological work needs to be authoritative, disciplined, scholarly, and so forth is precisely because it is unlikely to be popular. Once the allegations of 'sentimental Marxism' – or whatever – have died away the work needs to impress. The striking difference between the sort of agenda one might write for sociology today and the agendas people like Booth wrote in the 1880s is that ours has to recognise sociology as a *polemical* enterprise. In many other respects they might be remarkably similar. Above all, the sense of helplessness which Booth found to be the motivational source of sociology is still plainly in evidence (1887, pp. 326–7)

> It is the sense of helplessness that tries everyone; the wage earners . . . are helpless to regulate or obtain the value of their work; the manufacturer or dealer can only work within the limits of competition; the rich are helpless to relieve want without stimulating its sources; the legislature is helpless because the limits of successful intervention by change of law are closely circumscribed. To relieve this sense of helplessness the problems of human life must be better stated. We need to begin with a true picture of the modern industrial organism, the interchange of service, the exercise of faculty, the demands and satisfaction of desire.

What we have learned since the time of Booth is that our helplessness is in some senses even deeper than he imagined; we have learned that the best pictures we can paint of the industrial organism and so forth are most unlikely to be seen as true pictures; that the whole question of the nature of the truth of the organism is contested far beyond the level of fact at which people like Booth hoped to display truth. And in painfully, but rightly, dismantling that sort of positivism we have made life very much more difficult for ourselves. I have not come across a single professional sociologist in Britain who now believes in the sort of direct relationship between knowledge and action which inspired the monumental labours of

Booth as a serious possibility of our own contemporary social order.[16] And I would suggest that in so far as sociology has a crisis to face it lies precisely in our failure to work out a relationship between ourselves and the domain of public action which could satisfactorily replace the lost innocence of positivism. As I read the recent history of British sociology it has left us curiously disqualified to do that: the residual expectation of straightforward usefulness (sociology in the manner of the Webbs) is too strong; the institutional fabric of merely professional or academic sociology (sociology California-style) is too thin; our domestic intellectual conflicts are too wide-ranging and rancorous. Nevertheless, there are also certain resources. We are slowly, and notwithstanding the devotees of 'policy science', outgrowing our traditional attachment to usefulness and naively true pictures. We have a substantial reserve of professional self-confidence rooted in a substantial body of very respectable work – we have actually accumulated a great deal more defensible sociological knowledge than we give ourselves credit for. And our domestic conflicts are in some valuable ways sources of energy – and in any event no more searing or immobilising than those the Anglican Church or the Labour Party have in their time survived.

The analogy with theology should be taken seriously; not because sociology is a matter of faith but because, like theology, it has to be an *argumentative* discipline. Once it is realised that the truth of true pictures does not change the world, the sociologist is either a dilettante, a pedant, or a polemicist. Theology provides one among a number of highly respectable precedents for embracing the role of polemicist. The question is not whether an argumentative academic discipline is or is not intrinsically credible but which arguments we wish to pursue and with whom. For a number of reasons the 'school of '63' never got round to thinking about that question with the sort of concentration that has marked the history of more successful disciplines, however. I would single out two reasons in particular: the sheer rate of growth of sociology once the brakes imposed by the UGC were released and until the supply of cash and new students began to dry up around 1970; and the Marxist intrusion. The first made us indiscriminate, the second provided a focus of attention but one that proved a blinding distraction rather than a helpful point of concentration. The days of growth implanted a sense of not needing to decide issues of the nature and direction of sociology, a Wordsworthian youthfulness, and the Marxist intrusion forced those issues on us in a way which stripped us of our capacity to deal with them, plunged us suddenly into a dismally Wordsworthian maturity. My suggestion would be that as a result (or at least in large measure as a result) of these two experiences we have lost sight of certain defining properties of any essentially argumentative discipline and that in turn much of our chronic sense of crisis springs from that oversight rather than from more serious inadequacies or failures.

The rate of growth up until 1970 was of course phenomenal. Abbott

(1969) has calculated a 450 per cent increase in the output of sociology graduates between 1952 and 1966. And her total of 724 graduating students in 1966 had increased again to 1,768 by 1971 (Smith, 1975). Nor was it wholly unrealistic for proportions of around a third of those graduates year after year to expect and plan 'academic' careers for themselves; or for those who got on to the academic career ladder early enough to climb it with dazzling speed; twenty-eight new departments and thirty new chairs were created within a decade; as soon as the universities were saturated, polytechnics, further education colleges and schools opened up; lagging a little but then expanding almost as rapidly came research posts (but not careers) in both local and central government (Smith, 1975, p. 312; and cf. BSA, 1970). The BSA, which began life as a more or less private LSE salon, found its membership doubling every two or three years. Major publishing houses established sociology lists and went cap in hand round the new academics begging for titles.

Plainly such a rate of growth could not be sustained; a ceiling was bound to be reached; those who had come to take that sort of expansion for granted were bound to suffer a crisis of frustrated expectations. However, it is not the 'J-curve', relative deprivation, effect on its own that is important. Rather, I would stress two tendencies within the years of growth which combined to make the J-curve problem peculiarly acute when it finally arrived. I refer to the combination of intellectual eclecticism and technique-oriented professionalism which in my view provided the hallmark of the school of '63 and the patterns of sociological expansion with which it was associated.[17] On the one hand so many doors were open, sociology was so much in demand – and such an unknown quantity – so many talented young people were coming forward, that the new sociologists were to a quite remarkable degree left free to define sociology in any way they chose. On the other hand, though, the feeling that it hardly mattered what one did was balanced by a firm demand that one should do it well: for want of substance the discipline was defined on the basis of method – or rather, not on the basis of commitment to any particular sort of method, but in terms of the idea of standards of method. The SSRC in its early years provided a very striking illustration of both tendencies: on the one hand the Council – and perhaps most of all the Sociology and Social Administration Committee – was to be responsive, not directive, in supporting research, to accept its sense of worthwhile inquiry from the academic community at large; on the other hand this substantive permissiveness was counterbalanced by what it was hoped would be rigorous attention to methodology and a sustained drive to raise technical standards.

The pattern was nicely matched among sociologists in general by a simultaneous explosion of populism and professionalism: populism taking the form of a courting of lay audiences on a more or less indiscriminate basis by way of a shameless readiness to diagnose and prescribe for virtually every problem of the day; professionalism taking the form of an increasingly self-conscious effort to dissociate real sociology from the more spectacular embarrassments of populism by way of an adulation of technique. If the inner history of the BSA were ever written it would be seen that the years from 1960 to about 1966 were dominated by this latter development: the organising of a programme of method-oriented graduate summer schools; the founding of a Teachers' Section of the Association, the launching of the avowedly professional journal *Sociology*, the effort to formulate a code of professional ethics. By the end of 1966 the BSA executive committee reported itself 'concerned that the increasing popularity and the growing numbers of practising sociologists in this country should not proceed unaccompanied by questions about the professional standards of those involved' (BSA, 1967; Banks, 1967). And Alan Dawe was to put the general dilemma produced by the twin tides of populism and professionalism very nicely at about the same time: 'In the public mind', he wrote, 'sociology covers virtually any type of social comment and enquiry. Just about the only thing that does not count is the genuine article.' The danger as he saw it was that 'the producers and consumers of popular sociology will be allowed to determine the purposes and strategies of sociology for the profession', that the subject would become 'imprisoned in its sudden popularity'.

The great threat as Dawe and others understood it was to the 'autonomy' of the discipline; and for many of the more determined advocates of professionalisation the way to ensure autonomy was plain; there had to be a drastic technical up-grading to separate the real sociologists from mere pundits, pop sociologists and, as Banks was to call them, 'romantic dilettantes'. Dawe himself called for 'some agonising reappraisals' of standards of work and of the criteria of technical competence used in making grants and appointments in sociology. Graduate training he found 'grossly inadequate for a developing science' (Dawe, 1967). And in the same vein the BSA executive proposed that 'high levels of technical competence . . . should be obligatory on all who practise in this field' (BSA, 1967). On all sides in fact those who sought to create a profession and a discipline of sociology in Britain came to focus their concern on the issue of method and technique. The plea, typically, was for 'a recognition of intensive methodological training as being a first essential in the education of sociologists'; and equally, for 'the refinement of mathematical techniques in sociology' as somehow in themselves capable of constituting the discipline, of revealing and identifying 'the genuine article'.

I do not want to suggest that the demand for improved method was wholly inappropriate – especially as it is arguable that the theoretical and substantive diversities of sociology are such that standards of method are the only thing sociologists could hope to have in common. Nor would I argue that the call for technical up-grading was ever all there was to the movement for professionalisation – Dawe, for example, was quite clear that the menace of a brand of popularisation in which 'anything went' would not be met simply by insisting on higher standards of method within the profession and that there would also have to be, as he put it, more immediate 'correctives, books which demonstrate to a wide lay audience what sociology is really about' (Dawe, 1967). Yet I am fairly confident that the stress on method was the core of the effort to professionalise sociology – perhaps just because it was not at all clear what else one could possibly identify as 'what sociology is really about' on any general basis. And I suspect that this enthusiasm and emphasis itself drew fire from lurking embers of an older positivist expectation about the possibility of definitive social knowledge. Be that as it may, the move was at once academically respectable and politically uncontentious; it provided a standing excuse for the failure of earlier, less professionalised, sociological ventures to serve up the sorts of reliable knowledge various publics had expected; and it shelved potentially explosive questions, which some sociologists and many non-sociologists throughout the 1960s nevertheless went on asking, about what sociology was and what it was for.[18]

The rate of growth of sociology in this period thus contrived to foster an academic sociology anxious to dissociate itself from popular sociology on the basis of method. For a short while, indeed, it looked as though academic sociology might succumb as thoroughly to the 'misconception of technique' as academic psychology had already done.[19] It was largely the Marxist intrusion that saved it from that fate. The postwar history of sociology had of course run parallel with the history of British Marxism for some time. The popularity of sociology and the explosion of quasi-sociological works addressed to lay audiences in the decade on either side of 1960 had a great deal to do with a series of authentic crises within the socialist movement which left large numbers of the most thoughtful socialists looking for new intellectual bearings. And because sociology was briefly so wide open it seemed not impossible that appropriate bearings might be found in some sort of sociology. The parallelism was turned into a convergence. The move towards professionalism on the strength of method was engulfed in a tide of new, substantive and much more exciting debates about just those theoretical, substantive and practical matters which professionalisation had held discreetly in check. John Rex, one of the favoured luminaries of the school of '63, had, in a work as emblematic of the school as any, called for a sociology of conflict, and whatever else it offered, Marxism was the only serious candidate so far as the theoretical frame and substantive content of such a sociology were concerned (Rex, 1961). The modest invitations of Rex, Bottomore and others for Marxism to be taken more seriously by sociologists received an avalanche of acceptances. Yet the acceptances were from the first noticeably ambiguous. Marxism, itself proliferating into many modes, became a dominant mode of sociological theory. But it was not at all clear what the relationship between Marxism as a theoretical and political practice and sociology as a theoretical and political practice was – in large part because the professionalisers of sociology had so carefully left those matters vague. For some, sociology seemed to be a field to be conquered by Marxism; for others it came to be seen as an alien mode of social analysis to be eschewed and contested; to yet others it was an enterprise with which some sorts of qualified collaboration were possible.[20] But on whatever basis, the ascendancy of an a-theoretical, or at least theoretically reticent, professionalism was rapidly, even if in turn quite briefly, displaced by that of a compelling entanglement with theoretical (and substantive) issues defined very largely in terms of the concerns of Marxism. The ambiguity of the relationship was such that by 1978 one observer could see sociology as a profession entirely staffed by Marxists all entirely devoted to proving that sociology was a form of bourgeois ideology – an army consisting only of a fifth column, as it were.

I am not concerned here with the substantive analytical merits of Marxism, in any of its forms. For myself I have always found it the most compelling single intellectual tradition within the corpus of resources available to Western social analysis. But whatever its merits, the effect of the Marxist intrusion on academic sociology in Britain (a relatively minor matter but one that happens to be my concern in this chapter) was, given the already established effects of very rapid growth, profoundly disconcerting and distracting. The intrusion was itself remarkably rapid and comprehensive. It is difficult now to appreciate just how remote from one another sociology and Marxism were until the 1960s. In effect they occupied separate worlds. In Ginsberg's two volumes of sociological essays (which in 1960 were still prominent in a very short list of British works from which one could hope to learn in general terms what sociology 'really' was) Marx, K., enjoys only two index references; and in both cases the reference is to the author of a discredited theory of stages of social evolution (Ginsberg, 1956). In 1953 W. J. H. Sprott in another widely recommended work, *Science and Social Action*, was still treating Marxism as significant for sociology only as an example of the sort of 'grand manner' evolutionary philosophies of history from which sociology had arisen by reaction (Sprott, 1954). Although Sprott seized on the notion of contradiction as the analytical crux of a possible Marxist sociology he did not find it necessary or appropriate to pursue the idea since Marxism was for him axiomatically a pre-scientific enterprise. The only Marxist text he discussed in any detail was Stalin's *Dialectical and Historical Materialism*. And in his textbook, *Sociology*, Sprott again managed to treat Marx and Marxism as essentially irrelevant to the enterprise (Sprott, 1949). Marx is mentioned in Sprott's chapter on social stratification – but only to establish the inadequacy of 'this simple scheme' (the point being made by showing that the percentage of income devoted to salaries had been increasing in postwar Britain relative to that devoted to wages). And in an equally representative work of the same period, *Testament for Social Science*, Barbara Wootton (1950) similarly found it adequate to discuss Marx exclusively in a chapter entitled 'Two blind alleys' – the other one was dependence on 'muddled biological analogies'. Against the background of this sort of principled but largely unconsidered separation of sociology from Marxism the appearance at the gates and within the doors of the discipline of Marxisms deploying sophisticated theory and armed with research of high methodological calibre had much the effect of the appearance of Attila on the frontiers of Rome. Panic, confusion and flight ensued. Esoteric religions (the transformation of sociology into linguistics) flourished. A few joined battle but most retreated to their private estates.

Metaphor aside, there plainly was a period when it would have been difficult to establish that British sociology was very much more than the academic wing of British Marxism. Of course there was a good deal of misrepresentation and fantasy involved – the coverage provided in the columns of *The Times* early in 1969 of the establishment of a 'sociological tripos' at Cambridge is a rich source of both – but any considered conspectus of the most evident thrust of sociological work and of the main burden of discussion among sociologists between 1970 and 1975 would have to conclude the the Marxist intrusion was our dominant reality. The interesting and important thing to note, however, is that that intrusion did not produce an institutional crisis of significant proportions. Despite a good deal of threatening noise, the attempt to de-institutionalise sociology has been and to my mind will continue to be a very minor affair. By contrast it did produce certain very obvious intellectual troubles. And those in turn could have institutional effects.

In a market society the tendency of those in power is to leave things to the market. If British sociology is seriously eroded institutionally it will be, I suggest, because British sociologists have colluded in eroding the market demand for their work. This is not to suggest that the market is a neutral arena or to deny the very real effects of knocking advertising and other 'unethical' forces in turning prospective consumers away from our wares. But it is to emphasise the need to be willing to enter the market with some sort of persuasive and positive account of what we have got to sell. And that in turn, to put a complex problem in its simplest possible terms, means finding a way of reconciling the sort of professionalism, a professionalism of method, which marked the first stage of the growth of contemporary British sociology, with a recognition of certain substantive intellectual necessities. The two most compelling of these would seem to be – now that the character of the second, and in quantitative terms perhaps the last, stage of the growth of contemporary British sociology is over – first, to find a way of living with Marxism as a cogent mode of social analysis within the academic establishment of a capitalist society, and secondly, within the same framework, to accept the unavoidably contestable and contested nature of all particular items of sociological knowledge – although not necessarily of the broad message of sociology in the round. I believe that that can be done, and a 'saleable' account of sociology accordingly worked out, on the basis of a certain kind of understanding both of sociology as an intrinsically argumentative discipline and more specifically of the sort of argument we, collectively, want the discipline to promote. My own suggestion, which I shall not elaborate here, is that the argument could best be about the social conditions for a rational humanism. Assuming the discipline, having absorbed professionalisation and Marxism, could mount some sort of sustained argument of that sort, I would think it inconceivable, at least in the medium term, that it would suffer either institutional or intellectual collapse in a society such as our own.

There are, however, two other ways in which sociology might be seen or encouraged to collapse and I would like to conclude this chapter by saying something about each of them. This brings me back to Shakespeare and to Marx. The 'Shakespeare theory' proposes a wastage of sociology based on the absorption of any valued work done by sociologists into the domain of commonsense or of some other discipline. In so far as the concepts, perceptions and findings of sociology are judged to be of interest or use they are appropriated by everyday discourse and to that extent lost as sociology. Moreover, in so far as sociology seeks to promote argument about society *in* society, sociologists can not only not legitimately complain about this appropriation of their tools and terms of art – they are doomed to work positively to achieve it. But in so far as they succeed, in so far as status and role and relative deprivation and a relational understanding of poverty and the sort of account of inequality developed by sociologists all become part of the common stock of social consciousness, what is left to be identified as distinctly sociological, as not just common sense, are precisely those achievements of sociology for which nobody else has any use. The discipline suffers from a process of selective perception in which its successes tend to be defined away from it – for example, as research on ageing, or education or industrial relations or poverty rather than as part of a corpus of sociology – leaving its failures, oddities and most introspective theoretical activities as an esoteric residuum to 'live after it' and effectively constitute sociology. Without too much exaggeration I think one can also discern some tendency in many quarters to assign research one dislikes to sociology while identifying welcome research simply as research (or even as psychology, industrial relations, anthropology, history, and so forth); here the term functions quite simply as a negative label. But short of that the suggestion that sociology as a discipline peculiarly addressed to society is bound to be in some degree self-liquidating does seem to have a certain force.

One of the principal difficulties facing any attempt to isolate the social impact of sociological knowledge is quite simply that there is typically no point or moment of impact; rather, there is a diffuse osmosis in which – to take the most striking example – research on the social determinants of educational achievement is filtered into policies designed to minimise educational selection in an extended political and social process from which the research as specific items of knowledge cannot be separated. And in the more usual instances the problem is even more acute because the way in which sociology has worked to change assumptions and perspectives does not include any requirement for the new assumptions and perspectives to be recognised as specifically sociological – on the contrary, the form of the argument is likely to have been a request to recognise facts, logic or reason, not sociology. We can hardly complain if, when such arguments succeed, we find that they are denied a specifically sociological identity. Any discipline that seeks to change lay consciousness rather than to dominate it on the basis of a monopoly of esoteric knowledge – in the manner of, say, physics – is doomed if it is at all successful to suffer a constant erosion of its distinctive intellectual territory. It is not so much that the good sociology does is interred with its bones as that it vanishes into the soil of conventional wisdom.

The argument implicit in my quotation from Marx is in effect a different and stronger version of the argument about self-liquidation. G. A. Cohen has developed the general point trenchantly in *Karl Marx's Theory of History*, emphasising that for Marx of course the redundancy of social science arrives only with the advent of socialism (Cohen, 1979, pp. 329–38).

> By unifying social theory and social practice, socialism suppresses social science. It makes intelligible in practice spheres of human conduct which had been intelligible only through theory. When social science is necessary men do not understand themselves . . . Capitalism is obscure. Only science can illuminate it. But in the bright light of socialism the torch of the specialised investigator is invisible.

But non-Marxists have also seen the special task of social science as one of illumination and of demystification and have assumed that that sort of process could be carried to a high pitch even within the world of capitalism. Granted that 'relations between human beings under socialism are transparent and intelligible' and again that 'socialism would render social science superfluous' since 'it has no function in a world which has abolished the discrepancy between the surface of things and their true character', a question has to arise as to whether that sort of superfluity could not also be achieved under other social conditions, say, those of capitalism. One could agree with Cohen that 'the true content of social interaction must be hidden for social science to assume a role' and that 'there is a gulf between appearance and reality only when the explanation of a state of affairs falsifies the description it is natural to give of it if one lacks the explanation' and concede that sociology has grown up on the basis of that gulf and on the attempt to bring to light the hidden content of social interaction, and *still* ask at what point we might expect the gulf to be bridged and at what point sociology in the sense of 'independent social theory' (as Cohen puts it) rather than 'data gathering and data processing' might put itself out of business by bringing the true content of interaction entirely into the open (Cohen, 1979, p. 336).

For Marxists, of course, the answer to such questions has to be that the moment of superfluity can only arrive with socialism; capitalism is necessarily a masked social order; efforts to unmask it either simply substitute alternative masks or they move towards socialism. But I am not sure that we can automatically accept that answer. Admittedly the history of British sociology as a body of independent social theory from Rex's *Key Problems* to Giddens's *Central Problems* can easily be read as a renewal and deepening of mystification. But there are other histories. The history of the empirical research on inequality, industrial relations, education, even race and gender carried out under the auspices of sociology over the same period is much more ambiguous – and could be read as a history of quite dramatic demystification.

My own view is that the dialectic of mystification and demystification is much more complex and persistent than Cohen's reading of Marx suggests, that what we have seen of experiments in socialism so far should not encourage confidence in the imminent redundancy of sociology but rather suggest that the struggle for demystification is likely to have to be renewed in new forms and contexts for some time to come. Sociologists are likely to find themselves sharing the fate of Sisyphus rather than that of Hercules – the great rock of mystification will roll downhill as fast as we push it up; no imminent heroic rest need be expected. As we put ourselves out of business by clarifying some forms of social interaction, we and others will continue to generate new darknesses which will need to be illuminated and seen through by sociologists. In sum, I am enough of an optimist to believe that even under socialism some mysteries will remain – at least under any of the forms of socialism likely to be established at an early date. And I am also enough of an optimist to believe that even under capitalism, perhaps especially under the confusions of 'late capitalism', some demystification can be achieved, some sociological work will prove definite and not need to be done again – in that sense there will be a continuous collapse of sociology as defined by its traditional tasks. But I am not enough of an optimist to see beyond that to a point where sociology as a whole will collapse because we all, hunters, fishers and critics alike, see the social world directly, as an unmasked reality.

The chronic 'crisis' of sociology thus seems to me to reflect the constant and progressive movement of the task of demystification: nothing deeper and nothing more indicative of intellectual superfluity.

Notes: Chapter 4

1 *New Society,* 24 January 1980, pp. 196–8.
2 S. Cohen, *New Society,* 24 January 1980, p. 196, and cf. P. Hamilton, *Times Higher Education Supplement,* 23 January 1980, and D. Walker, *THES,* 21 March 1980.

3   *Guardian*, 19 March 1976, 30 August and 5 September 1977; *Daily Telegraph*, 12 October 1978.
4   *Guardian*, 22 August 1979.
5   But compare the *Annual Reports* of the Social Science Research Council for 1973–4 and 1978–9 for evidence that it did nevertheless happen to sociology.
6   But unlike sociology, Marxism has flourished on its own disarray; cf. P. Anderson (1976 and 1980).
7   See, for example, P. Hamilton (1976 and 1980).
8   It is clear that an important moment in the eventual frustrating of the closure proposal was the ability of staff at NELP to secure a forum for discussion in which authentically academic, intellectual and educational issues were restored to the agenda. It is to be hoped that now that the immediate threat has receded the mass of documentation circulated privately about the NELP crisis will be made available for public use to supplement the patchy but dramatic record kept in the columns of the *Times Higher Education Supplement* through February and March 1980.
9   P. Abrams, J. Eldridge, A. Glasner and J. Wakeford visited Dr Boyson on behalf of the BSA on 18 March 1980.
10 British Sociological Association, minutes of an informal meeting with members of the SSRC Sociology and Social Administration Committee held on 6 July 1979. I am grateful to the BSA executive committee for permission to draw on their files.
11 British Sociological Association, minutes of an informal meeting with members of the SSRC Sociology and Social Administration Committee held on 11 January 1980. These minutes are reproduced in *Network* no. 17 (May 1980).
12 BSA, *Network*, no. 15 (September 1979); and see the correspondence and statements of M. V. Posner and others in *New Society*, 7–21 June 1979.
13 How does one 'reference' silence – except by saying that one has found nothing to which to refer?
14 *Times Higher Education Supplement*, 4 January 1980: a subtler version of the argument was put to the BSA executive committee by representatives of SSRC at the informal meeting held on 11 January 1980.
15 S. Cohen, *New Society*, 24 January 1980, p. 196.
16 During the academic year 1979–80 I interviewed a sample of fifty fairly senior British sociologists in connection with an SSRC-funded research project on 'the uses of sociology'; my sense of the collapse of Booth's sort of positivist utilitarianism is thus somewhat more than a casual observation.
17 On professionalism see the contribution by J. A. Barnes in this volume; on eclecticism consult any or all of the surveys of British sociology in this period conducted by M. Carter, A. Little, E. Krausz, J. Jackson, J. Banks, R. Kent, and the celebrations of 'diversity' in Berry (1974), Cuff *et al.* (1979) and Thompson and Tunstall (1971), or the many matching laments for lost cohesion of which Gouldner (1971) is merely the prime instance.
18 See, for example, the symposium 'Aspects of sociology' in *Encounter* (1970).
19 The 'misconception of technique' was of course originally discovered by F. R. Leavis in a quite different context. Its brief ascendancy in British sociology is perhaps symbolised by the first edition of S. Cotgrove, *The Science of Society* (1967), which for a few years dominated the education of students discovering sociology at A level.
20 The debate is particularly well presented and assessed by Therborn (1976) and by Shaw (1972 and 1974).

Part Two

**Sociological Knowledge:
Creation and Practice**

5

The Social Construction of 'Positivism' and Its Significance in British Sociology, 1950–80

JENNIFER PLATT

It has become one of the platitudes of sociological teaching and conversation in Britain that we have now passed through, or transcended, an earlier positivistic phase; the point of transition is generally taken to be around the late 1960s. The request for papers for the 1980 BSA conference was quite representative in offering as a topic 'Positivism and after', with the implication that we had had positivism but that it is now dead, although it is not yet clear what is to replace it. This chapter poses the question of whether this is a correct historical account, considers how prevalent it has become and what is meant by it, and discusses some of the implications.

As soon as the question is addressed as an empirical one, a serious difficulty arises: what is 'positivism'? It is not appropriate to lay down a correct definition of the term, since the use of the term is a part of the object of study; it has become relatively commonplace to observe that it is used in loose and varying senses and that Comte's positivism has no clear connection with the practices nowadays associated with the term (Bryant, 1975; Fletcher, 1971, pp. 816–23; Giedymin, 1975; Keat, 1980; Mennell, 1974, p. 37). The matter is therefore approached by analysing the definitions given in some major sociological and social-scientific sources which make extensive use of the term. (See Appendix for method.) The common themes which appear most frequently in such abstract definitions are these: (1) belief in the unity of science, the general applicability of natural scientific method; (2) assertion that knowledge can only be gained by observation, or through the senses, that only material things are real; (3) an emphasis on externals, and lack of interest in actors' meanings; (4) belief in the possibility of an a-theoretical observation language, and hence of empirical tests of theoretical propositions; (5) emphasis on the existence of, or need for, general laws and deductive theory.

There are some obvious problems in attempting to assess how far these principles have been followed in practice, not least in that those writing on specific topics do not usually overtly take up such generalised positions. Principle 1 is vacuous, since it implies the existence of a standardised and generally known method in the natural sciences. Principle 2 also raises problems. To make *any* use of externals, to treat *any* material things as real or the senses as the source of *any* knowledge are not sufficient to qualify as instances of it. At the level of practice, therefore, as distinct from programmatic statements, it would enable one to identify unequivocal non-positivism (*no* knowledge – claims grounded in observation, etc.) but not positivism. Principle 4 is unclear, since it is hard to tell whether non-acceptance of it implies rejection of the very idea of empirical research, or merely of the idea that fundamental positions, not just specific hypotheses, can be tested. The principles seem more relevant to abstract discussion than to sociological practice, where it is hard to see how they can be applied.

There is, however, another and perhaps more instructive way in which the question of what writers mean by 'positivism' may be approached, and that is by observing which works they categorise as positivistic. A fairly systematic search of works making considerable use of 'positivism' as a category reveals remarkable variation on this. At one end are what might be regarded as the historical purists, who list only Comte and those directly associated with his ideas, plus perhaps Durkheim; at the other end Filmer *et al.* (1972) include Popper, Durkheim, Lundberg, Homans, Mannheim and Wilkins, Parsons, Marx, Rex, Percy Cohen, Merton, all demography, all attitude researchers and the whole British empirical tradition.

The rationale of the historical purists is clear: they are including only those writers who themselves accepted the description, and thus using a narrow but historically meaningful category. Numbers of other writers concentrate on the philosophical authors, and are in fact concerned with the school of logical positivism; one may note that their degree of philosophical sophistication is shown by whether or not they count Popper as a member of the school. The difficulty here is in defining the applicability of their discussion to sociology, since they do not mention works by sociologists.

The next group is that which ascribes positivism to all modern sociology, or to the dominant tendencies within it, without more precise specification, or at any rate without specification of any empirical works or authors primarily known for them; the lack of precise reference makes this hard to discuss. Finally, there is the group which classifies very large bodies of identified work as positivist, although it is different work in different cases; very broadly, this group may be subdivided into those of Marxist and those of phenomenological or ethnomethodological tendency, each calling 'positivist' those works from which they wish to dissociate themselves (see Bryant, 1980; Cohen, 1980; Stockman, 1977). Both this and the previously described group are applying the category to authors who have not applied it to themselves, and classing together authors who often regarded themselves as differing sharply. The polemical functions of this are clear, but such polemical uses are not necessarily descriptively helpful or historically meaningful.[1] Nor, more immediately, are they of any use to someone who wishes to find a practical, consensual definition to use in some simple historical research, without advance commitment to one of the positions in controversy. Even if there were consensus on the general themes first quoted from abstract definitions, there is clearly no consensus on which works they are exemplified in.

It seems safer to fall back on more pragmatic and less tendentious criteria, even if they cannot be so easily documented. The decision was made, therefore, to use the vulgar criteria of sociological gossip and book review imputations, as experienced in the author's participant observation, for the practical purpose of counting instances. This should not be taken to beg the question of whether there is any necessary, or even contingent, connection between the practices thus labelled and the abstract philosophical principles; it is sufficient, for the purpose in hand, that there is commonly felt to be some. The eventual decision was to note the following features: (1) the extent to which quantitative data were presented (with extent ranked impressionistically as 0 = virtually none, 1 = slight, 2 = heavy); (2) whether mathematical models were employed; (3) whether the writer claimed to be testing one or more hypotheses – which was regarded as a minimum condition for subscription to norms of 'scientific method'; (4) what main types of data (survey, participant observation, official statistics . . .) were employed. The concrete historical question of the significance of 'positivism' in British sociology in the period 1950–80 has been addressed by attempting to look systematically at research, teaching and general books.

For research, the data considered are the articles published in the main British journals (*British Journal of Sociology*, *Sociological Review* and *Sociology*) since 1950. These data have their obvious limitations, in particular three: (1) much research is published in books rather than articles, (2) other journals are also relevant, and (3) not all research is published. The first point is important; books have not been systematically studied both because of the sheer magnitude of the task, and because their more complex structure and less standardised format makes their contents harder to categorise. In mitigation, it may be pointed out that much research which eventually appears in books is also published as articles. The most dangerous possibility is that article format constrains the presentation of material in ways relevant to the distinctions here being made; is 'journal article' as a genre inherently positivistic? On the second point, one may assert with some confidence that these three journals are generally recognised as the central distinctively sociological ones, and thus at least as in a meaningful sense representative of the mainstream; however, general knowledge suggests that there may have been an increasing tendency for sociologists, especially those who see themselves as less positivistic, to publish elsewhere. Both these points can only be borne in mind in interpretation. The third point would only be worrying if more or less positivistic work was less likely to get published, and there is no way of finding this out. However, the commitment implied by submission to these journals, and the recognition implied by acceptance for publication in them and thus entry into the corpus of publicly shared knowledge, are sufficient to give their contents a central significance even if they are not fully representative of the whole range of work being done.

Not all types of article could sensibly be analysed in the same way. The choice was made to focus on 'empirical' articles, defining 'empirical' very broadly, in order not to beg questions, as including any article whose central point appeared to be to assert something about the world. A sample was then taken of the 'empirical' articles by British-based authors in alternate years over the period 1950–79. (For details, see Appendix.)

Within this sample, then, the aim was to identify any trends with respect to 'positivistic' practice. In inspecting for trends it seems reasonable to summarise the material by decade, since the supposed trend away from positivism started in the late 1960s, and so might be expected to be showing itself clearly in the journals by the 1970s.

Table 5.1   *Quantification in Sample of Empirical Articles*

	1950s				1960s				1970s			
					Degree of quantification							
	0	1	2	N	0	1	2	N	0	1	2	N
British Journal of Sociology	17	4	10	31	15	4	13	32	14	2	9	25
Sociological Review	5	6	6	17	9	5	10	24	25	10	13	48
Sociology	—	—	—	—	1	1	4	6	13	3	16	32
All journals, percentages	46	21	33	48	40	16	44	62	50	14	36	105

What, then, does the sample show? In each decade between 40 per cent and 50 per cent of the total were non-quantitative and between a third and a half were heavily quantitative; the change appears to be negligible (see Table 5.1). Only two articles with mathematical models were found in the sample, both in the 1970s. There is a small but steady increase, rather than decline, in the proportions claiming to test hypotheses, from 13 per cent in the 1950s to 25 per cent in the 1970s (Table 5.2). Since many of the hypotheses tested were other people's, this could as plausibly be accounted for by the existence of a greater body of work by other people at later dates as by any change in methodological preferences; it could also reflect an increasing level of controversy.

The analysis of main data sources must be rather more complex, since it is not so obvious which it is conventional to count as positivistic. We shall

Table 5.2   *Numbers Claiming to Test a Hypothesis (sample of empirical articles)*

	1950s			1960s			1970s		
	Yes	No	N	Yes	No	N	Yes	No	N
British Journal of Sociology	4	27	31	7	25	32	7	18	25
Sociological Review	2	15	17	3	21	24	12	36	48
Sociology	—	—	—	2	4	6	7	25	32
All journals, percentages	13	87	48	19	81	62	25	75	105

take it, however, that postal questionnaires, surveys[2] and official statistics may be counted as positivist types of source, while fieldwork or participant observation, non-survey interviews, documents and diffuse general knowledge may be counted as non-positivist types of source. On that basis, in each decade the non-positivist sources predominated, although to a slightly lesser extent in the 1960s. This is as near as we come to a confirmation of the thesis that a dominant positivism has now retreated (Table 5.3).

Table 5.4 shows the proportions 'positivistic' or 'non-positivistic' on all three criteria simultaneously, and suggests two conclusions: (1) there is no evidence for a non-trivial trend over time of the kind suggested, and (2) the existence of a clearly defined 'positivist' style is highly questionable.

The general conclusion must be that, as far as these data go, there is some limited evidence of a very slight increase in positivistic characteristics in the 1960s, falling away again in the 1970s; the evidence is quite inconsistent with a picture in which there was a solid dominance of positivism which was eroded in the 1960s and had been undermined by the 1970s.

Ideally it would be desirable to add some data on the extent to which teaching, as well as research, was positivistic over the period. Systematic data on this are harder to come by; available secondary or indirect sources are (1) published textbooks, (2) the list of details of then current courses on theory and methods compiled by Peel in 1968, and (3) the list of research methods syllabuses compiled by Wakeford in 1979. What, then, do these show?

There only appear to have been five general textbooks on research method published in Britain by British authors over the period: Madge (1953), Mann (1968), Stacey (1969), Ford (1975), Hughes (1976). There are immediately obvious differences between those before and after 1970. The earlier ones start with an account of 'scientific method', taken as a good thing, and then go straight on to such matters as data sources, questionnaires and interviewing. The later ones, although they cover many of the same topics, are actively concerned with epistemological issues, and make it clear that there are alternatives and choices to be made. Although they are, in my judgement, much more difficult than the earlier ones, they claim equally to be addressed to undergraduates and beginners; clearly

Table 5.3   *Main Data Sources (in sample of empirical articles)**

	Questionnaire	Survey	Official statistics	Fieldwork, participant observation	General Interviews	Documents	Knowledge
1950s							
British Journal of Sociology	—	9	3	—	2	15	3
Sociological Review	2	1	2	—	4	10	2
All journals	2	10	5	—	6	25	5
1960s							
British Journal of Sociology	2	7	4	3	3	10	4
Sociological Review	3	9	2	4	1	5	2
Sociology	—	3	1	2	—	—	—
All journals	5	19	7	9	4	15	6
1970s							
British Journal of Sociology	2	2	4	3	2	10	4
Sociological Review	4	8	3	12	8	16	3
Sociology	3	7	3	5	8	7	3
All journals	9	17	10	20	18	33	10

* Where there was more than one main data source, each was counted.

Table 5.4   *Proportions of Articles which Were by All Three Criteria ...* *

	Positivistic	Non-positivistic	N
1950s	2%	35%	49
1960s	11%	31%	61
1970s	13%	40%	104

* Only one data source was counted for each article.

there is no longer felt to be a simple orthodoxy to transmit, even to novices (see Perrucci, 1980).

Actual teaching, of course, did not draw only on British books, or only on textbooks from among British books. Something about the content of courses may be gleaned from the collections of syllabuses, even though the data are crude. A very rough analysis shows that: (1) 'scientific method' was more often taught uncritically in 1968 (27 per cent to 8 per cent) and more often not taught at all in 1979 (62 per cent to 42 per cent); that is, at the later period it was covered less often, but when treated was more frequently taken critically; (2) the research methods taught were more often predominantly survey techniques in 1968 (38 per cent to 3 per cent); (3) the possibility of epistemological alternatives was much more often taken seriously in 1979 (54 per cent to 12 per cent). These findings certainly fit into the picture of a tendency away from 'positivism' in the teaching of research methods. It should also be noted, as perhaps the most striking change, that in 1968 not one of the courses used the category 'positivism' to describe or organise its material, while in 1979 about one-third of them did.

The information we have about teaching, therefore, unlike that on published research, does suggest both a trend away from 'positivistic' practice and an increasing perception of 'positivism' as one, tendentious, approach among a number of alternatives.

A third source of relevant data comes from the general books published over the period. A complete listing has been attempted of (1) monographs on general theory, (2) histories of sociology, (3) general introductory textbooks and (4) works on method (whether textbooks or not), first published over the period in Britain. The books listed have been examined to see whether 'positivism' appears as a chapter title or subheading, and how frequently it appears in the index. (Journals were also searched, and only four articles with the word in the title found.) The findings, using this crude criterion of the extent to which 'positivism' is defined as a significant category, may be summarised thus: (1) in monographs on general theory only Rex's *Key Problems in Sociological Theory* before 1972 makes conspicuous use of the category (except in reference to Comte), while after 1972 uses are heavy and frequent; (2) in the small group of histories it is only the two most recent (Hawthorn, 1976; Bottomore and Nisbet, 1979) that use the category heavily; (3) it hardly appears at all in introductory texts (except in reference to Comte); (4) in works on method it appears heavily in those from 1973 onwards which concern themselves with philosophical issues (Hindess, 1973; Ford, 1974; Hughes, 1976), but not in those mainly concerned with techniques.

The pattern, therefore, is one where 'positivism' is conspicuous after about 1972 in the books on more philosophical themes and addressed to more advanced audiences, while it has continued to play little or no role in those on more technical themes and addressed to beginners. One of these points is more or less tautological, since 'positivism' is a philosophical category; the point of interest to be drawn from the finding is the extent to which books are still being written which do not raise epistemological issues in relation to research methods or theories. The beginners/advanced distinction may be accounted for by the widely felt need to teach relatively dogmatically at early stages (Bernstein, 1971; Kuhn, 1962); some of the general texts listed are probably aimed primarily at sub-degree-level students. Time did not permit any attempt to analyse authors' viewpoints. Paradoxically, however, it makes sense to treat the mere use of the word 'positivism' as an indicator of hostility to the ideas it is used to denote, so the findings may also be interpreted in that sense. These data, thus, fit well into an account which sees an increasing trend away from positivism and towards a consciousness of it as merely one approach among others, if not clearly a superseded approach.

The general pattern revealed in the data presented is one where there is an increasing use of the category 'positivism', and advocacy of alternatives to it, but no apparent decrease in 'positivistic' action in research. For the purposes of this discussion it must be assumed that the data are not misleading. How, then, can this discrepancy be accounted for?

One possibility is that positivism *has* been, intellectually or socially, defeated, but that those whose ideas were formed at an earlier period, or who are at the intellectual periphery, do not yet appreciate this and so persist in an outdated mode. This has been explored by looking at the professional ages of the authors of the sample articles, comparing the graduates of the three decades. The numbers available are not such that firm conclusions can be drawn, but results may be taken as suggestive. The 1970s generation are overwhelmingly non-positivist on every criterion – but they are only nine, and have only published in the 1970s. The broad pattern of differences in the 1970s shows successive generations as less positivistic, although since the two older groups change over time, not always in less positivistic directions, the total effect is neither one of consistent generational difference nor one of a trend affecting each generation in the same way. However, these generational differences could go some way to account for the popular version of history, especially when it is recalled that the relative sizes and ages of the generations are such that a small shift among the 1960s generation bulks large in the profession as a whole, and positions strongly held by 1970s graduates will only have started to be reflected in publications. However, this line of interpretation still has the problem that it assumes the existence of a coherent and meaningful positivist school or position.

Another possibility is that patterns of intellectual hegemony are not adequately revealed by the mere fact of publication, so that it is respect or influence which should be taken into account. Citations are not unambiguous, but provide a tolerable measure of this. The citations in the up to four years following publication have been counted for those articles covered by the *Social Science Citation Index* which were either both quantitative and hypothesis-testing or non-quantitative and did not test a hypothesis. The average number of citations per annum was 0·45 for the first and 0·41 for the second group. This is clearly inconsistent with the hypothesis of non-positivist hegemony.

Another possibility is that a simple mistake has been made in treating British sociology as a unified whole; the paradox vanishes if it is seen as consisting of different sectors, some concerned mainly with philosophical/ theoretical issues and others mainly with empirical research, developing in intellectual independence of each other (Menzies, 1979). This seems painfully near to at least part of the truth;[3] it is noticeable that those who write on philosophical issues are not often active in writing anything else, and vice versa. Expressions of discomfort over theoretical attacks from those involved in empirical research are common enough, however, to suggest that this is simplistic (Platt, 1976, pp. 30–1, 39).

Many of the criticisms of 'positivism' have been entirely negative in character, and do not hold out any alternatives not open to the same criticisms, so that they are really attacks on the very idea of empirical research. This consideration leads us to another possibility, which is that in so far as 'positivism' means anything precise all convincing empirical work is necessarily positivistic, whatever the researcher may proclaim about the matter in the abstract. ('Positivistic' here, obviously, is not being used in my crude operational sense.) I have considerable intuitive sympathy for this position, although time does not permit a systematic attempt to demonstrate it by analysis of supposedly non-positivistic work (see Bell and Newby, 1977; Goldthorpe, 1973). Even the exercise of empathy or intuition requires looking *at* or listening *to*. If one wishes rationally to convince anyone else of a proposition about the external world, it requires the production of evidence, a concept which can scarcely be made independent of the externally observable, whatever the possible relation of that to the unobservable. If one does not wish to make justified statements about the world, there are other games to play, with their own attractions – but they are *other* games, not an alternative way of playing the empirical one. It is possible to argue plausibly that an extreme philosophical positivism is untenable, and indeed impossible to put into practice. To the extent that this is true, the attack on the philosophical position cannot be an attack on actual practice, though it may be relevant to statements of intent. This does not, of course, make the attack on the philosophical position any the less justified, merely less relevant to research practice.

It seems possible that the main *practical* difference between 'positivist' and other methodologies is in the degree of explicitness with which they state in principle, and describe in individual instances, the intellectual procedures that they employ at different stages of research rather than in their ontological and epistemological assumptions. I suspect that the difficulty experienced in classifying particular pieces of empirical research as more or less 'positivist' by the criteria various writers have used to define positivism was more than a merely technical difficulty, and that it arose from the fact that the philosophical distinctions made have no clear operational meaning, and so no practical implications. (It is interesting that Halfpenny's recent paper, 1979, arguing persuasively for a 'deep relativism' in relation to different theoretical approaches, none the less recognises that varying epistemological assumptions do not operate autonomously at the level of research practices and so do not provide a basis of choice between them.) It would be foolish to deny that there are different styles of research, and profound cleavages among researchers on the ideology of methods; my scepticism is about whether the positivist/non-positivist distinction pinpoints them correctly.

The question then becomes whether, or under what circumstances, 'positivist' is a meaningful label.

For 'positivist' to be a useful category, those described by it must have in common more than divides them; acceptance of that principle would clearly still leave room for argument, though it is hard to see any way in which Marx, Parsons and all demography could fit together under the same umbrella. If one is to take seriously the question of how, or whether, to divide sociologists into schools, it raises some quite general issues of method in intellectual history – although one cannot take very seriously the kind of history that takes Durkheim's *Suicide*, which only became available in English in 1951, as the paradigmatic study of a parochial Anglo-American tradition already well established in the 1930s. 'School' concepts, when they do not represent members' conscious identifications, are likely to operate as a Procrustean bed distorting the distinctive positions taken by individual writers, and often imputing to them positions on matters where they have stated none; for the correct imputation of influence, one must demonstrate not merely some similarity of ideas but also that some influence actually took place, or at least that its occurrence is more plausible than that the similarity came about for some other reason. To concentrate on an idea or theme in itself, without placing each instance in its social context, is to run into serious danger of creating 'spurious persistence' (Skinner, 1969, p. 35).

It must be noted that those writers most commonly identified as sociological positivists (Durkheim, Lundberg, Homans) are those who have made general statements of an abstract position; vast numbers of others have been counted in with them without any similar evidence of what their abstract position is, or any detailed analysis of their concrete practice. It is perhaps unimportant to point out that the authors of research do not necessarily have a worked-out philosophical position, since it may none the less be argued that it exemplifies such a position even if it was not consciously held; it is careless, however, not to make the distinction between the man and the work, and runs a serious risk of committing the fallacy identified by Skinner (1969, pp. 16–19) of imputing coherence, or a standpoint, where none was present. The fact that certain theoretical positions could have generated particular research does not mean that they in fact did; it is possible both that it is also compatible with other (and perhaps less schematically polarised) positions, and also that it is simply research which has not succeeded in exemplifying the position held in principle rather than an exemplar of a bad general position. (It is naive to assume that proclaimed theoretical positions are necessarily put into practice.) Perhaps it is impossible for there to be research representing no theoretical position. But, even if this point is conceded, so long as it is not taken for granted that research must arise from a theoretical position already developed, research may be current whose implicit theoretical position has not yet been stated in abstract form. (It is, indeed, desirable that this should be so, since it must be one of the main sources of distinctly sociological creativity; see Kaplan, 1964, p. 11; a tacit theoretical position must, by definition, be operational, while one stated in the abstract need not have clear, or any, practical consequences – that is, it is likely to be a philosophical rather than a sociological position.)

As Merton (1967) has pointed out, sociologists are prone to confuse the history and the systematics of sociological theory. If we may take it that the historical aspects of the use of 'positivism' as an organising category have been dealt with, let us return to the systematics. It is a matter of judgement whether what one set of ideas, A, has in common sufficiently distinguishes it from another set of ideas, B, to justify describing everything in A by the same name. If, however, B has no internal homogeneity except that which is implied by being not-A, that suggests not only that B is not a useful category but also that a simple division of the intellectual world into A and not-A is uninstructive. It is just such a simple division that writers taking up polemical positions within sociology have tended to adopt: on the one hand the positivists, and on the other ourselves. Since, however, who 'we' are depends on who is writing, this division is either not comprehensive or uses the same word to make different distinctions. Those not taking up polemical positions, but attempting a relatively impartial survey of alternatives, have distinguished different non-positivist approaches, each a school with a name; one must note, however, that the *non*-positivists are usually authors who have overtly identified themselves with schools, while the 'positivists' are usually a motley collection of everyone else, identified with no particular name.

In so far as there is a reality to which the title corresponds, it is that of a diffuse attachment to the idea, or at any rate the name, of 'science'. Many standard textbooks have an introductory chapter on 'scientific method', usually a vulgarised and outdated version of philosophers' discussions without reference to their differences; there is no indication of how this method could be applied in practice, and it does not reappear after the first chapter.[4] Many journal articles, especially American ones, claim to test a hypothesis, but it is notorious that this mode of presentation often misrepresents the way in which the research was really done (Becker, 1966; Gusfield, 1976; Weigert, 1970). To treat such work as seriously guided by 'scientific' norms is to pay attention to form and to statements of principle rather than to substance and to practice; as in other studies of the relation between attitudes and behaviour, it is naive to assume an automatic correspondence (Wicker, 1969). The presence, however, of such vague and watered-down statements of a 'scientific' ethos provides a basis for allocation to a theoretical school of the otherwise unallocable, once the decision has effectively been made that everything must be placed in some school, and because self-styled positivists have claimed science for themselves the label is positivism. Our review of the British journals suggested that the actual practice of British sociologists has not been dominated by the American model, so perhaps one contributory factor in the false historical picture that has been built up has been an exaggeration of the degree of American hegemony.

When considering the division of writers into schools, a distinction needs to be made which depends upon the purpose of the exercise. For philosophical or analytical purposes, the connections between the ideas making up the intellectual positions distinguished should be of logical necessity, so that each 'school' has a logically coherent position. For historical purposes, however, it must be recognised that groups working together, or having much in common, do not necessarily possess a logically coherent position, or at any rate may share ideas and practices whose connections are empirically contingent rather than logically necessary. To look for logical connections which are not present, or to impute those coherent positions which have been worked out to authors who did not hold them, is the natural habit of a tidy academic mind, but as fallacious and historically misleading as it would be to treat the concatenations of the great system-builders as fortuitous.

It has been shown that the category 'positivism' has been increasingly used in British sociology as a way of organising teaching and thought in general. Very frequently this use forms part of the historical account in which there has been a positivistic phase, which is now over. The evidence reviewed suggests that this historical account is a highly misleading one as far as empirical work is concerned. If the simple operational definitions which permitted that conclusion to be reached are put aside and actors' uses considered, it appears that the term only has anything like a consensual meaning when used in the most abstract way; when applied to concrete cases it is commonly used polemically, with referents that vary with the polemical purpose, lumping together as 'positivists' writers who did not identify themselves as such and have in common only that the author wishes to be dissociated from them.

In casual conversation among people with known and shared intellectual positions such elastic terms have their functions, but there should be no place for them in careful professional writing. There we need to do both better history and better systematics, and to distinguish the two. Whichever is being done, it should be borne in mind that the intellectual world is not necessarily divided up into neatly distinct schools.

The concern here has been to refute some prevalent misconceptions, and hence most attention has been paid to counter-evidence. There is, however, an element of truth in the popular historical account. There has been an increasing hegemony of non- or anti-'positivist' positions in purely theoretical work, even if this has not obviously affected empirical work. Perhaps one of the reasons for the popularity of the dubious historical account is the easiness of reading statements of principle rather than observing the complexities and ambiguities of practice. To the extent that empirical and theoretical work are done by different people, and that the theoreticians adopt positions hostile to all or most empirical work, it should not be surprising that the two diverge in character. Whatever the reasons, the time has surely come to give up the use of an unhelpful category.

Appendix: Research Methods

(1) *Definitions of positivism*
Dictionaries, encyclopaedias and twenty-four theoretical and methodological works were consulted. The most commonly appearing themes were isolated, and their frequency of occurrence recorded. A list of works and fuller details are available from the author.

(2) *General sociological books*
In principle all general sociological works first published in Britain in the period 1950–79 were listed. 'General' is for this purpose defined as including all textbooks, general works on theory and/or method, and monographs or collected essays on theory or method. Excluded are works on particular methods, studies of particular theorists or theories, primarily philosophical works and those mainly about social sciences other than sociology. Included when they might otherwise have been excluded are a few particularly well-established works first published elsewhere (e.g. in the USA), works specially translated for British publication and (because of their wide diffusion) Penguins. Also included are all those found by Clarke

to have been used three or more times as required reading in first-year sociology courses (Clarke, 1976) and those referred to as relatively general works by Scott (1976). The lists were compiled from a search of the *British National Bibliography Cumulated Subject Catalogue* under appropriate headings, supplemented by general knowledge. Those works which could not be seen, because they were not in the libraries used, were not classified; there were nine, and it seems likely that most were not aimed at the university market. A complete list is available from the author.

(3) *Journal articles*
All articles published in the *British Journal of Sociology*, *Sociological Review* and *Sociology* from 1950 until the latest available issue for 1979 were listed. Research notes and correspondence were omitted, as were critiques of previous articles and replies to them unless they seemed to amount to articles in their own right or be treated as such editorially. (*Sociological Review* practice on layout in these matters was sometimes ambiguous, and here length in effect became the criterion.)

The articles listed were classified by their predominant tendency. Where empirical data made only a brief appearance as an example, the article was not treated as empirical; on the whole, however, ambiguously empirical cases were treated as such, since the prime purpose of the listing was to create a sampling frame, and to code as many cases as possible as empirical was the conservative strategy in relation to the argument of the chapter. Articles on the history or current state of sociology were counted as empirical if they were descriptive or analytical rather than normative. (One article, in the latest volume of *Sociological Review*, was omitted as unclassifiable.)

The sample used took every issue of each journal in even-numbered years. From each issue, articles were chosen from among those classified as 'empirical' in this way: where there were only one or two, all were taken; where there were three or more, the articles within the issue were numbered in order, and the odd-numbered articles taken from odd totals and even-numbered ones from even totals. From this list, those known to be by authors based at foreign institutions were deleted; since not all the issues give authors' affiliations, it is possible that a few which should have been deleted remain in the sample.

In deciding whether or not an article was to be counted as testing a hypothesis, the conservative strategy was followed of including even those cases where the author did not state that this was being done, but might have done so. Thus all instances are included where the structure of the article was to state an initial position and then to investigate whether it appeared to be correct in the light of further information.

In classifying main data sources, two unconventional categories were found necessary. 'General knowledge' was used for those cases where the author had (or appeared to have) collected no data specifically for the article, and did not refer to sources by others. 'Secondary documents' was coded where the sources referred to were of data systematically collected and analysed by others, and the author used their conclusions; instances of this were not counted for the tables, since the nature of the data of the original authors was usually not indicated and so these were unclassifiable.

In the analysis by age, ages of first authors only were taken when there was more than one. Professional age was regarded as more relevant than calendar age, and so age of graduation was taken; where the first degree was not in sociology and a later one was, the later one was used. When only the birth date was available, twenty-one years was added to it to estimate graduation; this was done in seventeen cases. Data were collected from the journals, BSA membership lists and published reference works. No data could be obtained on the authors of 62 of the 213 articles; it is known, however, that a high proportion of these were non-sociologists.

Notes: Chapter 5

The support of a Leverhulme Foundation Research Fellowship during the period when some of the preparatory work for this paper was done is gratefully acknowledged.

1 See Skinner (1974) for a discussion of the range of ideological strategies which may be involved in the definition and redefinition of terms.
2 The general understanding that surveys should be regarded as inherently positivistic, while participant observation should not, seems extremely odd, since participant observation entails direct observation of *behaviour*, while surveys commonly collect verbal data on *attitudes*. Treating surveys in this way is, however, perhaps more understandable in Britain, where unsophisticated descriptive/demographic types of survey have played a larger role than in the USA.
3 Worsley (1974) argues that there is now within British sociology a 'theory valuing community' which does not wish to know about society. It is striking, and paradoxical, how far this account of anti-positivists corresponds to Mills's account of abstracted empiricists, 'more concerned with the philosophy of science than with social study itself', and 'stuck way up on a very high level of generalisation . . . and they cannot get down to fact' (1970, pp. 67, 86).
4 This is asserted impressionistically, on the basis of preliminary work on a planned study of textbook ideas of 'science'.

6

The Anti-Quantitative Bias in Postwar British Sociology

CHRISTOPHER T. HUSBANDS

As cognoscenti will already know, the discipline of sociology in Britain lacks the sympathy to quantitative approaches that marks the subject in the United States. It is not difficult to provide indications of this orientation in British sociology – indeed, in some measure to quantify its prevalence, if I may be ironic for a moment. The recent compilation by Wakeford (1979) of syllabuses of undergraduate methods courses in British sociology departments has a distinctly diverse character; from courses where there is indeed a considerable quantitative emphasis, these syllabuses range along a continuum to the very opposite position of some courses where subjects like the philosophy of science and linguistics not merely predominate, but dominate to the exclusion of virtually any other aspect. This sort of content in what are avowedly courses in sociological method seems highly perverse when one considers the harshness of the economic climate into which most contemporary sociology graduates go. Most obviously at the present time, but also during most of the 1970s, there have been increasingly fewer teaching jobs within sociology as well as rapidly declining opportunities for graduate research. Thus, sociology graduates currently go into a world where – if they are to use their sociological knowledge and training at all – it is going to be in some research capacity in a part of the private sector or (even now) the public sector. In a competition for employment in this sort of economic situation, even a modest acquaintance with quantitative techniques, with the execution of social surveys, with data analysis and with their interpretation is a commodity that is rather more marketable than an exegetical knowledge of Wittgenstein or hermeneutics (whether single or double) or even a total understanding of why people say 'Good morning' to each other.

Even those university sociology departments that have made a commitment of some sort to a quantitative methods course have often done so only as a concession. Such courses are frequently taught in the first year

– before students are properly aware of, or committed to, their subject – in order to 'get methods out of the way'. The number of sociology departments that offer higher-level methodology courses as an undergraduate option, let alone as a course requirement, must be exceedingly few; encouragement to take appropriate courses offered in other departments of the same university is also rare.

Some of the consequences of this type of orientation have been dire, though equally there has been a refusal to face the reasons for them. A curious belief has long suffused much of British academic sociology that a good undergraduate degree is a sufficient prerequisite for undertaking full-scale independent graduate research. In reality, of course, the possessor of a newly acquired first degree in sociology is little more than wet behind the ears. Hence, over the years, many research degree students in sociology have simply lost their way when expected to progress on their own with only the often spasmodic assistance of a supervisor, whose control over, and ability to discipline, the research initiatives of the student concerned are frequently limited. The non-completion rate among graduate studentship holders in sociology in particular has, one suspects, been disconcertingly low, probably especially so in the one-time years of plenty when quota studentships were readily available to any holder of a II(i) degree who was at something of a loose end after completion of his or her first degree and was not immediately attracted by any of the other alternatives that he or she faced.

The Social Science Research Council has collected data on postgraduate completion rates in sociology and social administration that in general accord with this suspicion; the information was presented to an SSRC-organised conference on graduate methodology teaching in September 1979 (SSRC, 1979). A preliminary analysis based on twelve questionnaires returned to the Council, while not necessarily fully typical of the position in all SSRC-award outlets, showed a completion rate of 39 per cent among PhD-registered postgraduates who had received SSRC awards between 1966 and 1975. Moreover, in another data-gathering exercise organised by the SSRC, thirty-three quota-award-status departments had a completion rate of 51 per cent among those working for a doctorate whose registrations started in 1972/3, 29 per cent among those starting in 1973/4 and 20 per cent among the 1974/5 starters; not all of these would have been SSRC-supported. The completion rates for those registered for a master's degree by thesis were: 25 per cent in 1973/4, 22 per cent in 1974/5 and 16 per cent in 1975/6. Even when one takes into consideration the fact that some of the non-completions may eventually complete and that some were undoubtedly part-time registrants, these rates do not speak too well of the nature of graduate programmes in British sociology; it is difficult to escape the conclusion that the quality of supervision and training received by postgraduate registrants bears at least some of the blame. In any case, even a part-time master's degree by thesis should not really take more than five years to complete if supervision and training are adequate.

It now looks as though this general situation will be 'solved' by default, since extrinsic economic and political pressures have reduced to a trickle the availability of postgraduate studentships, but it is regrettable that the 'solution' has had to be the result of such factors, and the axe may well fall all the harder because of the manner in which so many intending graduate researchers fell by the wayside during the years of plenty. The chairman of the Social Science Research Council has recently made clear before the House of Commons Public Accounts Committee that the Council intends to adopt a more assertive and interventionist strategy in order to try to improve graduate completion rates, a strategy clearly likely to be more *dirigiste* as far as the content of postgraduate research training is concerned (*The Times*, 16 May 1980).[1]

These observations about British sociology's negative orientation towards quantitative methods and about the consequences of this for graduate training have been made despite the fact that much quantitative research is and has been done in this country and that a not inconsiderable proportion of the content of the major British sociology journals is devoted to quantitatively based studies. Even here, however, all is not quite what it seems; articles of varying quality by little-known Americans and Canadians from relatively minor institutions comprise a disproportionate part of the content of at least one of the three principal British sociology journals. Table 6.1 indicates to what extent American and Canadian sociologists have occupied the pages of these three journals during the past decade. Even allowing both for the fact that the percentages include a few marginal or special cases (e.g. Daniel Bell's Hobhouse Memorial Lecture in one issue of the *BJS* and a couple of articles by American authors who had done graduate work in this country) and also for the slightly greater tendency to multiple authorship among American and Canadian sociologists, the message embedded in the figures of the table is a troubling one. Only the *Sociological Review* – arguably the least well known if not necessarily the least prestigious of the three – has remained almost wholly immune to the trans-Atlantic bacillus. The situation concerning *Sociology* gives cause for some concern, although there is no obvious upward trend in the figures. On the other hand, the American and Canadian presence in the pages of the *BJS* until at least 1976 is remarkable, even if there is a trend – hopefully a propitious one from the point of view of British sociology – towards a decline in the percentage.

Of course, some of the major work in British sociology since the war – major in the senses both of frequent subsequent citation and of attempted theoretical input – has been quantitative. One can think of David Glass's study of social mobility, of the Nuffield team's recent follow-up study, or perhaps of the work of Butler and Stokes on British electoral behaviour. However, many such works have attracted criticism that has been directed not so much at their theoretical purpose and content as at straightforward aspects of their choice of method. To be sure, the issues of methodology and

Table 6.1   *American and Canadian Authorships of Full Articles in the* British Journal of Sociology, *the* Sociological Review *and* Sociology *from 1970 to 1979, by Location of Authors' Institution of Affiliation**

	British Journal of Sociology		Sociological Review		Sociology	
	No. of Authors	*% American or Canadian*	*No. of Authors*	*% American or Canadian*	*No. of Authors*	*% American or Canadian*
1970	36	39	20	5	24	8
1971	33	24	26	4	20	15
1972	38	34	27	15	21	0
1973	38	39	30	10	21	0
1974	34	35	34	6	25	20
1975	33	36	42	2	20	5
1976	33	42	26	0	17	6
1977	29	28	37	3	24	21
1978	32	16	35	6	19	11
1979	33	18	42	0	20	10

* Single authors and multiple co-authors have been given equal status in the calculation of these figures.

theoretical content are related and so there is appropriateness in the focus of some of these criticisms; however, they are not always fundamental and in any case the theory-dependence of concepts and categories (e.g. Hindess, 1973) is as widely accepted by quantitative as by non-quantitative practitioners of British sociology.

Forms of Hostility to Quantitative Approaches

British sociology has not rejected using some primitive quantitative techniques when the relevant data have been relatively 'hard' and essentially descriptive (e.g. Blackburn, 1967; Westergaard and Resler, 1976). Instead, it is at the more subjective level that suspicions about quantitative techniques have been expressed. There are two basic forms of this hostility: (1) that which is based upon premises about sources of bias in univariate measurement and which particularly excoriates large-scale questionnaire and survey procedures; and (2) a form of hostility based on a causal epistemology which is fundamentally different from that necessarily used in most types of analysis of quantitative data.

Let us consider each of these in turn.

Measurement
Questionnaire procedures are based on a fundamental premiss (which is in the last analysis unprovable but equally is also unfalsifiable) that the questions and items being administered to a sample offer the same stimulus to each respondent and are perceived by each to be doing so. If the assumption is true, differences in responses can be interpreted

unambiguously over the whole sample as being due to the different characteristics and personal circumstances of respondents – and to these factors alone if measurement error in the sample is randomly distributed. Responses may therefore, of course, be analysed in terms of different sets of aggregate personal characteristics within the sample. This is a basic premiss of conventional questionnaire research. If it seems feasible and plausible, or more or less so, such research may safely proceed. To the extent that the assumption seems improbable or implausible, use of questionnaires as a research procedure becomes increasingly indefensible.

Such a strong assumption has attracted well-known rebukes from the several 'non-positivist' schools within contemporary sociology. Interactionist and other *Verstehen*-based approaches to sociological analysis have emphasised that reality and each person's perception of it are 'negotiated', 'intersubjective' (Giddens, 1976), or are to be described as processes subsumed by some similar quasi-metaphorical epithet. The implications that such criticisms have for the use and interpretation of questionnaire material are well known: reactivity, for example, between the respondent and the process of measurement (such as interviewer bias and suggestion), idiosyncracies due to coding, and so on (Cicourel, 1964, pp. 73–120; Phillips, 1973, pp. 17–57). Of course, most of those who use questionnaire techniques have not been so perverse as to deny the possible existence of these problems, even if their significance has usually been played down. Interviewer bias, for example, has been a continuing concern of quantitative researchers and there have been attempts, of course (Webb *et al.*, 1966), to develop non-reactive quantitative techniques. Even so, the usual quantitative way of confronting these problems has been to rely on the appropriateness of procedures that are intended to randomise any such error, while the whole point of the interactionist critique of questionnaire use has been that the essentially adventitious character of such difficulties implies their intractability to solution (Cicourel, 1964, pp. 82–7): random assignment of interviewers, rotation of items from respondent to respondent in Likert-scale-type item grids in order to avoid response-set bias – such procedures assume that measurement error at the level of the individual respondent is self-cancelling in the aggregate.

Building on another common critical theme, Robin Blackburn (1967) has developed a rather differently based attack on one particular piece of quantitative research, but there is a general criticism that is more than implicit in what he says. This is his now well-known critique, based on 'The Vauxhall episode', of work by Goldthorpe, who argued that up to 77 per cent of the Luton car workers whom he had studied had a 'co-operative attitude to management' (Goldthorpe, 1966). This conclusion was reached on the basis of questionnaire data and Goldthorpe saw no reason why this attitude should not persist because of these workers' now sociologically notorious instrumental attitudes to their work. Of course, shortly after this research was published, there occurred an incident of substantial militance among the workers concerned. The deficiency in the particular questionnaire approach used by Goldthorpe – so Blackburn argues – is the former's use of a measurement device that has been abstracted from its situational framework and therefore belies any meaningful contextual interpretation.

> Their [the Vauxhall workers'] consciousness is likely to become volatile as a consequence of even quite minor adjustments of established understandings. An economic relationship which formerly seemed 'one of reciprocity and interdependence' comes to be seen as 'one of coercion and exploitation'. In the Vauxhall case, the very attitudes described by Goldthorpe are those most likely to produce a violent response if anything untoward occurs. (Blackburn, 1967, p. 51)

Apparently, then, an attempt at attitudinal measurement should not be conducted, according to this perspective, without that attitude having immediate and direct relevance to the circumstances prevailing at precisely the time when measurement is attempted. Although it is conceivable that questionnaire research can be conducted in situations of immediacy, the practical problems of organising such studies mean an inevitable temporal divorce between an attitude when measured and the past circumstances to which it may relate. Of course, the difficulty is by definition all the more intractable when measuring attitudes that may relate to some possible future circumstance whose occurrence is indefinite. Such a separation in time may – it must be conceded – seriously compromise the sociological analysis by questionnaire of some issues, and perhaps industrial relations, with their exceptional volatility, are an area where this is the case. However, it would be unnecessary to impose the lesson of this criticism upon questionnaire research in all subjects and on all issues. In any case, the procedure which it implies as one alternative – questionnaire-based 'action research' – has unfortunately not always had the happiest outcome in practice. For example, the National Opinion Research Center's attempt to conduct such research in 1966 in Chicago at the time of widespread riots found co-operation enough from rioters and those living in riot areas (in return, of course, for anonymity) but found it difficult to acquire financial support for the research after the event.

Marcuse, in *One Dimensional Man* (1964), develops a more fundamentally conceived attack upon 'empiricist' research that derives from his critical concern with the aspects and processes of advanced industrial capitalism which illegitimately 'reconcile or unify opposites' and which 'repulse distinctions' that are seen by Marcuse as real and necessary. Like the grammar and syntax of contemporary manipulative language, 'empiricist' social research is accused of translating individual statements into general functional forms that submerge in a blander version the sharpness and idiosyncrasy of the original. Because of the manipulative consequences of its procedures, such 'empiricism' is held to be ideological (Marcuse, 1964, pp. 84–120).

Causal Epistemologies

The basic causal model of much (though not all) empirical and quantitative social science is what Heise (1975, p. 111) has called 'cross-sectional statics'.

> It is presumed that a single basic causal structure is operative for numerous separate cases and that each case is observed after its inputs have been set and held constant long enough for all causal consequences to be realized. Thus, for example, the socioeconomic achievement of individuals might be studied from this perspective, presuming that essentially the same system of personal, social and cultural operators applies for all persons studied, that key inputs are set at some point early in an individual's life, and that observations of the individuals are delayed until they have actualized the full consequences of their inputs.

Even more central is that quantitative sociology's major conceptualisation of causation is as a probabilistic relationship revealed by different degrees of concomitant variation between dependent and independent variables. It is precisely this aspect of quantitative sociology about which many Marxist critics, for example, harbour doubts and they frequently combine these doubts with the belief that the most sociologically significant causal processes are resistant to quantitative, especially probabilistic, presentation. Macro-sociological structuralist analysis of a single society – which is, of course, the basis of analysis of much recent Marxist theory – is not compatible with large-case-based approaches.

Even some of the more 'empirical' contributions of contemporary Marxism do not imply a probabilistic conception of causation – or at least it would be fair to say that it is difficult satisfactorily to recast them in such terms. One example suffices to illustrate this point: Poulantzas's widely debated approach to the conceptualisation and operationalisation of social class (Poulantzas, 1973 and 1975). Poulantzas's contribution is essentially at the level of classification and largely concerns the criteria to be used for this purpose: his emphasis, as has been widely discussed (Wright, 1976; Nichols, 1979), is upon the distinction between productive and unproductive labour and he imposes two ancillary criteria of the distinctions between supervisory and subordinate and between mental and manual labour. These criteria combine to differentiate particular sections of the class structure, and such classes as the 'new petty bourgeoisie' can be further differentiated internally into 'fractions' by the resolution of various ambiguities in the relation of the class as a whole to these criteria. While this exercise has attracted controversy and criticism because of the emphasis it gives to its chosen multiple criteria, it is unexceptionable as a piece of classification *per se*, providing as it does categories that are internally homogeneous in relation to the criteria.

However, a difficulty does arise when Poulantzas justifies the significance of his classification, for he implicitly but incontrovertibly rejects a probabilistic notion of the causal impact of these structural locations; precisely by virtue of seeing them as structural, he conceives their members behaving uniformly as social aggregates. His writing in *Classes in Contemporary Capitalism* overflows with examples of this usage. 'The labour aristocracy in certain conjunctures takes up class positions that are in fact bourgeois' (p. 15). 'One can be led to an *a priori* restriction of alliances, by reducing this petty bourgeoisie to capital and ignoring the opportunities it presents, depending on the conjuncture, for alliance with the working class' (p. 331). Thus, though 'conjunctural' factors may affect the direction in which a class or a class fraction can 'jump', it seems also to be implied that the whole of that class or fraction will 'jump' in the same direction. One major purpose of the notion of 'class fraction' is apparently to accommodate the possibility of a differentiation of political orientation within a whole class at a particular conjuncture. This, however, merely modifies but in no way confounds Poulantzas's central perspective, for fractions define themselves by properties inherent in class position. The possibility that some part of a class or class fraction might adopt one political outlook and another part (even if only a minority) might adopt a different outlook, and that this divergence might be related to factors having little or nothing to do with class definition, is scarcely admitted by Poulantzas's perspective. In general, the only non-class-related factors recognised by him as determinant are historical ('conjunctural') ones. Although his conceptualisation of class uses three criteria, its implied invariance (to adapt a term of Willer, 1967, p. 76) or total determinism reduces it to a form of monocausality.

When examining any phenomenon, all Marxist sociological perspectives of causation, even if not strictly monocausal, are obliged – if they are to offer any distinctive approach – to give priority to one causal factor at the expense of others. Causal factors are thus hierarchised according to preconceived theoretical prescriptions. The more usual alternative of most techniques of quantitative sociology is to construct priorities according to temporal criteria (for example, by the structuring of 'causal chains') or to statistical criteria (by use of measures of the separate contributions to explained variation of each independent variable). The latter procedure is especially likely to produce tut-tutting noises from theoretical adversaries but, in the frequently perfectly defensible absence (at least for many *explicanda*) of preconceived theoretical criteria for according one causal factor a priority before others, statistical yardsticks are indeed as appropriate as any.

Of course, not all recent Marxist contributions adopt a rigorous monocausal epistemology (e.g. Wright and Perrone, 1977), nor is it only

Marxist sociology that uses this perspective. Durkheim, the *grand homme* of positivism, is explicit and aggressive in his assertion that 'a given effect has always a single corresponding cause' (Durkheim, 1964, p. 128). However, Durkheim, in elaborating a criticism of Mill, has a mistaken notion of multicausality as conceptualised in probabilistic terms across a universe of cases. Durkheim criticises the feasibility of regarding a phenomenon, say, Y, as being in some cases a consequence of one cause, say, X_1, and in other cases that of a second cause, say, X_2. This is, however, an inappropriate specification. If the occurrences of only X_1 and of only X_2 both somewhat increase the likelihood of Y, and if the joint occurrence of X_1 and X_2 then greatly increases the likelihood of Y, this latter outcome is because of the presence of both X_1 and X_2 in all cases where Y occurred, not because of the effect of X_1 in some such cases and of X_2 in the others. To take Durkheim's favourite example of suicide and its causes: egoism/altruism and anomie/fatalism may be antinomies with mutually exclusive categories, but egoism/anomie, for example, is not. Thus a Protestant committing suicide after an economic reverse or success might – even in Durkheim's terms – be operating under two simultaneous influences.

Sources of Hostility to Quantitative Sociology

In discussing the sources of the hostility to quantitative sociology one embarks upon an interesting sortie into the sociology of sociological knowledge in Britain. True, there have been the epistemological sources of hostility associated with particular schools within sociology and some of these were discussed in the previous section. However, this observation in a sense evades the crucial issue of what are true cause and effect. Since the 1960s parts of British sociology have been susceptible to what were initially American reactions against quantitative sociology as practised widely in the United States – to symbolic interactionism, phenomenology and ethnomethodology, in particular. There has also been an equal or greater susceptibility to French-derived structuralist Marxism (as opposed to the fundamental empiricism of the Anglo-Saxon variety of Marxism). However, the existence of these different susceptibilities was merely a consequence of the ongoing rejection of the empirical style of some of the more famous British sociological production of the 1950s.

It is incontrovertible that in the 1960s empirical research, even if it claimed to be theory-based, ceased to be a high-status activity within the profession. Its claims for policy relevance were seen as often disingenuous, or even sinister, by many of the practitioners of a discipline whom external events had made increasingly suspicious of the alleged ideological functions of much of the immediately preceding legacy of their subject. Even empirical research whose liberal policy relevance could less easily be gainsaid (for example, in the field of education) was none the less of low status within the dominant hierarchy of values of the profession. This sort of work, it was felt, could be left to the likes of social administrators, of whom the best-known within their subject are in consequence now far more widely known and respected by the interested lay public than is true of the best-known contemporary sociologists.

The anti-quantitative orientation may have seemed to derive emotional as well as theoretical support from a partial and imperfect reading of C. Wright Mills's famous critique of American sociology (and, by extension, the great bulk of postwar British sociology that seemed to be cast in the same mould). Had not Mills reduced paragraphs of Parsons's *The Social System* to a few sentences? Had he not dismissed Lazarsfeld as an 'abstracted empiricist'? Of course, Mills's position was really rather different from its vulgar image and he was always conscious of the value of the quantitative skills he had acquired at the Bureau of Applied Social Research.

> The specific methods – as distinct from the philosophy – of empiricism are clearly suitable and convenient for work on many problems and I do not see how anyone could reasonably object to such use of them. We can, of course, by suitable abstraction, be exact about anything. Nothing is inherently immune to measurement.
>
> If the problems upon which one is at work are readily amenable to statistical procedures, one should always try to use them. (Mills, 1959, p. 73)

Still, there may also have been a more deep-rooted source of hostility to quantitative sociology since the war – a source that partly transcends and predates the epistemological and theoretical currents which became dominant within the discipline during the 1960s and one that is also independent of that specific ideological rejection of quantitative techniques which derived from the suspected use to which the results of such research activities could allegedly be put. This further source of hostility lies in the origins of the academic discipline of sociology within this country. For much of the major quantitative work of the late nineteenth and early twentieth centuries that is associated with the beginning of an empirically oriented sociology in Britain was conducted by researchers who did not fully see themselves as sociologists, or, to the extent that they did, not as sociologists with any great wish for, or claim to, academic accreditation. Neither Charles Booth nor Seebohm Rowntree, of course, had a university post and A. L. Bowley, credited with the introduction of sampling procedures in social surveys, who held university positions first in economics and later, more famously, in statistics as the first professor of that subject in the University of London, had no formal connection with sociology: in a recent biographical summary of his life and work, Dahrendorf and Crouch seem almost to feel they need to justify their attempt to summon forth an interest among sociologists in his work on wages (Bernsdorf and Knospe, 1980, p. 52).

The work subsequently produced by later academic sociologists within the framework of this empirical tradition and the conception of social structure that such work implied remained very much a specialised minority interest and activity – and one that failed to leave any significant impression upon the discipline after the 1950s. Perhaps Carr-Saunders and Caradog Jones's studies of the social structure of England and Wales (3rd edn, 1958), which employed a basic demographic approach, best exemplify this sociological style. Their work has passed into desuetude since the 1950s partly, of course, because of its empirical obsolescence. However, there must be other reasons for such a fall from favour since the ready availability of relevant subsequent data from census and other government-sponsored compilations, as well as the enlarged facility of suitable computer hardware for the necessary analyses, mean that the production of an updated work cast within the same tradition and describing current British social structure would be a simple matter. However, sociologists have apparently been content to leave work within this framework to the Central Statistical Office, publishers of the annual *Social Trends*. No updated volume fully in the Carr-Saunders/Caradog Jones mode and prepared by an academic sociologist has appeared; perhaps the closest is the edited collection summarising twentieth-century trends in British society prepared by Halsey (1972). Despite such a distinguished example, there is in general little trace of this mode of social analysis in contemporary British sociology and part of the reason for its virtual extinction is that it was always in any case a relatively minor current within British academic sociology.

A sociology owing its intellectual origins to social philosophy and its style of written expression to literary models has in general been more preponderant and prestigious within the academic confines of the subject. Almost by definition such a sociology has been assertively supercilious about numerically tainted approaches to the study of social phenomena. Many contributions to sociology during the present century have taken the form of *belles-lettres*, even if such contributions have had rather higher intellectual pretensions. This format survives most explicitly in the writing of a sociologist such as Edward Shils, the style of whose sociology (including a frequent disdain for referencing footnotes) was influential and infectious in the development of the subject in the late 1950s and early 1960s, even if its theoretical content was more exceptionable. British sociology's most distinguished name, L. T. Hobhouse, clearly embodies the intellectual ambivalence about a quantitative approach on the one hand and social philosophy on the other – an indecisiveness of orientation well described by Philip Abrams (1968, pp. 129–36). Hobhouse came into sociology with a philosophical background but wanted to reconcile this with a wish to use sociology for social reform. His resolution of the dilemma implicit in this situation was in the direction of social philosophy.

The comparative method, explicitly quantitative in its formulation, reached fruition in the middle years of his sociological production. Take, for example, *The Material Culture and Social Institutions of the Simpler Peoples*, published in 1915 with Wheeler and Ginsberg (Hobhouse, Wheeler and Ginsberg, 1915), whose very subtitle, 'An Essay in Correlation', reveals its approach; compare this with his later *Social Development: Its Nature and Conditions* (Hobhouse, 1924). The latter contains only the most brief and obscure reference to the comparative method.

Conclusion: On Rescuing the Quantitative Approach

How then ought one to react to such a situation if one hopes to convince sceptics of the usefulness of an academic sociology that has some sympathy for – or at least does not totally reject – numerical approaches. One must, I think, do rather more than Hamilton who, from a self-consciously radical perspective and well-meaningly enough, berates the frequent obliviousness of the American liberal and radical intelligentsia to obvious empirical refutations of their ideas (Hamilton, 1972, pp. 552–3). Nor is it enough, as Hamilton also (1972, p. 564) does, to try to play upon the sub-Marxist sympathies of this coterie by pointing out to them that the master himself was not above little attempts to dabble in empirical endeavours – the famous and perhaps justifiably maligned *enquête ouvrière*. Even less can one derive any lessons from the fact that the *enquête ouvrière* was, as a piece of questionnaire design, a hopelessly botched job. Mark Abrams, for example, seems to derive considerable *Schadenfreude* from this failure, almost as though such a state of affairs could be used to put one over on those contemporary Marxist sociologists whose attitudes, he implies, have played a considerable part in generating the suspicions with which quantitative techniques are viewed within the British discipline (Abrams, 1979). Even so, I accept the spirit and intent, even the anguish, of the rest of what Abrams says in this article.

Instead, the convincing of the sceptics requires that one can justify the use of quantitative measurement as the appropriate methodological approach to a range of sociological problems, that one can make clear the subject areas where such measurement is appropriate and those where it is not, and that one can show which sorts of theoretical interpretation are permissible from such procedures and which are not. In the task of establishing the significance of quantitative techniques for probabilistic causal attribution, one must delineate those situations where this approach is justifiable and defensible and, most important, one must also be able to argue for the essential sociological significance, the problem relevance, as it were, of these situations.

Measurement

The assumption by Moser and Kalton, British sociology's most famous recent quantifiers, of the existence of an 'individual true value' (ITV) surrounded by 'individual response errors' (Moser and Kalton, 1971, p. 378), is frequently thrown in the teeth of quantitative sympathisers who do not share the positivist dogmatism of these two authors. Crucifixion of all quantitative sociology upon a cross of 'ITVs' is an unfair and wrongly specified condemnation, for the rejection of the concept of individual true values each in theory obtainable from a universe of subjects does *not* imply the rejection *tout court* of the quantitative approach. Thus the present writer (Husbands, 1976) has used such an approach to question the existence of these true values ('true-in-the-eye-of-God values', as with intended irony he calls them) in that most positivist of exercises, examination marking – incidentally a practice apparently indulged in without undue qualm by many anti-quantitative sociologists. Catherine Marsh (1979a) has also recently argued persuasively that survey procedures in fact lack the inherent positivism alleged by their detractors.

There are, of course, areas of sociology where the available quantitative data are indeed suspect, either because of straightforward biases in measurement or because of definitional difficulties negating the concept of true value, or for both these reasons. However, one wonders how long those critical of quantification in general will continue attempting to score cheap points with that hoariest of old chestnuts, suicide statistics; Keat (1979) is only the latest of a long line of writers illegitimately seeking to generalise well beyond the lessons of this now notorious instance. Let us consider instead some more serious examples.

The use of questionnaire approaches to measure the aggregate character of public opinion (e.g. to provide supposedly absolute measures of the proportions of the public or the electorate with particular attitudes on this or that issue), while being widely practised not only by opinion pollsters and market researchers but also by many political scientists and some sociologists, is one area where a rational evaluation of the evidence has to allow doubts about full objective measurement. Many opinions within the mass public are extremely ephemeral and are consequently highly labile.

One major indication of this fact is the effect of question-wording upon aggregate response. However, this susceptibility to wording-effects of the distributions of responses to questions on certain issues is now a very well-known phenomenon[2] and Payne (1951), for example, has offered numerous instances. He also provides documentation of the readiness of some respondents to give substantive answers on matters of which they have never heard. The traditional method of accommodating this problem has been to assume that such propensities are present in equal degree within all subgroups of a population and to argue that, while absolute percentages of agreement mean little, relative differences between such percentages are interpretable. However, Schuman and Presser (1977 and 1980), in a recent resurrection of these subjects, have shown that some of these effects are in fact less dramatic than the legends about them and, more significant in the present discussion, that they vary in their occurrence from subgroup to subgroup within a population – the level of educational attainment being one powerful discriminator. Catherine Marsh's (1979b) suggested solution to question-wording problems is to use filter questions, probes on issue salience and perhaps certain of the less obtrusive questionnaire techniques, although – given the import of Schuman and Presser's work – I am more inclined to accept the objective unmeasurability of attitudes either in whole populations or in subgroups of them where question-wording makes any large difference to the distribution of response. Questions whose response distributions so behave are *ipso facto* inappropriate to the interest and knowledge of a large number of their potential respondents in the population or subgroup concerned and they therefore oppose what is usually a premiss of questionnaire research into attitudes.

However, this is not my invariable judgement, for there are in fact numerous research occasions when it is the uncertain and aleatory character of responses to questionnaire items that is itself important and substantive and itself the subject of empirical research. Much work on levels of consistency and stability among political attitudes has both demonstrated and also made theoretical use of this very lability. One might mention some of the work of Philip Converse (e.g. Converse, 1964) or the demonstration of changes over time in opinions on nationalisation and nuclear disarmament as analysed by Butler and Stokes (1974, pp. 277–85). Such research has used quantitative data to show the unacceptability for numerous issues of that style of public opinion measurement which is carried out with all the spurious confidence of quantitative certainty by some professional opinion pollsters.

Attempts by political scientists to quantify such matters as 'political alienation' also tend to believe in the possibility of its absolute objective measurement but, since attitudes on such a subject tend to be rather more firmly held than is the case with many topics of public opinion polling, the basis of doubt about the admissibility of such measurement has a different emphasis. In a highly egregious, if slightly recondite, example of this approach, Nielsen (1979) makes much of absolute percentages of responses to questions such as 'Do you think that the state wastes a lot of money we pay in taxes and duties, some of the money or only a tiny fraction?' and 'Do you think that the municipality wastes a lot of the money we pay in local taxes, some of the money or only a tiny fraction?'. Of course, questions on issues such as this, where not only the issue itself but the very phraseology in which it is discussed and understood have been so determined by media presentation and manipulation that they have come to constitute part of a dominant ideology, are not amenable to objective quantification and one must accept that it is a mistake to think they are. Attitudes to trade unions would perhaps be a similar example of this phenomenon.

Indeed, because of the form of question presentation, the quantitative results on some issues where public opinions have constancy and consistency cannot in logic be regarded as corresponding to the level of some collective opinion; the only theoretically appropriate interpretation of them is as a measure of the degree of penetration of a particular aspect of the dominant ideology. Butler and Stokes's work again provides an example. Substantial majorities of the British electorate since the early 1960s have answered positively and often very vehemently that 'too many immigrants have been let into this country' (Butler and Stokes, 1974, pp. 303–8). Taken at their face value, findings about levels of agreement with such a statement have little objective meaning – they are crude measures of individual racism in a social-psychological sense and an attempt at a literal interpretation of them raises impossible difficulties. The form of the question implies the existence in the individual consciousness of some maximum acceptable level of immigration. Do individual respondents really have any notion of what this level might be? One doubts it in many cases, given demonstrations of the widespread ignorance among most of the population of even the approximate number of black people in this country. Even if individuals do hold such a notion, how constant is it from respondent to respondent? However, as a measure of consensus racism (Husbands, 1979) – of the degree of penetration of media and other external influences – this form of question and its results are central, for the 'immigration debate' is almost universally discussed in the media and in much ordinary discourse among the public using this non-logical and emotive style.

Causal Epistemologies

It is a more intractable matter to justify to many sceptics the use of quantitative procedures and their mode of causal attribution based upon probability, for fundamentally different causal epistemologies confront each other. Even the potential mutual reconcilability of quantitative versus some other conceptions of causation may be only partial.

One recent and widely quoted attack on the use of probability in sociology (Willer and Willer, 1973, pp. 96–105) – in a chapter that was written by another author, Cesar Hernandez-Cela, and whose content in fact owes a lot to Popper – makes much of an issue that may be philosophically important but is sociologically trivial. The foundation of Popper's position, taken up by much of the chapter of Willer and Willer's book, is that there can be no falsification or confirmation that, for example, the probability of heads/tails when a coin is tossed is one-half because one cannot carry out an infinity of tosses to test this (Popper, 1968, p. 190). Thus, he says, 'probability hypotheses do not rule out anything observable; probability estimates cannot contradict, or be contradicted by, a basic statement'. In the strict constructionist sense, then, probability statements are not falsifiable, nor of course could they in any case be used – except in the limiting case of zero or unity probability – to falsify invariant statements. However, such a dogmatic view that only certainty constitutes knowledge and that mere approximation is empiricist illusion is wholly restrictive and unacceptable in sociology and even Popper's own position (1968, p. 204) is more subtle and flexible than the chapter of Willer and Willer's book implies.

Probability statements are therefore an essential tool for almost every sort of sociological inference, whatever the philosophers of science and their acolytes in sociology may feel. Departure from the use of this perspective implies acceptance of necessary-and-sufficient conditionality as the only conceptualisation of causation, and for some *explicanda* this can only be a different way of asserting monocausality. Such a viewpoint has to be rejected as excessively rigid since it condemns to inexplicability a whole variety of social phenomena, as Hirschi and Selvin (1966 and 1967) have shown in their discussion of criteria for causal inference in delinquency research. Finally, even those non-quantitative epistemological positions that might not insist upon the necessity-and-sufficiency criterion but would use supposedly scientific criteria to give causal priority to a particular factor need to defend the axiomatic basis of their version of science. For example, as Nichols (1979) for one has observed, Poulantzas's conceptualisation of social class is fatally tarnished if the labour theory of value is not in fact correct. Thus, if the axiomatic underpinning of a version of science is suspect, a less restricted epistemological alternative that is ready to accept the equal potential relevance of several causal factors is a more attractive position to adopt.

Notes: Chapter 6

1 The behaviour of the Social Science Research Council itself on the subject of methodology training and on the encouragement of quantitative methodologies has over the years been far from unequivocal. True, the Council sponsored various conferences intended to encourage the development of methods teaching in British sociology; it has also financed the Survey Archive at the University of Essex, although its subvention has been limited to software support and the Archive's ability to make necessary conversions to machine-readability is very limited. On the negative side, the Council closed the Survey Unit and thereby discontinued the summer school in research methods that the latter had organised. It is slightly ironic that the recently announced 'designated centre' based on the organisation, Social & Community Planning Research, seems likely to carry out many of the functions of the old Survey Unit, although the summer school is unlikely to be revived in its old format.

On another matter, one hopes that recently circulating rumours that the Council will discontinue its support of the ongoing British election study are ill-founded; the study of mass electoral behaviour using the frequently appalling and unsuitable data collected through commissions from newspapers, and so on, by some of the market research organisations would be seriously limiting.

2 Thus, it was well known before the 1975 Common Market referendum that the ratio of positive to negative responses could be quite markedly affected by the wording and symbolic content of the question asked. The Britain Into Europe campaign also commissioned its own private polls that demonstrated the same effect (Butler and Kitzinger,

1976, pp. 60, 257). Although one might have one's suspicions on the matter, Butler and Kitzinger present no evidence that the precise wording of the referendum ballot was tested against alternatives in order to seek question-wording effects.

7
Towards a Rehabilitation of Data

MAUREEN CAIN AND JANET FINCH

Introduction

In this chapter we argue, with some temerity, for the re-establishment of empirical research as central to the sociological task. We argue for a new standard of utility. In so doing we risk the suspicion and opprobrium of fellow sociologists so it is necessary to be clear. Our position is not the counterpart, from within the discipline, of the current ideological position of spokespeople of government agencies who fund the work of social scientists. These latter appear to demand increasingly that the discipline should legitimise its continued existence, and even secure its survival, through the practice of 'relevant' research which produces 'useful' knowledge. For example, the Social Science Research Council noted with satisfaction in 1979 that 'the direction of research funding in the social sciences has moved slowly but decisively towards endeavours that will increasingly be recognised as useful – helping to inform those who make decisions, public and private' (SSRC, 1979). The treatment of 'usefulness' as an unproblematic notion implies a view of both science and society as unified certainties. We firmly reject this view of sociological knowledge. Indeed in this chapter we argue, by contrast, that empirical research is necessary precisely in order to create a radical and critical sociology. The recent past has been characterised by a welcome advance in radical theory, and a consequent departure from mechanism and determinism on the left, as evidenced by the rediscovery of authors as disparate as Gramsci (1971) and Pashukanis (1980), and the profound and widespread influence of Althusser (1968, 1972 and 1976). But in our view the time has now come to match this with a corresponding advance in research.

None the less, we also find unacceptable some of the possible defensive responses to government interference, such as the claim to professionalism, that is, to autonomous control over occupational practices and knowledges (Hughes, 1958; Johnson, 1972). This means that the professional is irresponsible except in relation to colleagues in the group, and thus it is inherently undemocratic (Cain, 1972 and 1979; Foucault, 1979; Illich, 1977). A demand for an autonomous profession of sociology, which establishes and investigates its own problems, would therefore be a tactic to be used with caution. Such a tactic might also imply that knowledge generated purely from within the discipline is politically neutral or absolute (or even value-free!). We disagree with this position too. For us, to be human is to be political, to engage with others in co-operative activities to achieve purposes that are constituted in such activity. If politics is conceived as struggle through organisation, all social organisations have political (as well as economic and ideological) dimensions. The ways in which sociologists are organised cannot be conceived as politically neutral: these modes of organisation affect their power to constitute and convey knowledge, as well as the forms and content of that knowledge.

Given this stance towards sociological knowledge, what should be the status of empirical research? Is it possible? Can it ever be validated, or is it simply a tool in a political game?

Throughout the thirty years with which this book is concerned, sociologists have confronted both technical and epistemological problems in validating the knowledge they have produced. Typically they have sought to overcome these problems by either etic or emic approaches (Harris, 1968).

Etic approaches assume that the validation of knowledge rests with the knowledge producers, either in the ways they formulate and test propositions (Popper, 1959) or in the community of scientists (Kuhn, 1962). Althusser (1968) comes close to the latter position, although he later (1976) rejects it. Our objections to etic theorising are that it is a-historic and idealist (Cain and Finch, 1980). Moreover, its criteria of validation either depend on a notion of 'facts' totally divorced from theory, or rely relativistically upon the agreement of the community of scientists, that is, on a collective subjectivity.

Emic approaches, by contrast, argue that the criterion of validation is to be found in the subjects investigated, that their 'worldview' has ontological primacy over any interpretation the scientist might make (e.g. Winch 1958; Garfinkel, 1967). Emic theorising is unsatisfactory for a number of reasons. Within its own terms it cannot resolve issues of generalisability, of the boundaries of relevance, of the production of rules and standards for the practice of research, or of the impossibility of the sociologists' being culture-free. Furthermore, the limits of knowledge produced are the limits of what subjects know, and the conception of validation by subjects' minds is idealist, as is the pre-given conception of the subject upon which the whole edifice is built (Cain and Finch, 1980).

In rejecting both emic and etic theorising, we reject all certainties. Indeed we argue that the task of scholarship is a responsible one precisely because the scholar cannot deal in or produce certainties. We shall argue for the substitution of utility for truth as the aim of knowledge.

It will already be clear that it is our intention in this chapter to be prescriptive as well as critical. Our argument takes the following form. First, we discuss the process of data and theory constitution, the historicity of knowledge and its value-full character. Secondly, we consider the implications of this position for certain aspects of research practice. This leads on to a discussion of validation, and an analysis of the politics of knowing as central to this process. Finally, we draw together the threads of the argument and re-present the sociologist's task.

The Rehabilitation of Data

On the Creation of Data
A central tenet of our argument is that data are always created, never found or collected. Following and adapting Thompson's (1978, p. 210) presentation of 'epistemologically inert objects', we wish to draw a distinction between data and sociologically inert entities. The distinction indicates that data have *already* been given the status of an object-within-theory. Sociologically inert entities might be a remark heard, a remark recorded, another person, or a building. None of these is a datum, but all are capable of being reconstituted as data. Reconstituted sociologically inert entities are one constituent of data.

The process of reconstituting sociologically inert entities as data is a creative one. It involves postulating relationships between these entities and others and therefore giving them new context and meaning. There is no way in which this creative process can be avoided. The minutes of a meeting cannot be captured in themselves and then interpreted. They have to be *seen as relevant*, and this seeing of the relevance of inert entities is necessarily a creative act which constitutes an object and locates it in a web of relevancies, that is, an act which gives it meaning and context, a place in a structure. This is most obvious when data are being created by the sociologist in the form, say, of a field diary, or a set of answers to questions. But the process is the same when the sociologist is deciding which objects to constitute as data from among those left to us by the biases of time. Thus theory calls data into being while data shape the elaboration of theory.

The other constituent of data is theory. Theory too is reconstituted during the process of data creation. Theory should be an interrelated set of knowledge objects and concepts which is abstracted from the material world by the procedures of incorporation and transformation described below. The interrelated objects and concepts which constitute the theory are not fixed. Elaborations to take account of new data and elaborations in the process of creating data necessarily involve a *reconstruction* of the pre-existing relationship between objects and concepts within the theory. Theory moves and is internally transformed: its growth is not simply additive. This applies not only when theory is being elaborated and extended but also when concepts within the theory are being refined.

On the Historicity of Knowledge

Knowledge (elaborated theory) should be historical in three ways. First, theorists live and work in temporal structures. The discourses available to them are historically unique and historically constituted, as are their institutional (political and economic) settings.

More important, data are shaped out of sociologically inert entities plus theory: new theory is shaped out of data-plus-theory. So that theory is at one further remove from material existences, but that does not mean it can be elaborated independently of them. In this sense, too, theory is time-specific: the data in terms of which the theory is elaborated are concrete. The constituents of a theory, the 'facts' out of which it is made and of which it makes sense, have temporal existences. The inert entities themselves will change – although data, having a theoretical component, may not immediately express an actual change in the sociologically inert entity. Only now, for example, are we realising how much of a problem salaried white-collar service workers pose for a theory of classes.

Theory, then, although sociology does not exist without it even when it tries to, can be a conservative force. This is particularly so if the theory is elaborated in the proverbial armchair, insulated from the task of constituting ever-changing sociologically inert entities as data. For logical elaborations by definition must be consistent with the concepts which go to make up the theoretical standpoint. Such elaborations, in failing to incorporate the process of constituting data, take place independently of the movements of real life. As a result, their claims to validity can only be in terms of their consistency with what *was* since the theory, which is their starting-point, was formulated in the past and is locked into the moment of its initial creation, unable *of itself* to take account of real changes in the world.

Finally, theory is for its time: this is the third sense in which the correctness and relevance of theory are historical. This last argument depends upon our concept of validation.

This explicit espousal of historicism requires us to respond to the very serious charges which have been levelled against historicist approaches. We accept that empiricism, simple humanism, and the conflation of the superstructural instances with the infrastructure so that their independent efficacy cannot be identified or theorised, are all dangerous tendencies which lead by diverse routes to mechanistic accounts (Althusser, 1972, pp. 119–44). But we deny that these inevitably form part of historicisms. Indeed, Althusser's reappraisal of his own work (1976) has left his attack on historicism without firm foundation (Buci-Glucksman, 1980, p. 341–2).

The fourth criticism of historicism has been that science is treated as superstructural rather than as a privileged practice. This is indeed our position, and accordingly we attempt to identify criteria in terms of which science – or the scholarly enterprise – may be assessed.

On Values

A further implication of our concept of data is that data are not value-neutral. The very selection of particular sociologically inert entities involves an interpretation, and the process of constituting those entities as data is inextricably part of these data. Data are never collected but always created, and they are created in terms of an on-going historical discourse (Foucault, 1970 and 1972). The facts, the data themselves, are alive and full of the values with which that discourse is imbued, and in terms of which they are created: the data themselves embody and constitute this discourse. These values in turn are related to the social/political organisation which carries them.

The whole process of research is value-full. Research starts with preconceptions and moves to refined concepts; and it is only after this fundamental value-full work has been completed that one can examine empirically the relationship between concepts. Possible 'results' are contained in the prior and value-full formulation of the questions. Protestantism and capitalism may be conceived in such a way that the relationship between them is almost 'obvious'. There is nothing wrong with this: we consider it to be not only inevitable but also desirable. Paradoxically, perhaps, it is the value-full constitution of these facts or data which are to be investigated which makes possible their validation, that is, an assessment of their adequacy and appropriateness.

Thus we argue that data – the basic 'facts' – are riddled with values and that there is no escape from this. Because of this, however, the onus is on the sociologist to be both *objective* and *scholarly*.

From Epistemology to Methods

On Ideologies and Subjective Meanings

In so arguing for the constitution of data in terms of a theory we do not want to neglect the advances made within subjectivist traditions. Patterns of thought are and have always been crucial objects of sociological analysis. What we deny is that the subjects of these thoughts and behaviours can provide in themselves validation of the sociological correctness or of the absolute correctness of their thoughts. The thoughts and accounts of those investigated have no ontological primacy. Patterns of thought, in order to be objects of sociological inquiry, must be converted into data. Thus an account or an expression of opinion or an unsolicited response by a subject will only become a datum and available for sociological use if it is subjected to the value-full processes of data constitution described above. Respondents may provide many slants on the truth, but the discovery of what 'really' happened is not the purpose of a sociological investigation, nor can corroboration be deemed to bring one closer to the truth as it does in a court of law. Sociological 'truth' cannot be voted on. Moreover, it is the task of the sociologist to produce this 'truth', not that of his or her respondents. The first step in this production process is the creation of data out of subjects' remarks. The verbal signs with which people represent their thoughts are thus inert entities to the sociologist until he or she converts them into data by constituting the speakers as relevant subjects, or the remarks as part of a relevant discourse, and providing a theoretical context which these remarks can be deemed to have a bearing on and, when theorised, a place within.

Patterns of thought are thus *objects* of study to the sociologist, who gives them a sociological life as data. This does not imply a lack of respect for the dignity, individuality and autonomy of the speakers/thinkers (Barnes, 1979). Rather, in order to preserve these attributes (which are social after all, even the individuality) the sociologist must identify such patterns of thought and meaning and adequately demonstrate their existence. The existence of patterns of 'subjective meaning' must be demonstrated with all the technical rigour available precisely in order not to undermine these humane and social values.

Subjects' accounts must be mapped; it is here that technical rigour is essential, and here that new techniques are required. It is necessary to establish when an ideology has been demonstrated adequately. Here the language used and the concepts and objects within the natural discourse are of greater importance than the opinion expressed. Even more important and more difficult is the task of establishing boundaries between discourses. Foucault (1973) has attempted this for scientific and professional discourses, but there has been no attempt that we know of to develop techniques for distinguishing between natural discourses, say, between the discourses within a village of country people and holiday people (themselves ideological categories), or between the discourses of men and women in a specified setting. Technical competence is a crucial part of the process of the demonstration of an ideology. This does not mean that one wishes to impose a set of rules whose long-term effect would inevitably be conservative: rather it means that careful thought must be given to the practice of demonstration, and that the procedures used must be capable of being made public.

To sum up, subjects' accounts are objects of study. They are not self-validating, and they are not sociological explanations. They may be constituted as data; but that is all.

Actions and Utterances

Subjects' accounts have no special or primary explanatory status, although they are important objects of study. But for a number of reasons subjects' accounts rarely yield sufficient data for a sociologically adequate explanation. These arguments are familiar and can be dealt with briefly. They have bearing on the vexed question of whether it is better to watch or to ask questions which we consider have been improperly formulated.

The arguments for observation are as follows. People are social, in that they live within, and derive their being from, a set of structures. Moreover, what they say and do, and in a sense who they are, varies from setting to setting. It follows that the search for an 'essential' identity which is non-social is a search for something non-human, for an identity not conceived or reflected upon in language. The philosophy underlying much survey work involves just such a non-social conception of the individual: people are removed from the contexts in which their views have meaning, and moreover are told that what they say will be inconsequential. It is argued that such uncontaminated remarks are nearer to essentially true views than normal contextualised speech for which an individual is always accountable (Becker, 1970). Against this, it can be argued that, if you tell people that their behaviour will be inconsequential, why should they bother to 'tell the truth'? Furthermore, saying different things in different settings is a normal part of social life, rather than a sign of peculiar deviousness or the will to deceive: the researcher can learn a great deal from discovering what remarks are considered appropriate in what setting. Likewise, observer effects can be seen as normal, inevitable and potentially informative, whereas for those adopting the essentialist view it is very sad that the observer too cannot be eliminated, for all social influences are regarded as reprehensible.

Thus we regard what people actually do and are recorded as doing as harder data than what they say they do. Similarly, we would regard what they say in various social contexts as better evidence of the structure of ideologies than what they say in private. Observations, properly recorded, yield 'harder' data than interviews. Ideally, therefore, observation should be a component of all research projects. However, we recognise that in many research situations interviewing subjects and using pre-recorded materials are the only possibilities. Since all of these sociologically inert entities in conjunction with theory can yield data, the impossibility of observing does not preclude research.

On Eclecticism and Pragmatism

There are good theoretical grounds for preferring some kinds of sociologically inert entities and certain techniques in the processes of data constitution. But theory also directs the researcher to make use of whatever appropriate inert entities are available. Such eclecticism now becomes epistemologically possible because of the central place which we allocate to theory in the constitution of data.

Since initial theories constitute data, they also allocate a weight and a meaning to data constituted from different kinds of inert objects. The question of how to weight, or how to add together, a casual remark, a recorded minute, an answer to a question, an employer's personnel file and an observed gesture is overcome. As part of the process of constituting these objects as data they are evaluated and given meaning in terms of the initial theory, which is elaborated to take account of their confirmations and contradictions. *Only* if theory is given a central place at this very first stage, if the task is conceived as data constitution rather than as data collection, can these different kinds of evidence be related together.

Advocating a multiplicity of methods is not quite the same as advocating triangulation, which depends upon the idea that multiplication can of itself provide a validation. Advocates of triangulation assume that inert entities, or data at least, speak for themselves, albeit in diverse tongues; they assume that the perspective of the researcher is a biasing factor; they assume ultimately that the objective of sociological inquiry is the truth, that real world events have a truth (Denzin, 1970). But truth in this timeless sense is an idealist category.

Our reason for advocating a multiplication of methods is somewhat different (and certainly quite independent of our conception of validation). In constituting data by a variety of methods, one is not asking which is the true or best indicator of some absent essence but rather what these data, having been converted into evidence, have to say. What place can be made for them in the initial theory? How can it grow to take account of them? What refinements does this evidence necessitate and precipitate? These questions make a virtue of the qualitative differences between the items of evidence collected.

So answers to questions can be usefully accommodated, once their status as data is established. This applies to the whole range of sources from which data can be constructed. A further paradox, then, is that *theory makes pragmatism possible.* If one wants to know about the prior socialisation of playgroup leaders, then the only data which can be constituted are answers to questions about schooling, work experience, friendship networks, and so on. If one cannot gain access to discussions between Common Market officials and civil servants in the Department of Trade and Industry, to analyse the relationship between capital and the state, then one must use newspaper reports, official statistics and accounts given by anyone prepared to be talked with. The doctrine seems a comforting one. We consider it to be both realistic and theoretically correct.

On Validation

Basic Concepts
The word truth has too many connotations to make a reconception possible. So this term has perforce been jettisoned, and replaced in our argument by *correctness.* In choosing this term, we intend to imply that correctness, unlike truth, is not absolute; on the contrary, correctness is always from a *standpoint.* Moreover, whereas truth implies the ultimate stillness of the absolute, we intend correctness to imply action. Correct knowledge demands to be used, and in this sense the objective of an enterprise is knowledge with a use potential, rather than truth. We call this useful knowledge, but in our concept utility is identified *prospectively.* This

leaves space for an assessment of correctness or of usefulness to be proved wrong by events.

Validity is defined in terms of *the adequacy and appropriateness of theory and the adequacy and appropriateness of data*. This new conception is necessary because if 'truth' or correctness is temporal, then the unqualified use of the term validation, denoting guarantees of truth, must be abandoned. The problem is to identify criteria in terms of which the moment-to-moment varying knowledges can be assessed as, for the moment, correct.

Adequacy and appropriateness, correctness and utility, necessitate a *standpoint* from which such judgements can be made. A standpoint as we conceive it is not merely an attribute of a subject but also an aspect of structure. A standpoint is a crystallised practice, or more technically, a moment in a practice. Standpoints then are structural rather than personal; but like the concept of practice itself, the concept of standpoint is intended to grasp a unity between a structure and its bearers.

On the Adequacy of Data and Theory

The adequacy of data cannot lie in themselves but retrospectively in their constituents and prospectively in their use. The constituents of data are sociologically inert entities and theory: flour, eggs and sugar, plus a recipe and a cook. While in this formulation it may appear that the criteria we seek to establish apply to each separately, it should be clear from the metaphor we have chosen that the quality of the end-product is a function of the relationship between the two.

Plainly, sociologically inert entities in themselves cannot be adequate or inadequate, appropriate or inappropriate. But it is possible to assess in this way the entities which have been selected for an active role as constituents of data. Here the question of adequacy becomes a question of *representativeness*. This representativeness is in part relational, determined by the way in which the theory creates data out of sociologically inert entities (the way in which the boundaries and conceptions of such entities are specified in the theory), and partly technical, being a function of the way in which the researcher sets about the task of identifying and responding to hitherto sociologically inert entities.

Both the initial theory in terms of which the data are constituted and the improved theory – new knowledge – with which the investigation ends must also be assessed in terms of their adequacy and appropriateness. Adequacy in the case of theory is structural: an adequate theory corresponds broadly to what has been characterised as *objective* theory. A structurally adequate, or objective, theory is one in which the constituent concepts and the relationships between them are clearly defined, and in this way made open and public to examination by other people as well as by the original theorist. A second characteristic of objective theory is the consistency of the relationship between its concepts. But internal consistency usually implies a finished quality, whereas we insist that a structurally adequate theory must be unfinished. Consistency must be a constant objective which is never achieved, for the permanent historical motion of the other constituent, the data incorporating sociologically inert entities, will constantly challenge and disrupt the consistency achieved so far. This is why one uses the analogy of theology for closed systems of thought for the 'data' of theologies are constructed entirely out of thought (e.g. angels), so that the scholasticist task is indeed that of generating a perfection of consistency between the thought categories. Internal consistency must be the objective of theory, for otherwise knowledges would remain itemised and discrete, which would render them inadequate for most purposes, whether scientific or practical. But we also recognise that internal consistency can never be attained in a non-idealist theory, that therefore internal consistency should never be attained. This criterion of adequacy, therefore, must involve an examination of the theoretical categories in terms of their consistency, to see whether necessary inconsistencies have been generated by material movements (which is fine) or unnecessary ones by insufficient thinking. The task is to eliminate both kinds of inconsistency, but of course the world will have again moved on while the task is in its process of inevitable non-completion.

In sum, the structural adequacy of the theoretical constituent of data (as of the theory in which the data are eventually described and located) lies in the character of its inconsistencies and the extent to which it is consistent, and in its resultant publicity. A structurally adequate theory will be both inside and vulnerable to the passage of time. This is the case both because of the role of inert entities (via data) in its own constitution, and because the process which we delineate is in fact simultaneous; in other words, because of both its past and its present. Structurally adequate theory, therefore, is both objective and changing. But at a moment in time its structural adequacy can be assessed: we are not offering a new relativism.

On Appropriateness

Representativeness and objectivity (adequacy) are necessary but not sufficient conditions for the creation of valid knowledge. A further necessary condition, likewise insufficient unless the others are met, is appropriateness to a purpose, a prerequisite of utility. Purposes are not determined by standpoints, but are certainly specific to them. Thus we are arguing that the validity of data and of the theory which ultimately describes them is specific to a standpoint. A theory may be correct now for the women's movement or for the community movement or for finance capitalists. It is extremely improbable that a theory would be correct for all three.

The appropriateness both of the inert entities and of the theory used in data constitution is given by their purpose. That means this appropriateness can only be judged from the standpoint of this purpose and of those whose purpose it is. But from such a standpoint appropriateness *can* be judged. Do these data and the knowledge generated with them clarify our position, reveal our weaknesses, show us what an appropriate course of action might be? If so, the data and the knowledge created with them are appropriate. One of the criteria of validity is achieved.

Valid knowledge, then, is historically specific not only because inert entities change but also because purposes, and, indeed in the longer run standpoints themselves, change. And even at a historical moment there will be more than one valid knowledge because there will be many and contradictory standpoints. But this position is no more relative than it is absolute. That dichotomy has been transcended.

On the Politics of Knowing

A standpoint, being a moment in a practice, implies a position also in a political structure, in the sense defined above. Thus purposes of knowledge enterprises, including the sociological enterprise, are in our sense politically given. So not only theories intended to serve and further these purposes are imbued with values, but also the very data which the theories in part constitute and out of which they are reconstituted. The 'facts' themselves speak with a political voice and kick with a political boot. For us, however, the pregnancy of data with values is not a problem, for this political constitution of data from a standpoint paradoxically also yields the criteria in terms of which the data and the theory describing them can be validated. For appropriateness is standpoint-given, and indirectly adequacy (representativeness and objectivity) is also necessary because of the standpoint-specific purpose of knowledge.

Thus there are no guarantees of knowledge which are independent of material and historical structures. Despite this, professional groups may pretend that they or their theories can produce knowledge which is absolute, or at least knowledge which is produced for purposes which are politically neutral. Such claims could be made for sociology. Our argument, however, is first that sociology is a position in an ideological (a knowledge) structure. Sociology is also a position in a political structure of institutions, opportunities, and competition or co-operation to achieve or control resources, status and communications. As a set of 'jobs' sociology is also a position in an economic structure. As a complex and changing unity of all these diverse practices, 'sociology' could be a standpoint. It is an empirical question as to whether sociology in fact is a unified standpoint of this kind at the present time; at the same time that possibility raises political questions. Professionalism claims political autonomy as a guarantee of ideological autonomy. But political autonomy is itself a political position, quite aside from the empirical point that complete autonomy is never achieved.

Blume (1974) has demonstrated empirically how political structures create and filter knowledge. We have argued theoretically that standpoints affect the constitution of both data and theory and we have shown that professions are standpoints. Thus on two counts we claim both that sociological knowledge is political and that professionalism cannot rescue it; and that this does not matter.

But in spite of our welcoming acceptance of value-laden facts, and our happy-go-lucky eclecticism in relation to sources, we insist on theoretical objectivity and a high standard of scholarship involving both technical competence and methodological rigour. Indeed the very lack of neutrality and the qualitative variation which our position forces us to accept are two main reasons for our insistence on objectivity and scholarship.

Scholarship: The Sociologist's Task

On Purposes

To be correct, knowledge must fulfil the purposes for which it was constructed. Knowledge thus defined guides people about what to do next by describing and elucidating where they are now, and it enables policy to be formulated for a given standpoint. Such knowledge, for example, could tell one how to formulate appropriate policies for a government of which one approved and whose standpoint one shared, although many sociologists might for various reasons not wish to work from the standpoint of officialdom, and many official policy-makers might for various reasons reject our attempt to make usefulness theoretically possible.

Thus useful knowledge must be valid, in our sense. Courses of action cannot be usefully or successfully shaped on the basis of invalid (inappropriate or inadequate) knowledge, nor is it helpful to tilt one's lance at abstract as opposed to abstracted opponents.

If, then, the aim of knowledge is to assist in devising a strategy for action by theorising and comprehending developments in society, this can only be done if distortion is minimised. Publicity and debatability achieve this.

On Publicity

Publicity – openness to continuous critical reappraisal – is a fundamental criterion of scholarship. Publicity makes possible assessments of the representativeness (adequacy) of data, of the objectivity (structural adequacy) of theory and of the processes of data constitution. This is why publicity is the key to scholarship.

In part the way in which this publicity may be achieved has already been discussed. The objectivity of relationships between concepts and objects within a theory is crucial. Conceptualisation must be clear, rigorous and explicit. It is a responsibility of every researcher, therefore, to be a theorist. If he or she is not, valid data and knowledge cannot be created. If he or she is not, therefore, useful knowledge cannot be created. This leads on to a consideration of the other, more frequently neglected, part of the sociologist's task.

Theory breathes life into sociologically inert entities and data are created. The mechanisms by which this is achieved must also be public if the data and the knowledge describing and situating them are to be adequate and capable of being valid and useful which will depend on their being appropriate as well. Great care must therefore be taken to specify in detail all sources, whether of theory or of inert objects. Technical proficiency in accordance with rules which are made public must be shown in relation to how these sources are first identified and then culled. This relates particularly to the criterion of representativeness of inert entities, but also in a different way to the use and formulation of theory. It is for this reason that sampling theory, comprehensiveness of the search for written sources and the rules governing their selection, the manner of recording field diaries and, always, close specification of the data base are essential. It is important if the knowledge is to be valid and therefore useful, to know, for example, if a researcher spend twelve half-days in a court or a hundred and fifty-two, and in either case whether the days were consecutive or spread over as many weeks. It is important because it enables both the researcher and other people (not just sociologists) to assess the representativeness of the inert entities likely to have been available to the researcher, and therefore the representativeness of the data and thus the adequacy and appropriateness (validity) of the new knowledge for the purposes for which it was produced. This point is crucial. Sloppy research is dangerous because it can lead to wrong policy decisions. Sloppy research can only be identified, and politically ignored or counted as necessary, if *both* constituents of the data, of the fundamental 'facts' of the new knowledge, are open to public appraisal, evaluation, criticism and debate.

Technical proficiency is important, but it is apposite to regard the sociologist as a craftsperson (Mills, 1959) rather than a technician. For although sociological research practices must be governed by rules which can be made public, or the data produced will not be valid, these rules need not necessarily be fixed in advance. Indeed, the same arguments apply to these rules as we used in our discussion of idealist as opposed to historically vulnerable theory: if timeless technical rules are fixed absolutely and in advance they will end up being inappropriate to the ever-changing inert objects which they are supposed to reconstitute as data.[1] Technical rules, rules of practice, must often be developed by the sociological craftsperson as he or she goes along, though he or she would be just as unwise to ignore altogether the rules developed by previous craftspeople as to ignore altogether all previous theory. Both will be adapted in relation with the inert objects of which they are making sense. The good sociologist will not beat an egg with a wooden spoon just because he or she believes in wooden spoons. What is important is that he or she can tell us afterwards whether he or she used a fork or a whisk. The rules of technique, however newly elaborated, must be capable of public representation, and must be so represented.

Even quantification, that masochistic pastime in the modern sociological world, can now be advised to stand up and brush itself down and take its place with dignity amongst the legitimate practices of sociological researchers. For while repetition can never demonstrate truth, and *what* has been counted must always be assessed by criteria of appropriateness, quantitative distributions of data may well be important, and whether they are or not in a theoretical sense, it is essential that they be produced in order to meet the criterion of publicity. A statement of the order: 'I went to court on twenty-eight occasions when squatting cases were being heard. On twenty-one of these occasions such-and-such happened. In six of the remaining seven cases the squatters were students . . . (etc.)' carries more weight, it is averred, than 'courts are usually harder on immigrant and working-class families than they are on students. On one occasion the judge said . . .' This is obvious, but it is not often done. And we submit that an even larger number of cases would leave readers and users of the research in an even better position for judging its adequacy and appropriateness. Statistical tests of significance may well help in this process. If numeracy is one among many ways of achieving publicity, then these skills are welcome indeed in the battery of sociological practices. What we are providing is a new context of use for quantitative data. It must be apparent by now that the imperialism of any technique can only retard the growth of useful knowledge.

Our plea for scholarship is therefore based on the fact that good theory and knowledge, as well as data, are impossible without it. In sum, research must be scholarly, and theory must be scholarly and its relations objective, if the knowledge generated is to meet the criteria of validity which we have established. These criteria themselves are largely derived from the fact that knowledge is constructed from a standpoint and for a purpose. The criteria are: appropriateness to the purpose of inert objects constituted as data; adequacy of inert entities in terms of their representatives as guaranteed by technical proficiency and publicity; structurally adequate theory, that is, theory which is of and in time, aiming for internal consistency and objective; and appropriate theory in terms of the purpose for which the new knowledge is being made. Sociologists must be both scholars and craftspeople.

On Accountability

The sociologist emerges from our arguments as a highly responsible person. He or she is responsible for his or her own theory and research practices. He or she alone can ensure that the knowledge he or she produces meets the criteria of validity which will enable it to be used by him/herself and by others within his or her standpoint. Moreover, although we have established criteria, the sociologist alone can decide when his or her theory is consistent enough, when his or her data include sufficiently representative inert entities, and so on. And while we can offer no rigid tests or guarantees, we insist at the same time that because of this every aspect of the process of knowledge constitution must be public and open to debate. Our sociologist is at risk indeed.

We welcome both the risk and the responsibility, for they add dignity to our chosen task. For too long sociologists have evaded these responsibilities, first in the myth of value-neutrality, in the idea that the world properly approached will speak for itself, and later in the myth that the truths of subjects' worlds could be frozen and apprehended, and that subjects could and would validate sociologists' representations of their knowledge. For these so called 'objective' and 'subjective' tests we can substitute no certainties. The sociologist cannot abdicate from his or her responsibility for the knowledge he or she produces. He or she must validate it, and must assist the knowledge users, of whom he or she may be one, both in assessing it and in interpreting its political messages.

To the competent sociologist anything does not go, eclectic and pragmatic though he or she may be in his or her choice of methods and sources: only valid knowledge counts. These assessments of adequacy and appropriateness (validity) cannot be made entirely within science, and the truly scholarly sociologist should make sure he or she is vulnerable to the judgements of those sharing the standpoint from which he or she claims to be working. However, these external and changing criteria of adequacy and appropriateness necessitate rather than subvert the maintenance of clear standards of practice in social scientific research.

The sociological researcher is therefore both responsible and accountable. His or her accountability is not to 'the profession' but to those who need the knowledge, and from whose standpoint it was made. We have argued that sociology and all knowledge is political in a far deeper sense than Blume and the post-Kuhnians ever imagined; knowledge is intrinsically political, not adventitiously so. This makes scholarship crucial in a way that for the positivists was unnecessary, and for the relativists impossible. In arguing that the task of sociology is to provide useful descriptions of the world as it is, we reassert our confidence that, in the task of intellectual production, sociologists can, indeed must, be scholarly craftspeople.

Notes: Chapter 7

The authors would like to thank Steven Ackroyd, Jennifer Platt and Colin Sumner for their comments on an earlier draft of this chapter.

1   Here we take issue with Feyerabend (1975), despite our agreement that fixed technical rules can inhibit the growth of knowledge. The problem lies not in rules as such, but in the fetishism of already existing rules.

8

W(h)ither Sociological Methodology?: Generalisation and Comparative Method

PETER ABELL

Introduction

I do not wish to use the word 'methodology' in a very precise sense though the burden of what I have to say will fall towards what we might term the epistemological end of things. That is to say, I am not so much concerned with research techniques as with claims concerning the appropriate methods for gaining social and scientific knowledge. In the spirit of this rather loose interpretation of the word much of what I say will stray across that hazy boundary between methodology and theory – even meta-theory. Again I do not want to draw any boundaries; I am in what follows concerned with that activity in sociology which debates the relative virtues of alternative ways of conceptualising social reality and thus presumably attempting to gain knowledge of it.

My title poses both a question and an answer, or more correctly an aspiration – on the first count whither methodology, where should it go in the future? My suggestion is that it should diminish in importance from its present, in my view, inflated position in British sociology. The chapter is divided into two parts – first some rather general and polemical remarks concerning the role of methodology in contemporary British sociology; secondly, an analysis of what I regard as the central issue facing sociology at the moment – not so much what conventional wisdom would dictate, that is, positivism vs anti-positivism, but the role that generalisation should take in our inquiries. I am concerned that certain contemporary trends in methodology and theory seem, either advertently or inadvertently, to be legitimising the introduction of a non-generalising perspective into our discipline.

The Role of Methodology

How could we characterise the achievements and failures of British sociology over the past few decades? The first thing that would, I think, strike any observer even if he or she restricted his or her attention to the last decade or so is the extent to which the discipline is subject to what I can only term fashion and fad.

In the late 1960s functionalism was the reigning orthodoxy outside Marxist circles. This orthodoxy, however, was being challenged – particularly in its overtly positivistic interpretation – by a variegated collection of doctrines and we heard phrases like 'the practico-inert' ringing down the corridors of many departments. Since then the variety of doctrines which, in one way or another, have laid claim to embody all that is truth and virtue has been manifold. I could easily run off a series of catch-phrases, once the subject of heated and often acrimonious debate, which all seem to have died a natural death. The life expectancy of each rarely exceeds five years or so and all this is no less true of the various Marxist sociologies as well. Such a state of affairs would be all very well if, as a result, we could see the gradual emergence of a clearer picture of how we should conduct ourselves as social investigators and provide a body of attested sociological knowledge. In my view there is clear evidence of some achievement in the latter respect but it has, to a large degree (but not entirely), taken place in isolation from the fierce methodological/epistemological/theoretical debates. I draw the rather uncomfortable conclusion, therefore, that the debates have in some fairly evident sense been a waste of time. To put it another way – in so far as we have gained any knowledge whatsoever of the social world (and I feel that it is often partial and fleeting), we have done so largely without the help of received theory/methodological/epistemological dispute.

Why should this be so? To coin a phrase myself, it is largely attributable to the 'separation of theory and method on the one hand from practice on the other'. But before I document what I mean by this and some of its serious and debilitating consequences I should like to place my assertion in a wider context.

Methodological debate in sociology seems to be animated by an assumption to the effect that there is some method or set of methods of social inquiry, if we did but know it, which would give us the sort of knowledge that is resistant to conceptual criticism; that is 'knowledge' which is in some sense conceptually or logically correct or perfectly sound. Of course our theories and facts could still be 'true' or 'false' but at least they would be capable of so being since they would be logically or conceptually 'true' precisely because they are epistemologically informed by the correct method. Thus, for instance, positivism is criticised precisely because its epistemological assumptions are not adequate to the subject matter which it addresses. This is not the place to delve into the possible meanings of terms like 'truth' and 'logically correct', but what I wish to argue is that this assumption or objective is in all likelihood unrealisable and, thus, we find the wasted effort I referred to above.

Although it is perhaps unwise to draw too many conclusions for the social sciences from happenings in the physical sciences, a brief look at the same problem there might be instructive. I am prepared to say that a review of the history of the physical sciences leads one to the shattering conclusion that all theories (and the propositions expressing factual evidence for them) are open to conceptual criticism. That is to say they are, without exception, from the most vaunted to the most humble, in some sense conceptually unintelligible. Take, for example, 'force at a distance' – the Aristotelians were quite right when they proclaimed the Newtonian picture of the solar system unintelligible but who would be prepared to say that they were also right in rejecting it on these grounds? What would have happened to the development of physics if the Aristotelians had had their way and consigned the Newtonian physics to the rubbish bin of history?

The lesson I draw from studying the history of the physical and biological sciences is that all attempts to model or grasp reality are to some degree based upon a 'conceptual compromise' – sometimes explicit, sometimes implicit – but inexorably so. Now one may argue that the social sciences are (or should be) different; one may appeal to the logical discontinuity between the social and physical sciences (which I accept) and propose the view that what is true for one need not be so for the other. This may in turn be also true though it is difficult to see how the social sciences, which are universally held to be conceptually more complex than the physical sciences, could evade the same pitfalls. If we concede the point that any attempt to study (model) that complex thing called social reality will, to some degree, be based upon a conceptual compromise, where does that leave methodology and its twin sister theory?

A number of things seem to me to follow.

(1)   Conceptual criticisms *per se* will always and everywhere be possible. I would also argue, given the present level of development of sociology, that the ability to provide such criticisms is fairly widely distributed as it is not a particularly intellectually taxing exercise.
(2)   Conceptual/methodological criticism should not normally be carried on in isolation from attempts by the critic to erect and test an alternative model/theory which *by his or her standards* is superior.
(3)   I think this in turn implies that there should be no separate role in sociology for the methodologist and theorist *per se*. Theoretical/methodological debate (and hopefully progress) should take place in the context of empirical inquiries concerned to solve specific problems

– however macro or micro in orientation. There is a rider here: I believe that so-called social theory is so poorly developed that it is not an intellectually worthy enterprise when taken by itself. I find, when compared, say, with general equilibrium theory in economics or most advanced physical theories, the intellectual achievement (and demands) of sociological theory are trivial. In the early days of the development of physics, before the structure of physical theory became so demanding that it necessitated a specialist role, each individual was his or her own theorist working within the framework of received, often competing, theories which were also developed at the empirical end of things. Some argue that sociological theory is indeed taxing (anybody who has tried to tussle with Althusser, Habermas and Parsons, to name only three, may apparently, with some justification, say so) but my feeling is that when these authors are stripped of their verbal pretention the structures left are not of sufficient intellectual depth, complexity, or difficulty to warrant the role of theorist *per se.*

(4) These observations have some implications for the teaching of sociology. First, theory and methodology should not normally be taught in isolation from attempts to solve empirical problems (I exclude here research techniques). In particular the present practice of teaching 'methods courses' which are essentially philosophy of science should be severely curtailed. The alternative approaches to the gaining of social science knowledge (with their inherent conceptual compromises) should be studied in the context of empirical problem-solving. Students should be exposed to alternative ways of addressing empirical problems and asked to adjudicate between them in terms of their competing epistemological assumptions. But they should (and this in my view is essential) then be encouraged, if they find fault, to provide an alternative way of studying the problem (or even rejecting the problem as significant) which would overcome their criticism. In so doing they will encounter their own conceptual compromises and be socialised into the view that criticism on its own is not enough. The present practice of separating out special courses has the effect of instilling the idea in students that the role of methodologist/theorist *per se* is an intellectually tenable one.

In this respect the situation at postgraduate level is calamitous. I estimate that a very large proportion of postgraduates in the UK are involved in straight methodological/theoretical/conceptual inquiry, quite often designed to 'evaluate critically' some well-known theorist. For instance, I have encountered PhD students writing theses in this vein on Parsons, Habermas and Althusser. Not only is this a waste of time, as the authors in question do not warrant such attention, but even if they did, it is puzzling that a student with no experience of the conceptual compromises which one has to make in research should be so engaged. If the above 'theorists' and the like have over a lifetime's experience given us ideas of worth, then what possible purpose can be served by a relatively inexperienced doctoral student culling around to find conceptual inconsistencies? If the ideas are of worth then put them to work. Use them to solve a problem and encounter the inevitable conceptual compromises one has to make in research however one approaches it – as a positivist, a phenomenologist, or a Marxist.

All this might sound rather hard to take but let me emphasise that I am trying to put the case in a stark and controversial manner. Given more space there would be certain caveats I would like to make but I stand by the assertion that many (if not a majority) of the PhD theses written (unfortunately usually financed by public money from the SSRC) are of no real use. The fine-grained conceptual criticism involved (1) is so easy to do that it should not constitute 'original research' as required at PhD level and (2) distracts talented students into the second-order activity of criticising established theorists/methodologists rather than trying to solve empirical problems for themselves. How many postgraduate students, when asked what they are studying, give the answer X where X is a named sociologist?˙ This preoccupation is, of course, reflected in our journals and the welter of papers submitted to them.

Theoretical and methodological debate should emerge from the necessarily flawed attempts to solve real empirical problems; in this way we might hope for some cumulative theoretical development and the consequent attenuation of linguistic fads and fashion. Then the day may eventually dawn when the 'theoretical' problems are worthy of study in their own right and the role of social theorist will become an acceptable one. Meanwhile we should change our teaching and practice according to the dictates of the time.

Generalisation in Sociology

My second concern about contemporary sociology is the sometimes explicit, often implicit, attack on the use of generalisation.

Until quite recently, what we might term the conventional approach to sociological investigation was one which implored us to search for generalisations or patterns in social phenomena. In its extreme version it would have taken us a stage further, either seeking to identify these generalisations as 'laws' or subsuming them as empirical generalisations under Laws (usually causal ones) in accordance with the strictures of the hypothetico–deductive or probabilistic–inductive models of scientific explanation. Thus, sociology was to be interpreted as a nomothetic enterprise just like any other 'science' and explanation of social phenomena was accordingly necessarily associated with the process of generalisation (inductively or deductively). This approach has been rather imprecisely called 'positivism', though, of course, some have rejected these models as inappropriate even to the physical sciences.

There has in the history of sociology been an intermittent reaction to this general viewpoint, rejecting generalisation as the objective of sociology and variously suggesting that (1) social phenomena do not 'contain' generalisations; (2) even if they do they are not 'laws' in the sense required by the epistemics of the hypothetico–deductive or probabilistic–inductive models of scientific explanation and are, moreover, often trivial; (3) thus, that these models are inappropriate; (4) social phenomena need to be *understood* and explained (in some sense of this term) without recourse to generalisation.

Closely allied to these ideas is the view that meaningful social action is the centrepiece of sociological inquiry and, despite Parsons's valiant efforts, the concept has become closely associated with ideographic interpretations of social science.

Though the attacks on 'positivism', especially in their most recent variants (broadly speaking humanistic/phenomenological/ethnographic), are often concerned to reject more than a generalising perspective (for instance, they also reject measurement, causality, experimental method), it is not my intention to confront these issues here. Rather my concern is to defend the generalising perspective in sociology though, I must emphasise, not within what might be termed a positivistic framework. It will perhaps help the reader if I summarise the viewpoint I wish to defend before I provide an analysis of the conventional 'logic of generalisation' and its close cousin 'comparative method'.

If we adopt the view that the central subject matter of sociological investigation is the social action of individuals (and collectivities, but I will not consider these here) then much simple instrumental action may be described in the following general form (Von Wright, 1971; Abell, 1977).

(1) An actor in a situation he describes as C has objectives or intentions X_j.
(2) The actor *reasons* that if he brings about or does X_i (in C) then X_j will result.
(3) The actor intends X_i.
(4) The actor therefore brings about or does X_i.

This scheme of things is, of course, much more problematic where the word 'actor' alludes to a collectivity of one sort or another, but when and where it refers to an individual the four statements seem to capture reasonably well the idea of instrumental action, i.e. the doing of something to realise something else. Needless to say, C, X_i and X_j may be highly complex natural language descriptions and may not even be 'precise' or 'unambiguous'. But these complications will not alter my central argument. Furthermore, one may wish to extend C to include taken-for-granted assumptions. In the space available all I can say is that the present formulation is compatible with such ideas. Similarly, in what follows there are a number of points at which it is not possible to qualify or extend the argument further. For the moment we may note that in response to the question 'why does or did the actor in question do X_i?' (i.e. bring about X_i) we would quite naturally provide the answer 'because he intended to bring about X_j and reasoned or believed that his doing or bringing about X_i would "lead to" X_j.' Thus, at a first order of analysis statements 1, 2 and 3 provide an explanation of the actor's act in bringing about X_i. The 'therefore' in statement 4 seems to confirm this interpretation; statements 1, 2 and 3 comprise a rather rough and ready practical or intentional syllogism. Now if an 'explanation' of the actor's act (the bringing about of X_i) can be provided by recourse to a syllogism of this sort we might quite reasonably ask – whence the need for generalisations? For it seems evident that the syllogism (a) provides some sort of explanation of what the actor is or was doing and (b) does so without any overt reference to any generalisation whatsoever. We have no need to cast statements 1, 2 or 3 in general form to 'deduce' statement 4. It may perhaps be argued that the syllogism depends, for its explanatory power, upon a suppressed generalisation to the effect that 'people always do what they intend' – or at least attempt what they intend. This would, however, be similar to saying that the hypothetico–deductive model, when postulating a causal law between events, depends upon the assumption that 'every effect has a cause' – something that comes very close to tautology indeed.

The syllogism might, nevertheless, refer *indirectly* to a generalisation. For, if X_i and X_j are physical events then the actor's practical reasoning rests upon his model of the causal relations between events in the physical world. Thus, in answer to the question 'why does X_i lead to X_j?' one would have to resort to a classical hypothetico–deductive causal explanation dependent upon some generalisation either connecting X_i and X_j or enabling one to deduce the connection between them. But notice the *incidental* nature of any such generalisation to the explanatory scheme 1–4. It may be that statement 2 is true even though X_i does not cause X_j; the conjunction of statements 1, 2 and 3 still, nevertheless, provides an explanation of why the actor did or does X_i. The explanation is invariant to the 'truth' of the causal generalisation connecting X_j and X_i or, putting it another way, the validity of the explanation does not depend upon the truth of the causal generalisation explaining the connection between X_i and X_j. This generalisation is nevertheless *necessary* to any explanation of why the action was successful or not. We should as a consequence not be overhasty in expunging the hypothetico–deductive structure from the armoury of the social scientist for we may well wish to explain why certain courses of action are unsuccessful.

There is one feature of the syllogism 1–4 which does perhaps call for comment. Its explanatory force depends upon the 'truth' of the statements 1 and 3 concerning the actor's intentions. Many have argued, quite incorrectly in my view, that habitual and routinised human behaviour is not intentional in nature. That is to say, there is no mental event, under such circumstances, enabling us to ascertain the truth of the intentional statements. This is quite evidently a complex issue but let it suffice here to say that I wish to use the term intention in a way that does not necessarily imply conscious awareness. Thus, statement 1, for instance, could cover an unconscious or pre-conscious intention of the kind discussed by Freud. Further, as for habitual behaviour it is, I think, best to interpret the statement '= intended x' as true if = can, under 'truth telling conditions', ascribe to the truth of the proposition that he did intend x on the occasion in question. It is, of course, the claim of psychoanalysis that unconscious intentions can be made to fall under this rubric also. I cannot discuss these issues at length, but I would maintain that an extended concept of intention formulated along these lines enables us to establish that the syllogistic explanatory structure has a very wide if not universal applicability in social science (*pace* the hypothetico–deductive and inductive–probabilistic models in physical science).

If we can guarantee explanation of the sort under investigation without recourse to generalisation, why should we trouble our minds at all with the role of generalisation in sociology? After all, generalisations enter the hypothetico–deductive model with the expressed purpose of providing an explanation; that is to say, generalisations, according to this model and the inductive–probabilistic one also, are *necessary* to effect an explanation. It seems to me that the central issue in the so-called 'crisis in sociology' (or more generally social science) concerns the role of generalisation. Those of an anti-positivistic persuasion have, and in part rightly, shunned the hypothetico–deductive model as a necessary logical construct in the explanation of 'social phenomena' and in so doing highlighted the possibility of explaining (or understanding) such phenomena without reference to any generalised proposition. Thus it appears that there is some truth in the longstanding distinction which has been drawn between the nomothetic and ideographic sciences whereby a sharp logical divide is drawn between, on the one hand, those 'sciences' for which generalisations (usually causal – nomothetic – ones) are necessary to explanation and the social sciences where this is not so; hence the apparent collapse of the 'unity of scientific method'. Whereas in the nomothetic sciences generalisation is a precondition of explanation, in the social sciences, explanation is a precondition of generalisation. One explains (or understands) in the social sciences in order to generalise, not the reverse. How can this be?

If we return to statements 1–4 once again, let us concede that, despite certain reservations we might have, statement 4 is in some sense of the word explained by the formal conjunction of statements 1, 2 and 3. If this assertion is correct we could then adopt a syllogistic structure of this form as a general model for 'explanation' of instrumental acts where the X_i, X_j and C would, in the typical case, stand for more or less complex (natural language) descriptions. It is my contention that such first-order explanations, as I shall term them, can always be provided to explain what a particular actor is going to do or has done on a particular occasion but they are only part, although a necessary part, of the sociological enterprise. I incline to the admittedly metaphysical viewpoint that what individuals (and collectivities) 'do' could, in principle, if not in practice, always be 'explained' in terms of some sort of intentional syllogism. Thus, the history of individuals, collectivities, and so on, could in principle be both described and explained (at a first-order level) in terms of a complex and often interrelated sequence of such syllogisms. Needless to say there might be rather acute empirical problems in so doing, but that is another matter.

In one sense such a sequence, if it could be provided, would give an individualising historical description/explanation of the actors concerned; it would, as it were, give an account of 'everything they had done' – an action biography or narrative. It seems to me that such biographies and narratives form the phenomenal basis upon which both the social scientists, historian and ethnographer, should 'work' in their respective ways. It is the 'job' of the social scientist to locate generalisations either inter or intra individually in such action biographies and narratives. It might reasonably be asked why this should be accomplished, since such generalisations are necessary neither to describe nor explain the actions concerned.

The need for generalisations arises in a rather different way, namely, to explain what we might describe as *structural regularities* generated in the course of on-going social action. A number of social theorists, at least since Marx, have wished to explain social phenomena partly in 'structural' and partly in 'voluntaristic' terms, the latter depending upon the action and 'power' of individuals and perhaps collectivities. The central problem in social theory has always been to combine these two perspectives into a conceptually convincing and logically consistent general model, with applicability to a wide range of social phenomena. Unfortunately, of course, many so-called social theorists have opted for one view to the exclusion of the other, giving a one-sided view of things. And where attempts have been provided to combine the two the results seem to me to have been largely incomprehensible. In outline, my argument is as follows. Structural regularities should be *explained* by deductions of the following general form:

(5)   In situation C actor $=$ intends X_j.
(6)   Actor $=$ *reasons* that in C if he *does* X_i, X_j will result.
(7)   Actor $=$ *does* X_i.
(8) X_j 'happens' (i.e. becomes the case).
(9) X_j 'leads to' X_k (this 'leads to' may or may not be causal).

Abstracting from the agency of actor $=$ we have by deduction:

(10) C 'leads to' X_k.

Now if either (a) $=$ repeatedly does X_i (in his belief that it will result in X_j) in C,

or (b) a series of actors (in C) act in this way,

then we will be able to locate a 'structural regularity', 'if C then X_k', and provide an *explanation* of it in terms of the practical syllogism.

Let me emphasise that this scheme of things is highly simplified, but even so we can indicate two central problems:

(a)   Situation C may not be perceived as C, thus 5 would read 'in situation perceived as C, $=$ intends X_j. Effecting the deduction would then lead to the reformulation 'a situation perceived as C leads to X_k'. So the problem becomes – how can we incorporate Thomas's theorem into our scheme?

(b)   Precisely what is the logical and epistemic status of the copula 'leads to' in 10, it being deduced from propositions relating
  (i) C to the actor's intention (X_j),
  (ii)   the actor's reasoning that X_i leads to X_j,
  (iii)   the fact that X_j leads to X_k?

If we return now explicitly to the role of generalisation in this scheme, there is nothing inherent within it which actually requires generalisations – 'C leads to X_k' can be deduced as a singular proposition from the conjunction of 5–9, each again in the singular form. However, it seems to me that social phenomena are only of interest to the social scientist (as opposed to the historian) in so far as one can locate structural regularities, for example, statements in the *general* form 'if C then X_k'. Statements of the form 'C then X_k' interpreted either in a singular or general form are central to the sociological enterprise. For let us assume, first, that there was no relationship between any conceivable C and what an actor does (i.e. brings about); then this would be tantamount to saying that the actor's behaviour bore no relationship to his or her situation. This is, of course, both logically and empirically possible. There may be cases of action of this sort *where* no way can be found of 'linking' what an actor does to the situation. A first-order explanation of what he or she is doing can still be provided using an appropriate syllogism and indeed his or her intention X_j may well be deductively derived from a 'deeper lying' intention or purpose. Such an explanation is of intrinsic interest to the psychologist but defeats the purpose of the sociologist.

We should now contrast the scheme 5–10 with the classical hypothetico–deductive model. There are some superficial similarities, but the differences are profound. The first major difference is the one already alluded to, that in order to explain a singular event using the hypothetico–deductive model the axioms thereof must contain at least one universal proposition (usually a 'causal law') whereas the scheme 1–10 does not depend on any generalisation except perhaps implicitly those explaining the connection between events X_i, X_j and X_k. The point is that the syllogistic system establishes an explanation of a singular event without direct recourse to these generalisations or indeed any others. However, as social scientists we are not interested in singular events but general ones. The syllogistic scheme can then, as it were, be applied 'n times over' to account for the regularity whereby n actors, in situation C, bring about X_k. Looking at things this way highlights the logical differences between the hypothetico–deductive and syllogistic models. The explanation of a singular event with the hypothetico–deductive model requires one to *deduce* the statement describing the event from the conjunction of at least one universal generalisation and a set of instantial propositions. The explanatory system is essentially deductive, taking us from the general to the specific. With the syllogistic system, on the other hand, the explanation is again effected by deduction, but from the conjunction of singular statements. The process of *generalisation*, which is logically distinct from the process of explanation, is, on the other hand, *inductive* – the application of the syllogism to each case! The social scientific endeavour has thus a deductive explanatory mode and an inductive generalising mode; but each mode is, as it were, logically distinctive although epistemically tied.

Generalisations may enter sociological reasoning in other ways also. I have space only to list them here: first, in providing an 'explanation' of why individuals have or choose the intentions and objectives they have and secondly, why they *reason* the way they do. These turn out to be very complex questions, but if they can be answered they provide 'higher-order' explanations of the premises of the syllogism itself.

Let us return to the inductive use of the syllogistic scheme to explain a structural pattern 'if C then X_k'. What one is doing when one applies it 'repeatedly' to account for the structural *pattern* is to create an equivalence on all the acts that produce X_k. That is to say, one is postulating that the acts are *identical*. This is an over-strong requirement, for in the practice of any generalising science (which I am claiming sociology should be) one creates abstract equivalences which in turn enter generalisations in a rather more relaxed way than this.

If for the sake of expository convenience, but without loss of generality, we truncate the syllogistic scheme to the form

$$\text{if } C \text{ then act } A$$
$$\text{if act } A \text{ then } X$$
$$\therefore \text{ if } C \text{ then } X,$$

equivalences can be created in terms of (1) C the perceived situation, (2) the act A itself and (3) the 'consequence' of the act X.

In the extreme we can imagine a situation where every act is unique (as, of course, it is in the least temporal/spatial location) and thus 'co-ordinating' a unique C, A and X. The art of scientific activity, however, is one of imposing equivalence classes upon what initially might appear to be unique phenomena. I would claim that in analysing the relationship between explanations and generalisation along the lines I have outlined one is able to be both precise and creative in this respect.

The explanatory system 5–10 (or its truncated form) might well superficially smack of a stimulus–response, behaviourist methodology. However, this is not the case. The assumptions of stimulus–response methodology require that an explanation is established by subsuming a particular stimulus–response sequence under a general one (i.e. for the very hard-headed stimulus–response law, *pace* the hypothetico–deductive model). As I have repeatedly emphasised, my scheme departs from this viewpoint in at least two vital respects: first, the explanation of the individual C–X sequence is established without direct recourse to any generalisation, and secondly, it is the general C–X pattern that itself requires explanation through the inductive use of the syllogism.

Comparative Method

The possibility of generalisation using the hypothetico–deductive and inductive–probabilistic models of scientific explanation are inherently tied to the comparative method. To locate a causal 'law' of the form 'A causes B', and where we interpret A as only a *sufficient* condition for B, implies 'all A are B' – that is to say, there are no As that are not Bs. It leaves open, however, the possibility that not-As that are Bs or not-Bs. If we, further, require A to be a *necessary* condition also, then this implies all not-As are not-Bs or, what is the same, there are no not-As that are Bs. In practice, of course, where B is *overdetermined* (i.e. there is more than one *sufficient* cause of B), it is the set of *alternative* causes which is necessary and sufficient for B. Furthermore, we can also entertain the idea of a sufficient (causal) relationship between A and B in the face of some As that are not-Bs by requiring that it is the *conjunction* of A and other conditions (initial conditions in the parlance of the hypothetico–deductive model) that are jointly sufficient for B. The occurrence of overdetermination and 'initial conditions' permits one to contemplate a causal link between A and B even where all the four *logical* possible combinations of A and B occur.

But consider the straightforward case 'A is a necessary and sufficient cause of B'. Then, to *test* for such a relationship, one would seek out cases of A finding that they were B and cases of not-A finding that they were not-B. One compares, so to speak, As with not-As with respect to B. Thus we have generated the comparative method. We would not establish a necessary and sufficient causal relationship between A and B merely by inspecting cases of A and noting that they are B and in so doing excluding cases of A that are not-B. We also need to exclude cases that are not-A being B by establishing that all the not-As are not-Bs.

Where A is only a *sufficient* cause of B we still need to rely upon comparative method. Once again we must exclude cases of A that are not-B by guaranteeing that all A are B. But we do not exclude not-A that is B because if A is only a sufficient cause of B there is the possibility that other factors are sufficient to cause B. However, the comparative method is still required to establish that A is a sufficient cause for B. We need to establish that holding all other possible or sufficient causes of B constant, not-As are not-Bs. This objective is usually accomplished through the manipulation of 'variables' in the experimental method or statistically where such methods are impossible or inappropriate. So in so far as explanation depends upon the hypothetico–deductive model, it depends upon causal generalisation and thus on comparative method.

One of the central criticisms that has been levelled at what is loosely termed positivistic method in sociology implicitly revolves around its reliance on comparative method. It is variously argued by 'anti-positivists' that:

(a)   To describe and *explain* human action – which essentially takes the form that an actor does X because of C – does not require us to locate cases of actors who do not do X because they are not in C.

(b)   Furthermore it is lucky that it does not, for it may empirically be the case that there are no cases of actors in not-C, so if explanation was dependent upon comparative method we would be in an impasse. (This argument is probably most pertinent in the context of 'hegemonic' theories of culture which would have it that *all* are manipulated in one way or another.) And thus there are no non-manipulated individuals around to test the universal proportion concerning the manipulation. (Abell, 1977)

It should be clear from what I have said so far that I accept both these points, albeit in a special way.

This can be made clear by considering the syllogistic systems 1–4 and 5–10 once again. If one explains the doing of X_j by the doing of X_i (according to 1–4) then, as I have suggested, this explanation in no way depends upon any generalisation nor, accordingly, on comparative method. There is no sense in which we have to locate actors who did *not* intend X_j and 'did not do X_i' to establish an adequate explanation. If we switch to the more complex explanatory systems 5–10 then a similar line of reasoning holds, if we interpret statement 5 in perceptual terms, i.e. 'in situation *perceived* as C actor $=$ intends X_j'. Once again this and the following statements are in singular form and enable us to deduce statement 10. The explanatory force of the total deductive system does not, therefore, rest upon the use of comparative method. It stands in the absence of (a) others who intend X_j in C, and so on, and (b) others who do not intend X_j in the absence of C.

However, if we interpret statement 5 in 'objective unperceived terms' so it reads 'in situation C actor $\doteqdot$ intends X_j' (i.e. where the actor does not recognise C it therefore does not enter his practical *reasoning*), the link between C and intention X_j (and ultimately X_k) can only be established through generalisation by discovery that in situation C individuals characteristically intend X_j. Of course some would wish to exclude such discoveries from social science, dismissing them as either fortuitous or of no interest. I believe such an approach is dangerously debilitating, but we must leave open, if we accept such discovered generalisations as interesting, the extent to which they might depend upon comparative method. Our conclusions in this respect would revolve around the epistemic properties we wish to put into the link between C and intending X_j. It would clearly be dangerous to interpret it in classical causal terms, for then we would be suggesting that an intention was in some sense causally determined.

Conclusion. I have in the second part of this chapter sought to lay out in simple fashion – without specifying many of the complications – a framework for social investigation which is at the same time 'generalising' in orientation and non-positivistic. In the spirit of the first half of the chapter I would search in the future for a 'methodology' which enables us in the context of empirical problem-solving to generate theories which combine an understanding of social action with deduced consequences of a 'structural nature'.

Note: Chapter 8

The analysis presented in this chapter will be much extended and elaborated in a forthcoming publication *Action, Reason and Power* (provisional title). I am indebted to the SSRC for a personal research grant for the academic year 1978/9 which enabled me to undertake the research upon which the chapter is based.

I should also like to thank Phil Strong for some helpful remarks on an earlier draft.

9

Sociological Practice and Language

MICHAEL PHILLIPSON

The interest in Language as a topic of analysis in British sociology has emerged within the last thirty years and has developed in four general directions. First, the work of Bernstein (1974) offered a synthetic method for the exploration and constitution of the links between social structure and everyday speech. Secondly, varieties of conversational analysis grounded in the work of Garfinkel and particularly Sacks studied the systematics of conversational practices and the routine production of sense in language in use (Wootton, 1978). Thirdly, in the area of 'cultural studies' speech and language provided an area of focus in the analysis of subcultures and media processes (Glasgow Media Group, 1978; *Working Papers in Cultural Studies*, 1976); the emergence of semiotics also contributed to the interest in Language in this area and attempts have been made to develop a materialist-grounded semiotics which brings together Marxism, psychoanalysis and the sign on the common ground of Language (Screen). Fourthly, the influence of phenomenology and ordinary language philosophy contributed to the emergence of a reflexively oriented sociological practice which placed all analysis in the context of the relation between speech and Language (Roche, 1973; Sandywell *et al.*, 1976). Each of these approaches has taken Language as at least partially if not wholly constitutive of the social world as a sensible phenomenon, but all, with the exception of the last, have directed their questions outwards towards the social world as a phenomenon independent of itself; they have not explored the possible consequences for their own practice of a constitutive sense of Language.

While the distinction between language and speech is both a conventional and an essential feature of all these sociological approaches to Language (as well as of contemporary inquiry into Language) throughout this chapter I work within a further distinction, that between Language and language(s). The capitalisation of Language points to the ontological difference between specific languages and their possibility within Language. This distinction is a necessary feature of the constitutive sense of Language I am writing on behalf of here where Language is implicated with Being as the very possibility of concrete languages and beings. To preserve the distinction is to point to the necessary ontological reference or ground of all those discourses, sociology necessarily included, which treat the ontic as their subject matter, and to remind us that our writing and speaking always constitute themselves tacitly in a relation to Language and Being.

This period also coincides with and in part postdates the emergence of Language as the fundamental problem, across quite different paradigms, for philosophical inquiry. Linguistics, too, has developed as an independent discipline and has provided for the generation of structuralism and semiotics as cross-disciplinary methods for the analysis of social phenomena. So far this broader analytical concern with Language has had little impact on the mainstream of sociological work and the basic questions concerning theory and method. The analytical questions of philosophies, unless they refer explicitly to science, rarely seem to penetrate the social sciences and provoke radical rethinking of the latter's own practices. In sociology's case the strong and continuing commitment to an empiricist conception of science and its own practice, together with its close ties to the concerns of social policy, work to push to the margins any radical self-questioning concerning sociological practice and its relation to the social world within which it lives. Because the split between theory and method, provided for by empiricism, underlies theoretical practice itself within sociology, the possibility that practice could be grounded on another sense of sociological speech is precluded from the beginning.

But if the possibility of Language's constitutive character is taken seriously this would clearly require the inclusion of sociological practice as much as any other. Not merely is there no reason to exempt our own practices from the inquiry, but it is, rather, essential to include them if the practice is to be true to the founding sociological motive of showing the way that 'the social' is grounded on, or present in, all phenomena. For if Language is constitutive of the possibility of sensible worlds then sociology constitutes its worlds (the worlds of sociological discourse) in and through Language; the specific speech practices of sociology constitute the worlds of sociology. This is already to point to the crucial difference between speech and Language; we can only know Language through specific speeches which themselves have their possibility only within and in relation to Language. Language, treated as an object of knowledge, always eludes the theorist's grasp for each speech is contained within the very phenomenon it is trying to grasp. This is the heart of the hermeneutic problematic. Language provides for the possibility of relation itself. Everything that 'means' is in a relation to Language and has a social dimension; thus the speech practices of sociologists are inherently social and in a relation to Language. As social practices sociological speeches place themselves in their specificity in a relation to other social practices; sociological practice as a specific form of speech contexts itself socially through its forms. Each speech or text that presents itself within sociology thus does at least two things: it asserts its membership within sociological discourse and, through this, puts itself in a relation to other discourses. It both seeks and constitutes itself in and as a social relation. Conventionally, sociology, bound by its empiricist commitment, does not recognise its own speech practices as constitutive but treats its speech as in a simple correspondence relation to a pre-given independent reality and sees its task as the bringing of this extra-linguistic reality to sociological speech.

But constitutive senses of Language work with a different sense of truth than that of correspondence or isomorphism; as a beginning they suspend senses of truth that propose a non-problematic relation between their speech and its referents (in the case of sociology, the social world), that is, a direct 'literal' correspondential speech that is a supposedly neutral carrier of an extra-linguistic referent. Neutrality is to be produced here apparently via a suspension of the speaker's values or commitments. This sense of Language which dominates sociological practice is bound closely to its commitment to empiricism so that sociological speech is projected as an observation language; its aim is to be speech purged of all reference to everything except its topic and to produce a degree zero practice that, through its elimination of all rhetoric, is all referent. In literary critical terms it aims at an absolute 'naturalism' in which speech appears to deliver the 'things themselves' to the reader. This direct relation of speech to phenomena assumed in most sociological speech, especially that reporting on or making reference to specific 'field' researches, is necessarily eschewed by constitutive senses of Language. It assumes that phenomena are *first of all* independent of speech or Language (for example, the sense phenomena of empiricism) and that Language is simply a vehicle or instrument which undertakes a perfect translation (that is, with no 'change' in the 'essence' of the phenomena) from the senses into sense; imperfect translations occur when the speaker's 'values' obtrude in the account. How this process occurs is never explained.

In this view, then, Language and world phenomena (natural and social) are absolutely separate independent realms but it is speech's task to produce these phenomena as just themselves; conditions for accomplishing this are maximised for empiricism when the speaker manages to prevent any intrusion of self or what is other than the phenomena (bias) into the speech. Transforming the self from being one speaker among others into an observer (following the rules of good observing) is the means for achieving this; following these rules (found in any methods textbook) produces a speaker whose speech can claim privilege over others' speeches because it has more of the world in it than do the speeches of non-observers. This sense of the relation between Language and world predominates in sociological discourse because of the power of the metaphor of observation: this asserts that before he or she is anything else the sociologist is an observer of the social world. The commitment to empiricism overrides all others, in spite of the continuing insistence within the tradition that sociology is a theoretical discipline. Theorising and empiricism cannot finally be reconciled because the latter insists upon the primacy of observation, and hence the possibility of a speech that directly captures an independent realm of phenomena, that is, it gives us these phenomena 'as they are' ('in reality' beyond the observer's speech). That this stands in tension with the dominant tradition of theory construction in sociology (the generation of 'ideal types' which, as Weber showed us, are nowhere found in reality) only serves to remind us of the paradox of sociological practice, exemplified in the split between theory and method as separate moments within that practice.

Senses of Language that are wholly or partially constitutive trace back the very possibility of a concrete 'world' from the sense that Language allows us to hold in *common* – and that is concretised in speech – to Language as the grant. The taken-for-granted world is the grant of Language. Constitutive senses of Language require forms of sociological practice that re-site sociological discourse in its relation to other discourses and in that process replace sociology as observation with sociology as a specific form of theoretical practice. To say that Language provides for the possibility of the world is to say that everything is contained within it; it is to relate to Language as, in Heidegger's metaphor, the 'House of Being' (Heidegger, 1971). World phenomena (natural and social) take on meaning in and as their relation to Language, where Language is the horizon that provides for their very being as phenomena in the first place, and this being-in-the-world is inherently social through Language's grant of relationality itself. And because the sense of the world is constituted in speeches that themselves stand in a relation to Language, so theoretical practice, the activity of making sense, is ontologically prior to observation as a process of looking.

Observations only make sense within a tradition of meaning and a pre-interpreted context. But, as the developed metaphor for sociological practice, observation essays a withdrawal from theoretical practice into a pre-theoretical passive contemplation of the world and is understood as a process of looking that comes before meaning; the empiricist observer claims to be the receptacle for what appears and, as a passive medium, the observer disclaims any transformation of the phenomena received, claiming to deliver them in their pristine state (the 'facts') for theoretical contexting – hence the desire for a pure 'observation language'. Sociology's commitment to empiricism places the sociologist in the world as an observer first and foremost, thus ensuring that its theoretical practices are both subservient to and contained by observation. Thus theorising that is not tied in some way to this conception of the relation between the observer and the empirical realm is deemed speculative, abstract, out of touch, and so forth. The split between theory and method ensured by empiricism's influence, providing as it does for the relative independence of the two processes (speculative theorising and empirical observation), even provides for a double-think where the two can coexist side by side, occasionally meeting but for the most part remaining apart.

This double-think accommodates two contradictory senses of the relation between sociological speech and its referents: the indirect relation of theorising and the apparently direct relation of observation. When the two do meet (when theory is empiricised) it is the empiricist sense of the relation between the observer and the world that rules; that is, theorising is subsumed under the rule of correspondence and the theoretical account is transformed into its other. These two senses of Language displayed in the ways speech is related to its referent (the social world) show a central internal contradiction that partially defines sociology's relation to other discourses in society. Because the common culture within which sociology lives is itself primarily empiricist in character its version of authentic sociology coincides with that of the sociologist as empirical observer. The relevance, weight and influence of sociology as one discourse among others is judged in terms of its ability to assure those who might listen to it of its empiricist commitment, that it is first of all observation and reproduction of untransformed 'facts'.

A radically constitutive sense of Language avoids the contradiction between theoretic speech and observational speech generated within empiricist sociology by showing sociological discourse as one among a plurality of discourses; sociology is here constituted in and as its theoretical practices where method is not an independent stage in sociological work but is co-present in every theoretical practice. Theorising here is grounded in method in the sense that every concrete theoretical practice displays a methodic relation to the world it analyses and speaks to. Thus method defines the ways in which the sociologist, through his or her specific speech practices, constitutes a relation to the world; and this would be to understand sociological practice as always rhetorical in character, for fundamental to it as a practice is its desire to persuade others that it is the best way of speaking about the social world. It makes space for itself among discourses and puts itself in a relation with them through the ways in which it asserts the persuasive power of its own truths. Fundamental to this persuasive power is the metaphor of the sociologist as observer.

But constitutive senses of Language would show that truth is relative to specific discourses and communities, that is, that it has a communal basis rather than being ontologically prior to discourse or community. And every sense of truth, specific to discourse and community, would display, and seek to preserve through the speeches which performed it, interests and commitments specific to it; it would put itself in, and seek to display a relation to, other discourses the character of which it would seek to ensure. Relating to others always displays the interests of the speakers. In this way the surface truth of sociological discourse (what it tells us about the world putatively independent of it) has no extra-discursive claim upon us; we could only see its truth as superior by standing within its commitments and sharing its interests in preserving the truths of empiricism. Obviously these interests have a moral and political character. The rhetorical element in sociological speech, then, is concerned to protect specific truths not only in and for themselves but also on behalf of the commitment on which the speech rests. This is to point to the metaphoric character of sociological speech where metaphor names the way each speech holds two meanings together in tension.

Every sociological speech points outside itself to a world (we might say that it constitutes the sense of a possible world) but at the same time in the very ways that it is done (its method) it points to itself as in a particular relation to that world and to Language. This is to emphasise the 'practice' side of sociology seen as a theoretical practice, where part of that practice is the active performing of a relation to others (concrete others and other discourses); the practice constitutes a relation through its very ways in Language. A speech then tells us both about the world and recommends itself as *the* way to see that world; its persuasive powers, its rhetorical character, lie in the ways it tries to guarantee its truth as a prior truth, as a truth to which other as reader must be subservient.

Now if every sociological speech is indeed recommending itself, it is engaged in the politics of speech: what it speaks *for* is as important as what it speaks *of*. It is displaying its speech as a form of politics where the 'how' of its speech (speech's method) points to the kind of politics that it desires to found, the social relationships it speaks for. In the case of empiricist sociology, where the commitment to empiricism is directly continuous with the empiricism that partially constitutes the common culture itself, it appears as if the society which its speeches speak for is coterminous with that in which it has its present life. It offers us no radical version of the other society for its radicality evaporates in the ways that its own speeches display only elaborations and sophistications of that form of life which already rules. The very phenomena that should be prime topics for sociology, the distribution and structure of those speech forms and commitments which permeate the common consciousness in a bureaucratised instrumental social world, are absolutely excluded for it because they are the very forms which structure its own practices. Empiricism is constitutionally incapable of reflexivity because of the very ways in which it relates the observer to the observed and the world in which the observer's speech negotiates its place. The products of empiricism are ultimately not theoretical in character (although they rest upon and require interpretation) but informational; empiricism is committed to the production of information not analysis and it is in and through this that it relates itself to the dominant concerns of an empiricist culture.

In so far as a basic constituent of the empiricist commitment is its conception of the member as observer, an exploration is required of this sense of observing, the speech through which it constitutes itself and its relation to Language. This will also enable us to assert the primacy of sociology as a theoretical practice.

I have already suggested that in literary critical terms empiricism lives through a 'naturalist' version of speech that reports details of the world as 'precisely' and as 'accurately' as possible. Observation then constitutes itself in 'naturalist' speech which ultimately shares the same ground as the kind of speech in which information (for example, media 'news', bureaucracy's self-monitoring materials, description in everyday life, and so on) is presenced for us. If we consider the ground from which this speech is produced it requires a particular conception of the observer and his or her relation to the phenomena spoken of. To begin with it presumes that the observer must be 'present' at the events naturalised in speech; it thus situates the observer in a temporally synchronic mode and a spatially immediate or unobstructed relation with the phenomenon. But in order to eliminate the bias of the observer self has somehow to be dissolved, for to be present as an 'observer' is to be present as 'anyman' and not in terms of self-interests.

The selection and collection processes of method (transformed in empiricism into methodology – a set of rule-governed and supposedly context-free techniques) provide a 'frame' through which the observer's acts of observing are reconstructed and limited in a ruled way, and the aim of the frame is to transform the observer's 'presence' as a self into an absence while preserving the observer's presence as a pure witness. This presence gives access to the appearance – what can be seen by the observer's looking – of phenomena so that, for empiricism, appearances become the reality: what is seen via the restrictive frame of method, which expunges the self, is reality. Of course, when empiricism's topic is a concrete whole (a specific society, institution, or collectivity) then the observer faces a problem, for how can one observer be 'present' at the whole? The observer's presence 'at' the whole is existentially that of everyone else, so the observer has to rely on others as witnesses (one typical resource of empiricism is here the sampling frame); other people become surrogate or substitute witnesses. They have to be treated by the sociologist as metaphoric sociologists (think, for example, of the constructors of records, statistics and accounts, or of interviewees). Presence at the whole, then, can only be explicitly metaphoric in sociological speech; the apparently direct unequivocal character of the naturalism of empiricism here begins to be transformed into a form of 'realism', for the whole cannot be 'literally' described. But this shift is unacknowledged in empiricist speech.

The first tensions for the observer arise, then, from the empiricist need for presence and this generates a further tension through the 'nearness' that presence involves, for as a self the observer has to transform 'nearness' into 'distance'; keeping self at a distance while maintaining the existential nearness of the observer is a continuing problem of practical strategy for the empiricist. In the case of the concrete whole, as suggested above, none can claim privileged presence at it so all are equidistant from it. Because the whole cannot be 'seen' except indirectly through metaphor, the metaphysics of vision on which the metaphor of observation itself rests begins to lose its credence. Empiricism finds great difficulty in preserving a relationship between its required sense of the observer and the whole (however conceived) about which sociology desires to speak. The phenomena studied in observing are first of all 'seen' and then transformed into sociological speech. The primacy of 'vision', seen as an independent 'sense', confirms empiricism's commitment to a pre-linguistic, pre-meaningful realm of the senses and is shown as delivering the observables from the senses to sense for the bestowal of meaning. Observing's objects have to be transformed into speech so that speech here is secondary to seeing, and this transformation is hidden (that is, it is an unexplicated, unrecognised process).

Of course this problem is compounded when the so-called observables are themselves already speech, as is the case in most sociological research, for we do not observe speech but listen to it if we seek to constitute its meaning. If presence is foundational for the empiricist observer and presence involves place, for to be present is to be somewhere, then we might formulate the ontology of observation to begin with as the need to '*be-there*' to act as an authentic witness and to provide empirically 'true' accounts. Observing as 'being-there' has its ontological ground in being synchronically and spatially at the phenomenon, and is thus bound to the phenomenon through empirical conceptions of time and place, for the latter are conventional clock time and a concrete geographical space. When the observer is 'not-there' (as is the case with the bulk of sociological accounting in spite of its empiricist commitment) this is treated as a methodological problem for it interferes with the production of a correspondential truth; the observer has to hedge the account round with caveats which turn on the temporal and spatial 'distance' from the events in question (this is most obviously the case in 'historical research'). Being-there, then, provides the ground on which the criteria of adequacy of method can be constructed.

This is often reinforced by the observer's necessary reliance on others as surrogate witnesses, as substitute sociologists, where other has to be treated as if he or she were an 'observing sociologist'. Such an assumption about other is facilitated by the continuity between the sophistication and elaboration in sociological observation of the empiricism which already partially constitutes and sustains the common culture within which sociology has its life. Everyday life in this culture is sustained in and through its empiricist production and use of information produced through an essentially similar relation to the world as that of sociological observation. Sociology, as observation, elaborates and formalises in its practices a way of working and of relating to other which are already institutionalised modes of constitution in the wider culture; bureaucracies and communication media epitomise this in their production of news as 'information'. Observation is the routinely accomplished and accepted way of relating to others where others are to be accounted for in and through 'descriptive' information. The aim of 'being-there' is thus the production of (sociological) speech as descriptive information.

Sociology, through its empiricist commitment, far from standing outside the culture which it claims to take as its topic, actually exemplifies and speaks for it; its speech is not other to that world but of it, so that there is a fundamental analytic unity between sociologists' ways of working and speaking (the supposed transformation of the seen into the spoken) and that way to which the culture itself gives the greatest value. Thus a central question is how sociology can be true to its own commitment to comprehend the construction of the social world when it lives within and presences itself through a repetition and reinforcement of the very practices which routinely construct that world in the first place. Wherever the empiricist commitment holds sway over other senses of practice sociology lives within this tension. Observing, then, in making speech secondary, treats it as a neutral medium which merely channels information about what it takes to be (for the most part) extra-linguistic phenomena.

If we constitute a sense of observing through an analysis of its practices it can then be pointed in two directions, both towards its use and development in sociology and towards its place in the world of everyday life as a prime constituent of sense and being. To talk about sociology here is also to talk about the common culture by treating sociology in its observational mode as the overdevelopment of a routine social practice. I now want to offer some tentative suggestions concerning the possible ways a radically constitutive sense of sociological practice would reconstitute its relation to the discourses of the common culture through a conception of theoretical practice that would displace the empiricist commitment to observation.

In so far as the culture in which sociology is practised does not routinely provide for its own sense of its activities through a radically constitutive sense of Language but rather, as suggested, through the literalism of empiricism, it can be assumed that such a constitutive version would clearly display its difference to this literalism through the ways that its rhetorical practices re-sited the sociologist in relation to the world. In a constitutive version world is not first of all outside Language but is a possibility of it and all relationships within the world are constituted within and as a relation of Language. The constitution of meaning is a metaphoric act so that Language, as it is concretised in speech, is fundamentally metaphoric in character; metaphor, as 'the normal mode of development of a language' (Empson, 1949), is the bringing together of two or more realms in a single act of meaning (word, phrase, account, and so on) and provides for the openness of speech and the necessity of interpretation. Metaphor is located in the 'is' that names and constitutes relationality itself ('this is that') (Ricoeur, 1978). The descriptivism of observational speech and information has to hide its own metaphoric character to preserve its sense of a world independent of Language and meaning which it brings to Language in a supposedly direct non-transformative act of reference; this act of reference beyond itself to a putatively independent reality is understood from within a constitutive sense of Language as the metaphoric constitution of a relation to a possible world. The speech of literalism is thus a surface of dormant metaphors any one of whose metaphoric character can be re-animated at any time. Metaphor's creative confusion works in the case of literalism in the ways that every speech offers a dual sense of relation both to a world beyond the speech (its concrete reference) and the world of the speech as a relation to Language. Each speech thus performs this double act of relating which structures the relation of speaker to other.

For sociology the worlds it addresses are pre-interpreted; they live in and through the practices that sustain meaning routinely. Thus its metaphors cannot help but transform those lived-worlds in their transposition from the pre-interpretations that constitute the living flux of everyday life into sociological speech. Sociological transformations are *other* than the worlds they report upon; description does not reproduce the world but metaphorises it into another world. Further, in so far as, from within a constitutive sense of Language, the phenomena that sociology addresses are not first of all *things* to be seen (observables) but theoretical practices themselves, sociology is a meta-theoretical practice that is foundationally interpretive in character; hermeneutically, it has to engage in the very same procedures it is trying to grasp theoretically. The constitutive character of sociology can be located at the level of theoretical practice when it offers, on the basis of its observations, senses of realities behind appearances, underlying structures, and so on. These have to be claimed, within empiricism, as findings rather than constitutions, for empiricism can have no sense that *method constitutes the object of knowledge*. Such realities and structures, the very stuff of sociological discourse, in so far as they are not existentially 'there' in that very form for the subjects studied, *are constituted by sociological practice*; ultimately such realities and structures are metaphors for *relation* between subjects or collectivities.

A relation is nothing concrete, is not an observable 'just lying there' for the methodic eyes of the observer to find; rather it is constituted in and through methodic frames that give it a specific character and form. Social relation, the first topic of sociology, lies in the gap between subjects and it is the specific conceptual frame in use that constitutes the relation (as, for example, a relation of class, function, role, or whatever). If social relations are not 'there' independently of the interpretive practices which constitute them (those of subjects and sociologists) then the theoretical practices of sociology are constitutive fillings of the gaps between subjects with what the interests and conceptual frames of sociology desire to found as the

relating of self and other, of identity and difference. The social relation is
what holds two subjects or collectivities together and apart. But in so far as
there is no-*thing* between these two the work that fills that gap has to be
metaphoric; the bringing together of two is a constitutive act that relates
them in specific ways and in so doing displays its own desire in the way it
relates itself to them.

Theoretical practice in sociology then, as a metaphoric constitution of
relations, is *parallel* to the lived realities whose pre-interpreted meanings it
transforms. Formulating theoretical practice in this way begins to point to
issues in the politics of speech referred to earlier, for clearly no privileged
place can be claimed for such a practice in relation to other theoretical
practices; once the objectivism of empiricism, with its implications of the
moral superiority of the sociological as a presentation of the real, has been
transcended, sociology needs to re-define as a matter of practice its relation
to other discourses. I want to offer an understanding of the relation between
theoretical practice and metaphor which draws together some of the above
themes by subsuming observation under theoretical practice.

As an initial move, perhaps we can reverse the coventional attributions
of subjective and objective before abandoning them. Perhaps we can call
the concrete experience of an individual subject (that which the subject
takes to be indubitable for all practical purposes) – 'objective'. As an area
for analytic exploration this tends to be the traditional province of
metaphysics and attempts to define 'certain' knowledge of the ego. Against
this let us call the theorist's attribution of order, structure and method to
this stream of other's lived experience – 'subjective'; it displays the
theorist's vision of other. This juxtaposition can then be approached in
terms of the contrast between the metaphoric and the literal (remembering
that the literal when inquired into is revealed as dormant metaphor itself).

Individual concrete experience (always social through its relation via
meaning to Language) in its indubitability is 'literal/real' in and as the very
moment of its experiencing: it *is* the world as lived and understood for the
individual. The individual's speech (consciousness) indexes the movement
of this literal/real (objective) being. But the analytic attributions of the
theoretical practitioner to this experience of the other are 'metaphoric'
(subjective) in relation to it; these attributions however in their turn
constitute the practical experience of the theorist and are therefore concrete
or objective for him/her. Attributions to the other subject are the theorist's
objective mode of being as theorist. Thus every act of both the subject and
the theorist when they are in a relation is always at least a duality,
understood through the subjects of the relation; in this way the attributions
by the subject to the theorist are always also metaphoric, that is to say, the
subject becomes a theorist about the theorist's practices.

Each speech is, then, real *and* metaphoric: it is the real life of the speaker
as activity, as practice, and the transformed (unreal) metaphoric life of the
subject (other/others) who is spoken of and for. For any speech we thus

have to ask, of and for what, for whom and to whom, does it speak, in order to be able to locate the metaphoric limits of its real world. These metaphoric limits would be our sense of the speech's place and work where such limits are the relation between the metaphor and the literal. When theoretical practice adopts the same stance in relation to its own speech, that is, in the attitude of self-reflection or reflexivity, it takes up a metaphoric stance to its own speech. Every theorist's speech is thus metaphoric in relation to its concrete other, its topic, which is *other's real life for other as a matter of practice*, and it needs this other to live its life as metaphor for us. And while it is always only metaphor for us or another, in its being-lived-through it is the real life of the theorist.

The 'real' here, then, is the living-through-the-speech, the pre-reflective activity, while the metaphor (as 'unreal') is the form of life attributed in the theorist's speech to others' living-through-speech – it is a relation of transformation. The real is thus the unending flow of practices which practically and together create and sustain intelligible worlds, and the actuality of theoretical practice is to produce in its real practices metaphors for its subject, to produce its subject in and through metaphor. Theorising's real practical life is the production of metaphor; it literally produces metaphor, *that* it does is its literality, its literally real life.

In this way, to begin with metaphor as a formulation of theory's product requires that it be correlated with a sense of the literal to live its real life as metaphor. Metaphor's real life is in the moments of its production, the practices of the constitution and sustenance of meaning, the activities in which it is produced. Metaphor needs the real to be metaphor, but here the word 'real' as a theorist's category (mine) must be read metaphorically – the real is a metaphor in the theorist's speech for that which is other than his or her speech. Theory's destiny is thus *to be metaphorically*; theorising is metaphorising so that the telos of real theoretic practice is to real-ise metaphor, to real-ise itself metaphorically (its paradoxical life is to be *really* metaphor). To understand the site of sociological practice as a theoretical practice situated among other real theoretic practices we have to recognise that the sociological theorist is a meta-theorist in the ways he or she treats others' theoretical practices as topic; the real life of sociological practice is a meta-theoretical practice the realisation of which metaphorically transforms the real theoretical practices of others. Empiricist observing cannot see itself as such a transformative practice because it is blind to metaphor; a recognition by theorising of its foundationally metaphoric character enables it to transcend and displace observation as the criterion of sociological practice, as the definer of sociology's being-in-the-world. Once this reflexive turn, which attempts to grasp and display the relation of its own speech to Language and world, has displaced the primacy of observation, it has begun the turn towards the character of its own real life, its being really metaphoric, to show the difference that the displacement makes; one of its concerns is to show how being metaphoric makes a real difference to, is a real displacement of, the life of observing's literalism. It is other to literalism and stands for other possibilities of theoretical practice.

Metaphor knows itself to be always in a relation of tension with both its problematic (its topic or subject matter) and itself; it knows that its problematic is only approachable metaphorically so that its life as a problem is both given by the metaphoric act and yet eludes it 'ultimately' precisely because it *is* metaphor (metaphor is incompatible with 'essence'); and it is in tension with itself because it both is and is not what it says. That is, it knows that its own *real* life is to speak metaphorically of its problematic, so that when it makes itself a topic in the reflexive turn, it can only grasp its own real life metaphorically – it cannot know its own real life (except in its practice in and as metaphor). This process of a continual deferring of the real is what defines theoretical practice as metaphor, for the real is always that which is not present in the theoretic speech. The real is really absent.

Sociology's articulation with other discourses defines its cultural place and this occurs in and through the ways that the actual theoretical practices of sociologists attempt to structure and negotiate this place; the problem as I have developed it suggests that if sociology works within and accommodates to the conventional definition by others of sociology as empirical observation that produces information for use (where this definition fits with one central self-conception of sociology) then it fails to take a radically analytic stance towards either itself or those cultural practices that produce the culture itself as empiricist. It maintains sociological practice as superior 'technically' to other discourses and this technical superiority carries a latent morality that underpins the practice and represents its deep commitment (for example, that 'more information of the kind we produce is good in itself').

Now rather than the covert morality carried within empiricist practice the conception of theoretical practice outlined above speaks for a self-recognition by sociology of the practical-moral character of its transformations. This practice would understand its own metaphoricity in a recognition that, in speaking of the social world in specific ways, it is also speaking *for* an-other possible world: what it speaks *for* or on behalf of is its real reason for speaking, for it is a display of sociology's founding desire to speak for and thus constitute the 'social relation' as the ground of all relating. Thus every occasion of sociological speech is an attempt to display through a specific topic the deep reason for making the 'social' first in any understanding of our relationship to the world. This can only be done in specific speeches so that each speech is a rehearsal of the reason. Presumably the felt need to assert the primacy of the 'social' as the ground of being is continuingly enacted in sociological speech precisely because this sense does not ground most cultural practices which surround sociology. Theoretical practice thus speaks for that which is other than what is, for another society, another community grounded on an alternative possibility of discourse to that which conventionally constitutes cultural sense. Clearly a sociological practice that continued to work within empiricist conceptions of observation and speech could not display this alternative in its practices no matter how strongly it might claim to be speaking for this other; the form of the practice would here deny the concrete possibility spoken about – it would contain its own negation through the ways that the form continually acted to deny or keep at bay its hope in the very act of its expression.

The problem for theoretical practice, then, is to show the promise of the form of life it speaks for in the very form, the realisation, of its articulation. Not to do this is to suggest the impossibility of the formal break with the form of what is taken to be 'that which is'. It is to say: 'Here is what I would like to assemble but I can only show it to you from within the very practices and speech of its negation.' It is to say: 'I do not know what other form speech (practice) could take because all I have is the speech of "what is".' And the speech of 'what is' does not allow the display of the 'what is not yet' that is beyond it. In this way the denial of the break is formally maintained. The alternative that understands theoretical practice as metaphoric hears 'what is' as always metaphoric too; this provides for the display of 'what is not' in the 'what is' from the beginning. Positivism and empiricism, displaying the classical version of science, are the metaphors which conventionally ground sociological practice, but clearly alternative metaphors are available. Discourses which themselves acknowledge their own metaphoricity, contemporary science and art, for example, provide instructive models for the constitution of sociological practice on site other than that of observation.

Part Three

**Marxism and Feminism:
Radical Interventions in Sociology**

10

Sociologies and Marxisms: the Odd Couples

LESLIE SKLAIR

It is impossible to be clear about the relations between sociologies and Marxisms and the ways in which they have influenced each other without first sorting out the varieties of sociologies and the varieties of Marxisms spawned in the twentieth century. As my brief here is to look at the last thirty years or so I shall merely mention, as briefly as is compatible with the importance of forebears, the key figures in and around sociology and Marxism through whose interpretations of the subject matter most of us have come to the awareness that there is something very problematical about the relations between sociology and Marxism. To purists the matter may well have been settled by the sarcastic reference that Marx made to the recipes of Auguste Comte in *Capital* and indeed the contempt that some Marxists have for some varieties of sociology is exceeded only by the contempt that sociologists have for them. To balance this let me remind those who need reminding that the orthodox textbook of Marxism in the 1920s, written by that very influential Bolshevik, Bukharin, was subtitled 'A System of Sociology'. However, extreme reactions of outright hostile rejection or outright incorporation are quite uncommon and most Marxists and most sociologists have been and continue to be more interested in working out some unilaterally beneficial *modus vivendi*. The precise nature of these strategies vary with the varieties aforementioned, and so it is to these that I must immediately address myself.

I

First, let me construct a rather conventional but serviceable classification of sociologies, then one of Marxisms, restricted to the period (roughly) 1900–60. Soc. 1 will refer to the remnants of the nineteenth-century evolutionary tradition, incorporating attempts to locate whole societies in developmental sequences all the way from Durkheim's solidarities to Parsons's functional subsystems. Soc. 2 refers to the ideal-typologising aide of Max Weber and the systematic analysis of institutions. Soc. 3 refers to the formal social action side of Weber, Simmel and the interactionists who were to emerge, particularly under the influence of Mead, in the United States. Soc. 4 is the phenomenological approach, for whose several wings Alfred Schutz can be cited. Soc. 5, something of a residual category, I shall label (borrowing the term rather than the meaning from David and Judith Willer) systematic empiricisms, which includes some functionalism, some innocent fact-gathering and most data-based cross-cultural research. Now the practitioners of Socs. 1–5 have been, ideologically, a very mixed bag but the one thing that they have had in common is that as soon as it had been invented, they all were committed to Academic Sociology. This does not solely imply a commitment to scholarly publication and research but also a commitment to teaching a certain body of legitimised material, to working with other professionals in departments of institutions of higher education, sitting on committees to secure funding and recognition of such enterprises, and further activities in and out of the real world as are necessary for the progress of the discipline and the profession. As sociologists of science have demonstrated the creation of a new 'science' is a matter of proving both cognitive viability and institutional acceptance.

There are not so many different varieties of Marxisms, in my estimation, as sociologies, but there are a few. Marx. 1 will refer to the humanistic tradition of the 'early' Marx in which problems of alienation and the division of labour are paramount. Marx. 2, sometimes and not entirely without reason referred to as 'mechanical materialism', devotes itself to the analysis of the ways in which the economy determines everything in the last resort. Marx. 3, finally, refers to the post-Leninist attempts to grapple with the problems of power, consciousness, hegemony, natural questions for those whose hopes of revolutions that did or did not take place have been dashed. This, as I would be the first to admit, is a very arbitrary classification of Marxisms from *c*.1900 to *c*.1960 and is in at least one respect (epistemologically) quite confusing. However, my purpose here is not to give any sort of picture of the real development of Marxist thought but to highlight the ways in which Marxisms related (or failed to relate) to sociologies, and in this one respect the classification is, I think, helpful, in so far as it can be seen that while Marx. 1 appears to open the door to sociology, particularly Socs 1, 3, 4 and 5, Marx. 2 appears to render sociology either redundant or epiphenomenal. Marx. 3, on the other hand, as we shall see, in some ways tries to create a new sociology and fails. To this extent, we may identify Marx. 3 with the 'critical theory' of the Frankfurt school.

The formal and explicit links between sociologies and Marxisms before 1960, and particularly before the Second World War, were tenuous in the extreme. In the sociology textbooks of the period, most of which were rather more eclectic than nowadays, Marx and Marxism might well receive a mention but there are few, if any, examples of a systematic exposition and critique for the benefit of the sociology student or professional. In this, the lead of Durkheim and Weber was being followed. Weber's terse footnote in *The Protestant Ethic* against 'one-sided materialism' and his wishful thought that all that was best in Marx could be understood in terms of ideal types hardly constitute a serious attempt to come to terms with the ideas of Marx and Marxism. Durkheim, who write a whole book on *Socialism (and Saint Simon*, it must be added), makes what can only, and charitably, be described as curious references to Marx himself. Of course, neither Weber nor Durkheim was the ivory-towered sociologist that so many of their disciples turned out to be, and engaged as they often were in the rough and tumble of German and French political life, the question of Marxism was not purely an academic issue but a live and even very personal one for both of them. It is idle, though none the less interesting, to speculate that if the major work of sociological theory of the 1930s had, say, chosen Marx rather than Pareto or Marshall for a hundred-page treatment then the subsequent history of sociology in the United States and elsewhere might have been different. But this speculation *is* idle for there were political as well as cognitive reasons for Parsons's choices of *dramatis personae* in *The Structure of Social Action*. It seems to me to be a matter of the greatest significance that Parsons in the 1960s felt constrained to deal more extensively, but not I am bound to add, much more enlighteningly, with Marx than he had done in the 1930s, 1940s, or 1950s (Parsons, 1967, ch. 4).

The task of presenting Marx and the ideas of Marxism to sociologists, then, was not seriously taken up by sociologists themselves in this period and so by default the field was left open to political philosophers, most of whom were to some degree hostile. It is not the hostility, however, that is important here, but the fact that Marx was filtered through the prism of a usually liberal political philosophy, politically, socially and temperamentally unable to take dialectical materialism and Marx's critique of political economy seriously. This can be seen, albeit in rather different ways, in the elegant biography of Marx written by Isaiah Berlin for the Home University Library series in 1939 (now in its fourth edition), in various early works of Raymond Aron, in the books of the American philosopher Sydney Hook and, quintessentially, in Karl Popper's *The Open Society and Its Enemies*, Vol. 2 (first published in 1952 and still going strong). Perhaps even more influential was, and is *The Poverty of Historicism* where Marx lurks in the background casting his evil spell backwards and forwards in history. I would guess that for every one sociologist who actually read Marx (and Engels) themselves in the English-speaking world, and there were by 1960 many translations of their works available, there were ten who had read Berlin or Hook or Popper. To add to this there were dozens more or less influential introductions to the life and thought of Marx, some quite sympathetic but most on the level of political philosophy.

What of the Marxists? Not surprisingly it was in Germany and Austria and other German-speaking parts of central Europe, and Russia, where most intellectual and political ferment had been aroused by Marxism that the opportunities for an opening to sociology arose. The key event, in this connection, was the founding of the Frankfurt Institute for Social Research in the early 1920s, which, as Phil Slater demonstrates in his informative book, was intended to be an *Institut für Marxismus* but had to trim its title in the interests of formal academic recognition. For sociology (Slater, 1977, p. 149), despite the later prominence of Marcuse, the key figure was Karl Korsch. Korsch wrote two very important works before the Second World War, neither of which has received the publicity deserved in the English-speaking world. The first, which created a great storm in the Comintern in the 1920s, was *Marxism and Philosophy* (1923, reprinted in German in 1966, and translated into English in 1970), a seminal attempt to evaluate Marxism itself from the standpoint of the sociology of knowledge derived from Marxism. Mannheim, who must have known of its existence, does not mention it or anything else by Korsch in *Ideology and Utopia*.

Even more important, but just as neglected, from the point of view of sociology, was Korsch's intellectual biography of Marx, written in 1938 for a series in sociology edited by Morris Ginsberg. Here Korsch clearly elaborates the theme that has continued to structure the debate: can there be a Marxist sociology or does Marxist political economy displace sociology? However, as Tom Bottomore argues in his brief but instructive *Marxist Sociology* (1975, p. 39), few if any of the Marxists of the 1920s or 1930s considered the sociology of their contemporaries, the Marxist view of sociology being generally fixated at the level of Comte and Spencer. This neglect of the quite rapidly growing sociologies of America and Europe between the wars was, as I have suggested, reciprocated by the sociologists' neglect of Marxisms. There is at least one plausible reason for the apparently cavalier treatment of the sociologies by Marxists in this period and that is the view, most powerfully and provocatively expressed by Lukács, that Marxism was not the real empirical social science that positivist sociology aspired to be but, on the contrary, a methodology for the rational understanding of the historical process. This being so an epistemological critique of any sociology would do, as they were all tarred with the same brush. For the dialectical materialist the differences between idealism and empiricism are not very important. We may speculate that such arguments, coupled with the outrageous notion that the proletariat has privileged access to historical knowledge, did not endear Marxists to any of the varieties of value-free sociology struggling for academic recognition and corporate and government funding at this time.

This, then, is a bare catalogue of main items in the sociologies–Marxisms relationships, or rather lack of any systematic relationships, before the 1960s in the English-speaking world. I think it is too simple, as well as too crassly ideological, to argue that sociology rejected Marxism because

Marxism was political and not scientific; the early history of (especially American) sociology was notable for the political and social involvements (if not quite interventionism) of its practitioners (Reynolds and Reynolds, 1970, pt I). Marxism and communism were rather different. The Cold War was not entirely an invention of the late 1940s. Sociologies were already appropriating to themselves the right to speak for pluralist democracies, competitive capitalism and the science of society.

When the American and European (and Asian) universities erupted in the 1960s it was, as we all know, sociology that was held responsible for most of the 'troubles', and it was the so-called New Left, who had almost entirely rejected the claims of the sociologies, who were in the van of the various movements. Is this a paradox? And if so, how is it to be explained?

'Students often ask themselves what jobs there are in sociology and psychology. The facts are clear to one and all: there are many more students of social science than there are jobs awaiting outside, and this even after elimination of the examinations.' Contrary to appearances, this is not a gloomy report from some anxious Careers Advisory Service in one of the universities with oversubscribed sociology departments. It is the translation of the introduction to a leaflet 'Why do we need sociologists' put out by students at Nanterre in March 1968 and quoted by the Cohn-Bendit brothers (1969, p. 35) in *Obsolete Communism, the Left-Wing Alternative*. In America, in Europe, and in Britain, the phenomenal expansion of the social sciences in general and sociology in particular in the 1960s in the universities and other tertiary sector institutions had clearly not been matched, in general, by a similar expansion in employment opportunities for the graduates who were pouring out. As the Nanterre leaflet and other interventions (notably Martin Nicolaus's explosive 'eyes down, palms up') correctly pointed out, most of the new jobs available were in precisely those manipulative fields in which sociology could be seen to be in the service of the state and private capital (Reynolds and Reynolds, 1970, pp. 274–8). The economic contradiction of the reserve army of the unemployed, the creation of an intellectual lumpen-bourgeoisie, was therefore brought home to the student generation of the 1960s in most of the advanced capitalist (and some not so advanced capitalist) countries. Sociology graduates were soon to discover that, in the market place, 'sociological skills' were not nearly so generalisable or adaptable as mathematical or literary or even philosophical skills as far as earning a living was concerned. The Nanterre students make this point nicely in the sentence following the one I quoted at the beginning of this paragraph; they say: 'The concern which students feel about their future goes hand in hand with the concern which they feel about the theoretical position taken up by their lecturers, whose constant appeals to science only emphasize the confusion of their various doctrines.' Having been attracted into sociology for the obvious reason that it promised to help them make sense of the societies in which they lived and the world in which these societies were situated, the generation of the 1960s were disappointed in the lack of both coherence and revelation of sociology, and in the absence of jobs which would give opportunities to rectify matters.

Of course, relative to before (and sadly today) there were plenty of teaching and research and other jobs around for talented radical sociologists to make something of, but not nearly enough to satisfy the demand. So the psychologically devastating combination of potential relative deprivation and actual cognitive bewilderment created a real contradiction for most left-wing students seeking sociology jobs. There were, naturally, many national variations in these patterns but, on the whole, I think it is true to say that wherever there was significant growth in the institutionalisation of sociology this contradiction at the economic level emerged.

The political contradictions matured rather differently in the different countries. In America, from Berkeley to Columbia and points between, the civil rights movement and the anti-Vietnam War movement dominated the 1960s and structured the campus revolts; in France and Germany and Italy and Britain the opposition to the Vietnam War was often overlaid with struggles for university reform and rapidly growing disillusionment with the ineffectual policies of the parties of the official Communist and Labour movements. The profound effects of bureaucratic organisations and their capacities to numb people and make them apathetic have been very widely documented in sociological research; what is far less often noted and studied is the profound effect of radical organisations, especially those which enjoy success even if not for very long, on their members and the optimism and creative energy released even, again, if it does not last for very long. From New York to Rome, from Paris to London, and in a host of less well-known centres, student militants on the left achieved impressive feats of mobilisation, publicity and the raising of revolutionary consciousness, mostly short-lived but mostly of the stuff that myths are made of. The left-wing alternative to the 'obsolete communism' of the European parties and the other 'guardians' of working-class interests elsewhere came predominantly from Marxist sociologists, or Marxists who had come through some sociological training. The specific contents of these alternatives relate to the specific political condition of each of the countries involved and in some cases to the political conditions of the institutions involved. Nevertheless it is clear enough that in most if not all of the political programmes and enshrined in most if not all of the important organisations of the student left it was not the old-style democratic centralism of the Bolsheviks that prevailed but a very new-style and almost libertarian version of Marxism. The political contradictions, therefore, may be expressed as a thesis, an antithesis and a synthesis, as follows:

Reject the communism (social democracy) of the Communist (social democratic) parties.
Reject the liberal-sociological rejection of this.
Create a new left politics.

It is, consequently, not to be wondered at that elements of the thesis and the antithesis find their way into the synthesis and as the synthesis was, in fact, quite a variety of syntheses this is even less surprising. And this brings me to the ideological contradiction of the conjuncture of sociologies and Marxisms in the 1960s.

I should like to look briefly at two books of the 1960s, one very famous and influential and one not so famous but, as representative of a tendency, even more influential. The first is Herbert Marcuse's *One Dimensional Man* and the second is Bottomore and Rubel's *Karl Marx, Selected Writings in Sociology and Social Philosophy.* (Strictly speaking Bottomore and Rubel is a book of the 1950s, as it was first published in 1956 in hardback. However, it was reprinted in a second edition by Penguin in 1963, and in 1965, 1967 and 1969, and so its 'ideological career' is of the 1960s and thereafter.) Bottomore and Rubel represents the first substantial attempt to translate Marx (both literally and intellectually) for the benefit of sociologists. Indeed, in the second section of their Introduction, Bottomore and Rubel address themselves specifically to the question of 'The influence of Marx's sociological thought' and show, significantly, that in contrast to the 1900–60 period with which I have dealt briefly above, in the years before and around 1900 there was a good deal of contact between Marxist thought and sociological thought. It is ironic that Enrico Ferri had, in 1896, been pleased to report that the 'conspiracy of silence around Marx's social theory had now been broken' (Bottomore and Rubel, 1963, p. 45). The writings of Marx selected by Bottomore and Rubel have two rather novel features for the time.

First, they were much more balanced between the early and the later works than anything else published to that date; it must be remembered that the basic source of English translation of Marx and Engels, the *Selected Works* published in Moscow (1935 and reprinted often thereafter), had contained none of the early writings at all. In the course of the 1960s the importance attached to these early writings, especially for sociologists, by Bottomore and Rubel proved to be well founded for translations of the early works came pouring from the presses of Europe and America. To mention only the most important: *The Holy Family* and *The Poverty of Philosophy* were issued from Moscow in 1956 (ironic timing), the Martin Milligan edition of the *Economic and Philosophic Manuscripts of 1844* – probably the single most influential work of Marx for this time – was published in 1959; Bottomore produced his own version of these Paris manuscripts and other pieces in his *Early Writings* (1963), and in America Easton and Guddat edited *Writings of the Young Marx on Philosophy and Society* (1967). Something was obviously afoot! (To find out what was afoot we shall look at Marcuse in a moment.) The second novel feature of Bottomore and Rubel's selection was the fact that the reader (more often than not the student) did not have to plough through the masses of text replete with anachronistic references to long-dead controversies and the scholarly footnotes of Marx's fertile and detailed literary mind to catch the nub of the arguments presented. None of the hundred or so selections in the book is more than a few pages long and many are only a paragraph or two. A judicious use of the 200-plus item index might give, in a short space of time and with the expenditure of not a very great deal of energy, a quite serviceable idea of Marx's position on more or less all the important issues to which he had addressed himself. With such a sourcebook, sociology could no longer pretend that Marxism was irrelevant, or that it was an inaccessible foreign dogma, or that it was so discredited by the experience of the Soviet Union and Eastern Europe as to be immediately rejected. And it is this last point, the relationship between Marxist theory and Communist Party practice, that brings me to the meteoric history of Marcuse and *One Dimensional Man.*

The publication of *One Dimensional Man* in 1964 brought into prominence, and a prominence that must have seemed at first astonishing, a scholar with a solid if unsensational reputation in the development of Marxist thought in directions that were at the same time unorthodox and conventionally contemporary. *Soviet Marxism: A Critical Analysis* (1958) and *Eros and Civilization* (1955) were both, in their own ways, criticisms of political and personal authoritarianisms, but such criticisms in the mid-1950s, while nowhere near as plentiful as they were later to become, were hardly unique or seminal. Indeed, as has been argued by many commentators, the roots of these views can be found in the works of Marcuse himself and others connected with the Frankfurt school in the 1920s and 1930s. But what transformed Marcuse from a solid if somewhat obscure scholar into the intellectual inspiration of a veritable mass movement, the darling of the capitalist publishing world, and one of the most dangerous men in America?

There are three themes in *One Dimensional Man* that help us to answer this question. First, Marcuse argues that there is something in industrial society as such, as well as in capitalism in particular, that dehumanises people. Therefore, the book can be seen to continue, implicitly at least, the critique of Soviet society, from the left certainly, but in such a way that the absurdity that workers in 'communist' societies were spared the alienation from which workers in capitalist societies suffered need no longer be defended. Secondly, in a brilliant exposé of pluralism and the superficially rich variety of life in advanced capitalist societies, Marcuse seems to have put his finger precisely on a spiritual phenomenon to which young educated people could respond and he did this in a manner that no other writer on the left, perhaps since Marx himself, had managed to do. The brutalities of material technologies have conscious and unconscious consequences for us all. In this way, the groundwork of *Eros and Civilization* was exploited to the full. Thirdly, and politically most vitally, Marcuse pointed vaguely to the way ahead. The traditional proletariat and especially the organisations that purported to represent their interests had been totally discredited and it was the 'new proletarian elements' – students, ethnic minorities, and so on – on whose shoulders the decisive historical burdens were laid. It is worth quoting Marcuse (1968, p. 200) at this point to indicate the political potentialities that his book offered. He says: 'underneath the conservative popular base is the substream of the outcasts and the outsiders, the exploited and the persecuted of other races and other colours, the unemployed and the unemployable ... *their opposition is revolutionary even if their consciousness is not*' (italics added).[1]

Therefore, the opportunity to discover (or rediscover, as the case may be) the sociology of Marx and particularly the humanistic sociology of the early Marx, through Bottomore and Rubel and an ever-increasing body of other commentators and editors, and the example of a Marx-inspired (though not necessarily a 'Marxist') critique of society *as it now is*, combined to deal a blow to positivist sociology from which it has not yet recovered, and may never recover. The ideological contradiction of sociologies and Marxisms in the 1960s lay in this conjuncture of unprecedented institutional growth of the several conventional academic sociologies, which was the source of most of the money and other support needed to sustain this growth, and the explosion of Marx-inspired denunciation of these sociologies which was a main attraction for the heavy recruitment of the sociological student body which was at once the cause and effect of the unprecedented institutional growth. As I have said, a contradiction stated or even resolved is not a paradox explained and there is, of course, a very great deal more to be said on these issues – but not here, by me. Instead, I shall turn to a particular case, that of British sociologies and Marxisms in the 1960s and 1970s, in an effort to throw a little more light on the blow that the sociologies have been dealt. In the sense that this next section will be a medical history, the final section will be a recommendation for treatment.

II

The first thing to be done is to record the emergence of two more sociologies and one more Marxism in the 1960s, and I apologise in advance for a streak of provincialism here in that these are, perhaps, rather more relevant for Britain than for elsewhere. Soc. 6 is ethnomethodology which, in Britain at least, began its career in a refreshingly radical and debunking fashion but has not, as they say, maintained its early promise. Soc. 7 is 'conflict sociology', an invention of John Rex, David Lockwood and Ralf Dahrendorf, whose intellectual rationale was the perceived need to steer a path between the twin evils of Karl Marx and Talcott Parsons. Also influential was C. Wright Mills. Marx. 4 came from France in the shape of Althusserian structuralism and it is notable that the diffusion time for these new ideas was not the several decades or even centuries that sometimes have to pass for French intellectual innovations to cross the Channel abyss, but a few short years – the late 1960s in fact. Soc. 6 has had practically no influence at all in the sociologies–Marxisms affair and so I shall say nothing more about it. Soc. 7 and Marx. 4, however, were intimately involved, though in a political and in an ideological connection rather than in any cognitive relationship.

For some of the reasons already stated in the 1960s, Western intellectuals and particularly young Western intellectuals and even more particularly those in sociology and other social sciences became interested in left-radical ideas on a scale unknown since the 1930s, and because of the large increase of university students since then the absolute number soon reached a critical mass. By this I mean that left-wing, Marx-inspired, or actually Marxist students were now, collectively at least, a large enough constituency to form a political movement by themselves and that in several countries sociologists provided the intellectual and often the tactical leadership of these movements. This outcome was certainly *not* a direct consequence of the 'conflict sociology', Soc. 7, with which the radical 1960s had been ushered in, not only in Britain but also in the United States, and I think that it is of some interest to examine this a little further.

Despite their differences, which were subsequently to grow even wider, the early works of Rex, Lockwood and Dahrendorf shared a common reading of and rejection of the normative sociology of Parsons. Soc. 7 argued that conflict, not consensus, was the baseline of human relations and that any theory that was founded on consensus to the exclusion of conflict was bound to lead to wrong conclusions about how societies really worked. This crucial opening to Marx, however, was quickly closed off by the argument that, while it could not be entirely ignored, class conflict was by no means the only or even the most important form of conflict in the modern world, and that other forms, notably racial and occupational and national conflicts, which were not necessarily or at all reducible to class conflict, had to be given priority in sociological analysis. In the late 1950s and the early 1960s when all it had to push against was a flabby and ideologically suspect functionalism, Soc. 7 was rather successful and each of the three main protagonists went on to produce important substantive works but there was not a great deal of theoretical development of 'conflict sociology'. Significantly, the major theoretical development came from Lewis Coser (in the United States), whose amalgam of functionalism and conflict theory through an imaginative reconstruction of Georg Simmel served thoroughly to confuse the issue for almost a decade. By the end of the 1960s and the beginning of the 1970s when the *real* conflicts of race (immigration, the ghetto), occupation (student unrest, industrial strife) and national liberation (Vietnam *et al.*) were coming to the boil, not one of Socs. 1–7 seemed to have any very convincing set of answers to offer.

Three new phenomena forced themselves into the limelight at this time and each, in its own fashion, tells us something important about the ways in which sociology has coped with Marxism and vice versa. These were, first, the emergence of a New Left in Britain and the role of its intellectual inspiration through the *New Left Review*; secondly, the impact of Althusserian Marxism which followed it chronologically but, unexpectedly, not politically; and thirdly, the attack on Marxist subversion in sociology, spearheaded by the 'Gould Report', which drew the era to a close.

The most serious differences between the old and the new New Lefts in Britain in terms of their theoretical and political practice seems to me to have been their differing attitudes to the English radical tradition and their, in some cases connected, different attitudes to the Labour Party. The key dates of this series of ruptures spanned the years of hope and optimism of the left that in Harold Wilson British socialism had found a leader, perhaps from about 1963 to 1965. These were the years of Anderson's 'Origins of the present crisis' and Thompson's 'Peculiarities of the English' and of the *New Left Review*'s brief flirtation with, and root-and-branch denunciation of, Labour Party politics. We are fortunate in having both documentary and passionate accounts of this period (for example, Widgery, 1976; Thompson, 1978), and so I can simply sketch in some general points of relevance to my main theme.

In the first place, and to vulgarise, where the old New Left stands for the widest possible political platform commensurate with some sort of socialism, the new New Left appears more sectarian. Further, the old New Left is quite open to sympathetic sociologists and others; for example, Thompson's criticism of Smelser at the beginning of *The Making of the English Working Class*, far from being interpreted as a criticism of sociology as such, was enthusiastically picked up by many anti-functionalist sociologists. The new New Left, on the other hand, evinced unremitting hostility to more or less all sociology. With few exceptions what I have characterised as Socs 1–7 were tarred with the same brush in a typical essay by Robert Blackburn (1972).[2] Finally, whereas the old New Left marched under the banner of socialist humanism, the conviction that runs through their swan-song, the *May Day Manifesto* of 1967, the new New Left became increasingly concerned with epistemological questions and the contributions of continental Marxists, for many of whom socialist humanism represented rather a dangerous tendency. It was therefore not at all surprising that the book-publishing wing of the *New Left Review* (NLB) published the works of the most prominent French anti-theoretical humanist Marxist, Louis Althusser, and that a leading member of the *New Left Review* editorial board, Ben Brewster, translated and edited these works.

One might be forgiven for supposing that, thereafter, the *New Left Review* would have lent itself to the systematic dissemination of Althusser's views and the views of the schools that had grown up around him in Paris and soon elsewhere, as had happened in a modest fashion in the cases of Lukács and Antonio Gramsci, amongst others. However, in early 1971 the *New Left Review* printed a not very flattering paper by Norman Geras, and followed this in 1972 by translating a paper first published in 1967 in *Les Temps modernes* by Glucksmann, 'A ventriloquist structuralism', which was extremely hostile. Not one general defence of Althusser was printed – rumour has it that more than one was rejected as being unsuitable for publication in the *Review* – and the stream of anti-Althusserian criticism became a flood in which the *Socialist Register, Marxism Today* and the *Sunday Times* all played a part. There were, however, two new journals which began publication around this time and each with a distinctly Althusserian ambiance. These were the short-lived *Theoretical Practice* and the still surviving *Economy and Society*. While the first was an esoteric magazine making no compromise in its quest to politicise theoretical militants in Marxism in the new Althusserian mode, the second was a commercial journal aimed at radicals of all types in the social sciences. While the first was printed on a shoe-string by a small band of like-minded Marxists, the second was published by one of the premier sociology publishing houses in Britain and the editorial board comprised mainly sociologists on the left.

The link between *Theoretical Practice* and *Economy and Society* was the participation on both of their editorial boards of Barry Hindess and Paul Hirst, who later went on to write, individually and collectively, several books in which Althusserian Marxism was brought to bear on a series of problems with which sociologists in particular had been grappling. Hindess wrote extensively on problems of method, on the use of official statistics, against social phenomenology, amongst other topics. Hirst wrote on deviancy theory, on Durkheim's epistemonology, on Weber's sociological concepts, and so on. Therefore, while there was no attempt by them to construct an Althusserian *sociology*, indeed, such a project would have struck them as absurd, many of the main branches and problems of conventional sociology were being witheringly criticised in the Althusserian mode. The high point of all this was the publication, in 1975, of *Pre-Capitalist Modes of Production*, a book which, in a rather paradoxical way, filled a gap in the sociological literature. Most sociology courses try to teach something about pre-industrial (or pre-capitalist) societies, often in the context of comparative social structures, dealing with such topics as slavery, 'Oriental despotism', feudalism, caste, absolutism, and so on. As those who have taught such courses will confirm, there is no single sourcebook that can be recommended unproblematically to students in this area; in fact, the volume and variety of material for such a course is, by its very nature, vast. *Pre-Capitalist Modes of Production*, by taking the reader step by step through the primary modes of production, while rather confusingly denying the validity of any form of teleology and asserting that the 'study of history is not only scientifically but also politically valueless' (p. 312), does cover many of the problem areas of a sociology of pre-industrial societies. While the style of the book and some of its conceptual arguments might prove to be unhelpful if not downright self-defeating it does constitute an important intervention into the debates about the genesis of capitalism and the structure of other pre-capitalist modes of production which had begun to re-emerge with force in the 1970s as sociologists, and particularly Marxist sociologists, became bolder with historical materials.

It cannot be denied that Althusserian Marxism, which Hindess and Hirst were soon almost entirely to abandon, created for itself a definite space within British sociology. In many problem areas the 'Althusserians' (an extremely loose title at the best of times) engaged sociologists (and enraged sociologists), often Marx-inspired sociologists, in the name of the new orthodoxy. In political sociology, notably in the debate between Poulantzas and Miliband; in the sociology of education; in urban sociology, stumulated by the work of Manuel Castells and his colleagues; in the sociology of culture; in economic sociology; in the sociology of race; in historical sociology;[3] and elsewhere, there is now an 'Althusserian' presence. There are four main components of this presence – perhaps it is a little cavalier of me to assert it so straightforwardly though I have no doubt that it does exist and will develop.

First, and most typically, is the critique of all forms of empiricism in sociology. Each of Socs 1–7, to a greater or lesser extent, falls foul of this indictment. It cannot be too firmly stressed that empiricism and empirical research are *not* the same, and the awkward silence of Althusser on this vital matter has not helped to curtail confusion on this count. (On the contrary, I would argue, it is precisely in the critique of empiricisms of all kinds that empirical research in sociology can most reliably be based. This, I think, was the import of Hindess's insightful critique of official statistics in the Indian census.)

Secondly, and following from this in an as yet not fully articulated fashion, is the radical distinction between science and ideology in Marxism and, by implication, sociology. As an aspiration rather than as an achievement there can surely be no doubt that Marx and Engels, like the founders of modern sociology, laboured to construct an intellectual edifice that was to have the same status as the natural and biological sciences that were growing around them. The dogmatic assertion that we have already at our disposal a scientific Marxism or a scientific sociology is just that: a dogmatic assertion. The distinctive claim of the Althusserians is that the project is a scientific one and that scientific knowledge does deserve cognitive privilege.

Thirdly, and substantively, there is the conceptual apparatus of modes of production and social formations. Althusserian notions of modes of production and social formations are complex and open to a variety of interpretations and, in the case of Hindess and Hirst at least, have changed drastically in a very short space of time. Nevertheless, in recent years these concepts and the analytical procedures that accompany them have become an established part of the discourse in many important sociological problem areas. In one, the sociology of development, if not more, it is true to say that this approach is now the dominant trend.

Finally, implied in these three components, but important enough to merit special attention in its own right for its cognitive and political consequences, Althusser's Marxism is intended to be a science of structures – not in the usual sense of structuralism of the kind propounded by, say, Lévi-Strauss which renders itself eventually into biology – but a sociological structuralism. Thus it takes sides in the debate which used to be labelled 'sociological holism vs methodological individualism' on the 'sociological' side, it warns against psychologising (Althusser has some scathing remarks on psychology), and it wages a fierce battle against socialist humanism on the theoretical level. As I shall discuss in the next section, these uncompromising positions have not won Althusser many friends.

Taken together, these four components of the Althusserian presence in British sociology have, as it were, found a life of their own, cut adrift as they have been from the later developments of Althusser himself. It would be extremely difficult, and impossible within the scope of this chapter, to separate out the ways in which the general renaissance of Marxism in the 1960s paved the way for the Althusserian impact on sociology from the ways in which the Althusserian presence itself facilitated the process of Marxist entry-ism into sociology in the 1970s. It is precisely this process that constitutes the third phenomenon of the era, to which I now turn.

That the impact of Marxism on sociology at this time had been noticed by those who would not wholeheartedly welcome this development can be clearly seen in the publication of an extraordinary document entitled *The Attack on Higher Education: Marxist and Radical Penetration* in 1977. The author, Julius Gould (1977, p. 1) had written the report as the 'outcome of the deliberation of a Study Group ... on the penetration of extremist minorities and ideas in education and its effects on the liberal values of a pluralist society'. The academic members of the study group were all social science and philosophy teachers and four out of the seven were professional sociologists. The 'Gould Report' was published under the auspices (and extremely expensively – it cost almost 10p per page!) of the Institute for the Study of Conflict which ensured immediately that it would be regarded with extreme hostility by the left, suspicion from the centre and glee from the right (if I may be excused these old-fashioned categories).

It is quite difficult to convey the flavour of the report. It is a mixture of sensationalist polemic, guilt by association, solid sociology of knowledge and political theory, examples of each of which will help to illustrate how Marxisms and sociologies were increasingly interacting. The technique of sensationalist polemic is nicely illustrated by the cover of the report, in bright red, which highlights the contents as follows:

Challenges to our society
Departures from the scholarly tradition
Politicising social work
What is happening to students and teachers?
Marxist strategy and tactics
The Leftist minority: why it matters

If we added to this the fact that the first substantive page is in heavy type with heavy underlining, and that emphasis is achieved in the body of the report by the device of boxed quotations (in the *Encounter* style), we can certainly see (in my view rather welcome) 'departures from the scholarly tradition'. Throughout, the style is polemical to the extent that the author clearly decided that it was time to fight the left with its own weapons.

The charge of guilt by association (and this is a *charge* whereas the other three characteristics of the report I have noted are merely debating devices that academics use) can be substantiated with reference to the four Appendices. The first, 'A coda on publishing', addresses itself to the superficially curious phenomenon that most of the 'respectable' publishers in Britain – Gould specifically cites Macmillan, Penguin, Routledge and Heinemann – are feverishly publishing 'Marxist texts and tracts' (p. 48). Appendix II, 'Some illustrative case material', contains a university examination paper, some reading lists and an announcement of a meeting on the sociology of art and literature. This material is presented as if there was no question that Marx's work is irrelevant to the study of methods of social investigation; that the presence of works which have 'Marxist provenance' is in itself sufficient evidence of bias and indoctrination into irrational creeds; and that, absurdly, there is really something notable in the fact that a meeting on Marxism and Culture should recommend participants to read Raymond Williams, E. P. Thompson, Terry Eagleton and something on Gramsci (or perhaps I have missed the point here, I feel sure that I must have). Appendix III lists the speakers and sessions of the 1976 and 1977 Communist University of London (over 100 people) and educational activities of the Communist Party.

The Gould Report itself recognises that the charges of McCarthyism might be levelled against it but categorically rejects this by asserting (in heavy type) that the left extremists 'constitute a clear and present danger to the liberal mode. They thrive on perversions of theory and distortions of fact' (p. 47). The implication clearly is that the names and items immediately following this statement do, in some manner, relate to the statement and it was precisely this technique of raising an alarm and naming names in association with the alarm that was the hallmark of Senator McCarthy's activities. Despite the disclaimers in the report that all Marxists are bad, and the vague admission that some varieties of Marxism may be 'helpful', the overall impression of these Appendices cannot fail to be one of guilt by association.

These characteristics, sensationalist polemic and guilt by association, seem to me to indicate two things. First, they are a measure of the real threat perceived by *some* sections of the sociological establishment – members of other establishments, well represented by the officials of the Institute for the Study of Conflict, have been issuing dire warnings of communist subversion for many years. Secondly, and more relevant for my present argument, much of the actual documentation of the report does indeed demonstrate that the impact of Marxist ideas in the social sciences over the past decade has been considerable. This is the dilemma which runs through the solid sociology of knowledge of the report, namely, to differentiate the occasions when Marxists win the debates of theory and of fact by fair means (rational argument, balanced assessment of all the evidence, scholarly standards) from the occasions when Marxists win by foul means (terrorisation of opponents, suppression of uncomfortable truths, dogmatic assertion).[4] Despite some telling criticisms of some leftist tendencies, many of which echo the criticisms that members of the left continually make of each other, this problem is not resolved and, interestingly, actually mirrors the epistemological problems that I have already noted.

Finally, the report propounds its own political theories, the most important of which is the theory of the 'drip effect', which argues that radical ideas, though they might seem bizarre, can gradually penetrate (i.e. drip) into fields of practical activity through secondary literature, teaching, and so on. The fields chosen to demonstrate this thesis are social work training and teacher training, good choices as both the sociology of social work (particularly study of the welfare state) and the sociology of education (particularly study of the school) have been influenced by Marxist critiques in recent years. It is not my purpose here to evaluate the merits or demerits of this theory but to connect it with the question of sociologies and Marxisms. Once again, however we interpret for good or for ill, Gould's evidence does show the impact of Marxism on sociology, and through sociology on the social and political practices that academic sociology teaches, researches and sometimes staffs.

Despite the initial flurry of publicity in the media and much outraged indignation from the sociological profession, the Gould Report appears to have sunk into oblivion. To my knowledge there has been no further major attempt to warn us of Marxist subversion in the social sciences, and the attack on higher education now comes from the right – the actions of a Conservative government threaten to close down universities and polytechnics and have united academics in defence of their institutions – not from the left. This could mean that, as Gould and his associates feared, people simply would not listen and the insidious effects continue unabated; or that since and as a consequence of the report the tide has turned and Marxism is on the retreat; or that the whole affair really was a false alarm and that far from being an attack on the social sciences and higher education the Marxist influence has been invigorating and generally beneficial. The first of these alternatives seems to be unlikely, partly because of the vigilance of those who control our institutions and partly because of the general political (and economic) climate. The second seems entirely out of the question because the volume of Marx-inspired books and journals continues unabated, courses and reading lists show no signs of dramatic changes, and debate on the left continues to reverberate within sociology. The third alternative is, in my view, the correct one and I shall conclude this section of my chapter with a brief account of why I think this to be the case.

The mere fact that I can list seven more or less distinguishable sociologies strongly suggests that sociology's aspiration to something like scientific status has not been realised. For some this is welcome confirmation that sociology, like literary criticism, for example, is not and cannot be a science. Nevertheless, for most sociologists, the production of plausible theories and reliable knowledge about the world we live in remains a fundamental goal, similar to the goal of physicists to know something about the natural world and biologists to know something about the biological world.

For the scientifically inclined sociologists there have been two main paths open, and several minor ones. First, and most obviously, the various forms of systematic empiricism (Soc. 5) have appealed, especially to the philosophically more innocent, as more 'science-like' than the other Socs. This is not merely a case of the 'number crunchers' but also of the use of formulae, analytical typologies, mathematical models and other novel techniques. In all of the sociological tendencies I have labelled Soc. 1 to Soc. 7 there are some proponents of these models, utilised in the name of scientific rigour. In terms of institutional success – winning research funds, recruiting students, converting young professionals from other tendencies, in short, founding schools – some have done extremely well. The common factor which overlays (perhaps underlies would be closer to the truth) these is what can best be described as a 'commonsense epistemology' that masquerades as common sense itself; the world is out there and we can measure it, observe it, even order it conceptually and when it talks back to us (a special problem for the social sciences) we can develop ways to control this systematically. This broad consensus on the methodological problems of social research does cover a multitude of differences in particular interpretations, often interestingly reflected in different objects of research, but the key device of testing out hypotheses, pre- and post-Popper, clearly dominated in the social sciences of whatever tendency.

In order not to be totally misunderstood let me emphasise that I am speaking in very general terms, so general, in fact, that we can even include Marxisms 1, 2 and 3 under the rubric of 'commonsense epistemology' in so far as they actually engaged in social research. Again, a variety of epistemological and methodological claims might be made, and often were, but when we get down to it the procedure does not vary too dramatically in essentials. The problem for most scientifically inclined sociologists sympathetic to Marxism (pre-1960 at least) was the embarrassingly strident claim of historical materialists to be, unproblematically, scientific. The traditional, though not universal, modesty of the claims of sociologists in this respect only added to the already strong impression of dogmatism that Marxist social science exuded.

The massive and comprehensive success of T. S. Kuhn's *The Structure of Scientific Revolutions* in the late 1960s, just at the time when, to recall, the works of the early Marx were being so widely disseminated and discussed, is of prime significance here. The early Marx, in this version the inspiration of socialist humanism, impressed precisely because it avoided the strident claims of scientific privilege so jarring in most historical materialism up till then. The achievement of Kuhn was to marry the hitherto irreconcilables of cognitive relativism (more or less incommensurable paradigms) and scientific progress. Therefore, the confused or vacillating scientifically inclined sociologist could start to believe, on good authority, that theories in 'real' sciences could appear just as dogmatic and be overthrown with as much disdain as had always seemed to be the case in sociology and, further, rather than the theory (or the whole science for that matter) being a report of a reality 'out there', the history of paradigmatic science seemed to show that the theory and the concepts *constituted* what was 'out there'.

Now, to epistemologically sophisticated social scientists this was all philosophical old hat, but to many or most working social scientists it appeared to come as something of a revelation. Kuhn, it will be remembered, mentioned a (then obscure) French philosopher of science, Gaston Bachelard, as a precursor. Bachelard, as is now well known, provided some key methodological concepts for Louis Althusser's reinterpretation of Marx. My argument, therefore, is that scientifically inclined sociologists who become interested in the new humanist but scientifically ambiguous Marx in the 1960s were much impressed by Kuhn and his views on the growth of science which they rapidly assimilated to the case of the social sciences. This prepared an intellectual climate in which the theoretical-scientific claims of Althusser and Althusserians within sociology, far from sounding outrageous, actually seemed to meet a need that was painfully felt by those who wanted to participate in the construction of a scientific sociology, but not in the empiricist mode. Marxism, which had been carving out for itself a more respectable and acceptable position in the 1960s, had its obvious attractions for politically active sociologists (of the left, I had better add); for the rest, in an increasing number of problem areas in sociology Marxists were actually beginning to win arguments, positions of institutional power and, in a few cases, professional chairs in sociology and related disciplines.

A slow, incomplete and uneven development of an Althusserian presence in sociology in the 1970s was, in my view, an intellectual spearhead of this process. Marx-inspired sociologists, in the main, were against the Althusserian tendency, for fairly obvious reasons which I shall soon go into; nevertheless they felt it necessary to challenge and refute Althusser and to resist his influence. Soc. 7 (conflict sociology, later to be taken over by a mostly American-inspired radical sociology), and Marx. 1, 2 and 3 have all taken issue with Marx. 4 (Althusserian sociology) and the existence of a regular array of paradigm-clashes provides the evidence for my assertion, as I have argued elsewhere (Sklair, 1977).

Whether one regards this state of affairs as healthy and invigorating for sociology or as a gloomy indicator of decline is, of course, a matter of opinion. My opinion is that free-ranging debate is usually a good thing for any science, and particularly for sociology; that Marxism in general has released new creative energies in sociology and has opened many new lines of inquiry (often with rather than against non-Marxist sociologies); and that Althusserian Marxism in particular has injected an epistemological awareness into sociology that is a stimulant to theory and research. Why, then, it can fairly be asked, is there so much hostility, and that of an unusually virulent nature, to Althusserians? It is to this question that I address myself in the concluding section.

III

I think that there are two main reasons why Althusser (and his followers) are excoriated beyond the normal limits of academic criticism. First, there are problems of style, verbal complexity, dogmatic assertion, much of which is a consequence of Althusser's theory of reading and silences. As with C. Wright Mills's famous 'translation' of Talcott Parsons in *The Sociological Imagination*, there is no smoke without fire, but Althusser and Parsons are not the only writers whose works have their obscurities, repetitions, convolutions and other inelegancies in the literatures of philosophy and the social sciences. The second reason, for which the first is a convenient front, is the *type* of challenge that Althusser presents for both conventional sociologies and conventional Marxisms, namely, the dual attack on method *and* history. The theory of theoretical practices, and particularly the conceptual distinction between ideology and science and the pervading ambiguity about the role of evidence in scientific practice, does expose Althusser to charges of metaphysical abstractness against which no satisfactory defence has been forthcoming. The radical abhorrence of historicism connected with this has been transmuted, especially by Hindess and Hirst, into a total rejection of historical knowledge and a science of the past. In so far as Marxist historical scholarship in the West has traditionally earned higher prestige than any other Marxist academic undertaking, this Althusserian position has enraged many who might otherwise have had some sympathy. For those like E. P. Thompson and Eric Hobsbawn who could fairly claim decades of service to Marxist history and the cause of the labour movement to be told that their efforts were both scientifically and politically worthless by young men, whose own historical scholarship was undistinguished and yet whose works were being widely discussed, must have rankled considerably.

There is, naturally, a political dimension interwoven. Althusser has been widely accused of Stalinism in his own political practice (or lack of it) and as a corollary, of playing down the active role of the working class, indeed of any class, in historical change. A more analytic interpretation may be found in Gouldner's 'The two Marxisms' (1975) where he identifies this theme with the growing 'sociologism' of the mature Marx, a resistance to subjectivist accounts of 'man', and notes the 'intrinsic merits of this for a conception of a sociology' (p. 433). Gouldner is making a very telling point here and one that he himself does not fully elaborate, for good reasons. In a nutshell, Thompson's opposition to Smelser (and by implication Parsons) which I have already mentioned and Thompson's opposition to Althusser meet precisely at the point that Gouldner identifies with Althusser's opening to sociology, namely, the 'sociologism' of the mature Marx. Whereas the old mechanical materialism of Marxists resulted in an economism unacceptable to most sociologists, the complex structure of relations of production-forces of production-social formation makes possible a sociologism seductive to many sociologists. Further, those elements in Parsons which undeniably did have a powerful appeal to a wide variety of sociologists in the 1950s and 1960s, stripped of their ideological lumber and their tetramania,[5] reappear in the new Althusserian sociology. Accordingly, several writers (Turner, 1977; Mouzelis, 1978; Hirst, 1979) have noted the 'functionalist' tendencies in Althusser and the Althusserians and such is the state to which the once-hegemonic functionalism has fallen this is regarded as a damning indictment in itself. Functionalism too, it will be remembered, was widely criticised for being a-historical.

Althusserian sociology need not be obscure, metaphysical, or ahistorical and if it has to contradict Althusser to be clear, scientific and historical, then so be it. There are enough sociologists who acknowledge the primacy of the mode of production to constitute a sociological community which can take up these tasks seriously. The elaboration of the precise nature of the effects of the structures of different modes of production in their social formations, through the economy, politics and ideology, can be set out in such a way that all of the traditional concerns of sociology are located within a unified framework. This framework, to be scientific, cannot be closed and there are many missing links in the chains connecting modes of production and social formations. Althusserian sociology leaves many of the old questions about sociologies and Marxisms unanswered and some as yet unasked. The one firm conclusion that I can draw from the last thirty years of the encounters of Marxisms and sociologies is that, more often that not, they seem to me to have enriched each other. They may have looked like odd couples in their various liaisons, but perhaps odd couples have a better chance of survival in the long run.

Notes: Chapter 10

1   It is worth adding here that while Lukács, Sartre and Gramsci, to name only the most prominent, were and continue to be theoretically far more important, it was Marcuse who made the greatest political impact of the 1960s and early 1970s.

2   The exceptions, however, include the *NLR* influentials Perry Anderson and Gareth Stedman Jones.

3   Historical sociology is something of a special case. In the works of Barrington Moore, Wallerstein and Anderson, among others, there can be seen a certain convergence of interests if not exactly method between Marxism and sociology. The future influence of a reconstructed Althusserianism remains to be seen.

4   For a lurid account of events in one institution, see K. Jacka, C. Cox and J. Marks (1975). It may not be entirely coincidental that C. Cox and J. Marks both contributed to the deliberations leading to the Gould Report.

5   This term, which refers to Parsons's obsession with fourfold classifications, is introduced by Mike Lessnof in a review (forthcoming in the *British Journal of Sociology*) of Parsons's last works.

11

The Division of Labour Revisited or Overcoming the Two Adams

MARGARET STACEY

The Task for the 1980s

The Problem of the two Adams and the Deficiencies of those Theories
There appear to be two separate accounts of the division of labour: one that it all began with Adam Smith and the other that it all began with Adam and Eve. The first has to do with production and the social control of the workers and the second with reproduction and the social control of women. The problem is that the two accounts, both men's accounts, have never been reconciled. Indeed it is only as a result of the urgent insistence of feminists that the problematic nature of the social order related to reproduction has been recognised.

The problem arises because we lack a conceptual framework, let alone a theory with any explanatory power, which will permit us to analyse paid and unpaid labour in a variety of social institutions and social settings within one notion of the division of labour; which can encompass the domestic arena of Adam and Eve as well as the industry of Adam Smith; which can articulate the home as well as the market place and the state and relate the class order to the gender order; and which can comprehend the nature of the social relations involved not only when people work for others (personal service), but when they do work to others (human service or people work), whether that be a paid or an unpaid labour. The lack of a theory which relates these problems to each other matters not because one particularly hankers after an over-arching theory, but because it is clear, both theoretically and empirically, that relationships exist among these various factors although they have hitherto been dealt with discretely and under different theoretical conceptualisations. Aspects of the private domain have been discussed under the general heading of the family, the public domain under headings such as the state, the class structure, labour and industry, advanced industrial societies, monopoly capitalism.

The problem exists, I shall argue, because the classical theories derived ideas from and focused on industry, the market place and the state. All other institutions and processes were secondary and of relatively trivial importance. The theories were deficient in analysing the part played in the social order by non-waged work, by human service, by use value as opposed to exchange value. This thinking still dominated sociology thirty years ago when the British Sociological Association was founded: the division of labour as between the public and the domestic arenas and within the family was taken as unproblematic, as 'natural'. There was no recognition that this 'naturalness' was a social construction. No attempt was made to explain the two sets of divisions of labour in the same terms: the accounts of the two Adams remained distinct. The consequences of this division have not only been to hide women from sociology, but to leave sociologists of the 1980s with inadequate conceptual, theoretical and methodological tools to analyse or explain the shifts in activities between the domestic and public arenas. This problem emerges particularly starkly where the same tasks or services are undertaken in the private domain unwaged and simultaneously in the waged public domain. The emotional component of human service has been ignored by classical theories but is critical to it.

The challenge to classical theories has emerged particularly from feminism (see BSA, n.d.; Mathieu, 1977; Smith, 1973 and 1979), making it plain that it is urgently necessary to develop a non-sexist sociology if our discipline is not to play an inglorious role in reproducing ideologies which legitimate the oppression of women. That alone is reason enough for rethinking our approach to the division of labour. In addition, there have been social and economic changes since the classicists wrote such that the very social divisions upon which the theories were predicated have been considerably altered. There are therefore two problems: one about the limitations of the theories; the other about empirical changes in the social order which require identification and explanation.

The Legacy inherited by Sociology in 1950

Classical Theory derived from the Public Domain of Men
Our present problems stem from the early male domination of sociological theory which led to exclusive attention being paid to the public domain, to affairs of state and the market place which in the mid-nineteenth century were not affairs with which women were allowed to be concerned. Women were confined to the private domain of the home.

I should perhaps define my terms. I use the terms public and private or domestic domain to distinguish two arenas of action. They have nothing to do with the private and public sectors of industry nor directly with the ownership of the means of production. The private domain is the domain of the home, where social relations are based on family and kin, on mating, marriage and procreation. The public domain includes government and the market place. 'The public sphere is that sphere in which "history" is made. But the public sphere is the sphere of male activity. Domestic activity becomes relegated to the private sphere, and is mediated to the public sphere by men who move between both. Women have a place only in the private domestic sphere' (Smith, 1974, p. 6).

There has not always been a distinction between the public and private domains nor, once made, has the empirical distinction remained static. Not only was there formerly no clear distinction between production and consumption, both of which took place in the home, but in terms of government these domains were fused in the early Carolingian period, the government being run from the households of the noble families with women and men both involved (McNamara and Wemple, 1974, p. 109). It was as central state government developed and before production was separated from the home that a public arena developed from which women were excluded (see also Stacey and Price, forthcoming). The social order that was understood and legislated for was an order of men within which women and children were subsumed. When industry was also removed from the home the separation reached its height. *And it was in this period that the foundations of sociology were laid by men.*

The Dissolution and Invasion of the Private Domain
Classical theories were always inadequate to deal properly with the private domain and therefore were inadequate to deal with the whole society. In addition since the time when the theories were first enunciated major empirical changes have taken place in both public and private domains and most notably in the relations between them. Emerging in the late nineteenth and early twentieth centuries and taking on greater force since the Second World War with the establishment of the 'welfare state', some of the human services which were formerly provided in the private domain have been translated into the public domain and therefore into the waged sector. This was understood in another terminology as 'stripping the family of its functions'. This translation has also involved the transformation of the services into skilled activities for which extensive training is required. The social sciences have played an important part in this process, which can be seen in both education and health care. At the same time the private domain of the women has been increasingly invaded by experts, by representatives of the state and by men. The ability of the unwaged workers, parents and especially mothers, to perform their tasks and indeed their entire social roles without expert guidance has been increasingly called into question (Graham, 1979). There are educators, advisers and councillors for every facet of marriage and child-rearing. No longer are we allowed to believe that anything 'just comes naturally', except perhaps that it is still 'natural' for women to stay at home to rear the children they have borne and to do the associated service tasks. In so far as there is a private domain left it is not

exclusively a woman's domain yet little of the reproductive work of women has been collectivised. The so-called 'democratic egalitarian family' has ensured that while women are left at home to do the housework and mind the children, at least for some part of their child-bearing years, there is no domain where women's expertise is unquestioned (Goode, 1963; Gillespie, 1972; Stacey and Price, 1980 and forthcoming). At the same time the employment of waged workers in the home has declined, thus reducing the span of command of middle- and upper-class housewives.

The work which has moved from the private to the public domain or which lies uneasily between the two domains can be said to be 'human service' work 'designed to change the physical, mental or emotional state of the consumer' (Stevenson, 1976, p. 78) or 'people work', 'those kinds of work which consist in doing something for, or to, people' as Everett Hughes put it in the 1950s (1971, p. 305). These are activities in which the minds or bodies of people are processed and they take place in education, in health services and in the home in child-rearing. The nature of these tasks, of these services and of their potential abuse partly accounts for the failure of theories about occupations as professions to be satisfactorily discussed in relation to social class or the gender order.

Nineteenth-Century Concerns

But although their roots lie in the nineteenth century, on their present mass scale these are twentieth-century developments; what riveted the attention of nineteenth-century economists and sociologists were the immense changes which were taking place in the public arena and which altered the previously understood social order in ways which many found profoundly worrying and sought to explain, predict and, if possible, control. The theories, therefore, sought to explain these changes in the public domain: their authors were all men working in that domain and addressing other members of it. In so far as they considered changes in the private domain, it was from their stance as mediators of the private to the public domain.

Durkheim in *Division of Labour in Society* of 1893, looking at the family from a juridical point of view, argues that developments in the family over time had been associated with an increased division of domestic labour. He uses this as an example of the replacement of repressive by restitutive law, although the arguments he cites indicate rather that the social control of domestic relations and relations between the sexes had increasingly been left to the father and head of household in a process of privatisation of the family (1964, pp. 122–3, 156–8, 206–10). In the Preface to the 1902 edition he discusses how the corporation has substituted for the family, but neither here nor elsewhere does he discuss the implications for women, except that their misdemeanours in the organic society are punished by their husbands or fathers rather than the state: no mention of the punishment of husbands by wives. Organic solidarity emerged in the public domain and what the implications were for relatively undifferentiated domestic labour are not discussed.

In analysing the development and characteristics of rational-legal society, Weber makes much of the separation of the office from the home. In practical politics and in his married life Weber was remarkably pro-feminist for one of his era and certainly so in comparison with Marx (Marianne Weber, 1975, pp. 203, 371, 429), although somewhat equivocal: 'the patriarchal man [who] promoted the liberation of women' (Green, 1974, p. 128). His feminist concern did not extend to his analysis of the rise of citizenship. He failed to note that despite the establishment of equality before the law for all men and the development of rational-legal authority, women were still bound by traditional ties of loyalty and allegiance which he saw as inappropriate for the modern state. Mass democracy may have made 'a clean sweep of the feudal, patrimonial, and . . . plutocratic privileges in administration' (Weber, 1978, p. 984) for the men. It certainly did not do so for the women (Stacey, 1960, p. 136). When Weber discusses women, as in *The Religion of India* along with caste relationships, he discusses them as sexual objects, as objects of exchange (Weber, 1958, pp. 41, 114, 125), as potentially polluting and as subjugated to male gods (Bendix, 1966, pp. 144, 185; see also Turner, 1974, pp. 139–40).

Marx and Engels's recognition of the existence of the problem and their attempts to confront it have received wide comment and discussion. Engels made a most serious attempt to locate the sexual division of labour within a general theory of the division of labour giving a centrality to production and to the family. He failed, however, to recognise the persistence of patriarchy under capitalism (Beechey, 1979; cf. Eisenstein, 1979).

Sociology around 1950

Still Dominated by Concerns of the Male Public Domain
Sociology around 1950 was true to its nineteenth-century origins, addressed the public domain almost exclusively and assumed the 'naturalness' of the gender order. This I conclude from a study of the *British Journal of Sociology* and some critical textbooks of around 1950. (The new series in the *Sociological Review* did not begin until two years later, so I excluded it, and *Sociology* had not yet started). The textbooks, MacIver and Page, Lowie, Folsom, were in common use in teaching courses. Ginsberg's textbook (1934) does not deal with the division of labour, the gender order, or the family in any detail. Although Parsons had been publishing since the 1930s his great impact on British sociology came later, as a check of the references in British journals confirms.

There was other evidence, but it was largely ignored. For example, by 1950 Margaret Mead had long since published *Sex and Temperament in Three Primitive Societies* (1935) which for many of us at that time was exciting and sufficient evidence to show that the gender order and associated notions of femininity and masculinity were not god-given or biologically determined but socially constructed. Mead, still at that time something of an anthropological outsider, also published *Male and Female* in 1950. Klein had published *The Feminine Character* in 1946. It was about fifteen years since Eleanor Rathbone, one of the few women working in the public arena, had achieved the payment of family allowances to mothers rather than fathers and over ten years since Margery Spring Rice had exposed the downtrodden lives of *Working Class Wives* (1939). The entry of women into the public domain had been and continued to be slow, not surprisingly since there was no challenge to the institution of the family or alterative child-rearing arrangements made available, although generally there was an increase of women working in this period (Wilson, 1980). With a few notable exceptions, sociological theory and empirical work continued to be done largely by men. In particular theorists' attention continued to be focused largely on the public domain.

Aron's Society as a Whole: less than Half a Society
Raymond Aron's analysis in the first two numbers of the *BJS* in 1950 is an example in another theoretical tradition in which once more the only problems to be adduced are the problems of the public domain. Following Pareto and Marx, Aron addresses the question of the division of society by elites and/or classes but he makes no concession to division by gender. He distinguishes between class-based inequality and power-based inequality which later he concludes continues in the Soviet Union. He sees five elite groups in modern society: political leaders, government administrators, economic directors, leaders of the masses and military chiefs.

Aron's analysis, he argues, is a system of concepts which could be the instruments of a synthesis between analytical sociology, the sociology of social types and the interpretation of history. The analysis, however, does not uncover those facets of the social structure or social relations which are hidden from history. Aron does not mention the absence of women in all of his five elites, nor does he comment about the more than half of the population (women and children) who had at that time no effective share in either political or economic power. He is, of course, dealing exclusively with the public domain. But he extrapolates from that to 'society as a whole'. He has to mean 'the whole of the public domain of society', but he does not notice his mistake and in any case, the public domain cannot be understood without taking account of the unwaged labour upon which it relies for domestic work and for reproduction.

The Grading of (Male) Occupations
Empirical sociology also concentrated on the public domain as the same 1950 volume of the *BJS* bears witness. In 'The social grading of occupations' John Hall and Caradog Jones, seeking to show the chief factors responsible for social class differences and for class mobility,

concentrate entirely upon paid employment. Because of the confusions cause by entering females into such an occupational analysis, attention is in the end focused on grading men's occupations only: a partial analysis indeed, and a limitation still to be found in studies of occupational status. The Nuffield Social Mobility Survey of 1972 only sampled men. Wives were included in 1974. The only discussion of women in the book Hope edited is about the 'marriage market' (see Hope, 1972; Goldthorpe and Hope, 1974; Goldthorpe, 1980). It is clear that Halsey and Goldthorpe still do not understand how their topic choice makes women invisible to sociology. They fail to answer this point of Broadbent and Lockwood (*The Times*, 14, 22, 25 January 1980; ref. Bradley article, *The Times*, 9 January 1980).

MacIver and Page and the 'Natural' Division of Labour

MacIver and Page do not find it necessary to look further than 'natural differences' to explain the gender order. 'The family rests on biological differences between the sexes . . . These differences, natural and developed, show themselves in society in the *social division of labour*' (1950, p. 8, emphasis in original).

When they write of the family, MacIver and Page refer to the endless variations in the form of the family (p. 239). They discuss the history of the move from the patriarchal to the modern family, referring to the minor legal status of women in the eighteenth century, how in all households women and men co-operated in economic tasks now removed from the home. They then discuss 'the crumbling of the patriarchal foundations' (p. 251) – the decline of the authoritarian mores of feudalism and the religious concepts that went along with them; how the workshops and factories drew ever larger numbers of women. 'They [the factories] broke down the age-old doctrine – "man for the field and woman for the hearth" ' which they appear to believe in despite what they have just said about variability of family form. But the temporary employment of young women '*is rather a condition of than an alternative* to marriage and the family' (p. 254, my emphasis). The family '*alone provides a way of combining and harmonizing certain closely related functions*' (p. 263, emphasis in original), which are stable satisfaction of sex needs, production and rearing of children, provision of a home. The assertion is made (p. 264) and repeated (p. 276) without citing the evidence that in the family 'the nurture of children takes place within the focus of the home which, as considerable evidence seems to indicate, is a more favourable environment for them than that of a state nursery or other public or private agencies'. There was no doubt in the minds of MacIver and Page that urbanisation and industrialisation were liberating for women. Not a hint of isolation or privatisation is there, nor any suggestion that women's social conditions and freedom might vary by class.

Lowie's Relative Relativism

Lowie's (1950) views form something of a contrast as has already been indicated. He lists a number of exceptions to gender order rules found in various societies. Thus in Albania women can avoid marriage by a vow of virginity and thereafter they wear masculine dress, while among the Comanche men could avoid war by wearing female dress (p. 5). He is clear that 'sex . . . is an effective sorter, but . . . it fully determined definite associations only, or mostly, when coupled with age or some other factor' (p. 6). He recognises the importance of economic relations, showing how the introduction of stockbreeding profoundly affected the status of women among the Chukchi coast dwellers; women had not been allowed to hunt seals, but they could tend herds and came to own reindeer themselves (pp. 26–7). Lowie is much more of a relativist than MacIver and Page, taking the view that sex dichotomy is only partly dependent on biological differences and partly on the division of labour (p. 177). It is no simple matter of nature for him.

Folsom Recognises the Issues

Folsom with Marion Bassett in *The Family and Democratic Society* (1948) recognises quite clearly the subordination of women and that there is more to the sex hierarchy than 'lingering partriarchal attitudes', but again nature is the fundamental explanation. 'It is socially *natural* that most cultures should build their *most consequential* classification of human beings upon the chief biologically natural classification . . . To the dominant sex it gives the satisfaction of superiority' (p. 177, his emphasis on 'natural', mine on 'most consequential'). As with all other male writers of the mid-century (and indeed later, see Giner, 1972, p. 22) there seem to him to have been immense changes. Folsom discusses why men are opposed to the 'masculinization' as he calls it of women's dress and describes the great cultural changes, for example, men of 50 becoming used to looking at women in bathing suits, astride horses.

Folsom admits 'some legal inequalities remain' but he sees beneath the surface: 'Moreover, women are now placed in a position of inferior economic opportunity and opportunity of personality development. Their status in this respect may even be relatively lower than it was, but it is concealed beneath superficial phenomena which often give the false appearance of matriarchy' (p. 178). He reminds us that Lester F. Ward in 1911 called the family a device for the subjection of women and children.

While he thinks the two sexes, despite all the changes, still feel very different pressures, one thing is certain: women have become more differentiated among themselves, the professional woman being divided from the home-maker. He discusses the lack of specialisation in contemporary housework[1] and concludes: 'while factory work has become unsatisfying through extreme specialization and monotonous repetition of processes, housework has become frustrating through going in the opposite extreme' (p. 594) – a technological rather than a relational explanation. He is clear about the presence of class divisions: 'The home-making mother is economically rewarded according to her husband's ability and fairness, not her own ability. Hence class injustice is even greater among women than among men' (p. 597). There is a lack of psychological reward: 'To a large extent it is a pain economy . . .' (p. 598).

Furthermore, Folsom sees that the gains made by feminism are threatened. Why should it be the women who are blamed for any inconsistencies in aspiration and practice? he asks (p. 622). He blames a neo-familism and the caste system into which men and women are divided and finally he accepts the existence of a sex class struggle.

Everett Hughes and Symbolic Interactionism
Hughes's approach is rather different. He has inspired a great deal of fieldwork, much of it undertaken by women, but he too takes the gender order as 'given' and 'natural'. He is sensitive to its consequences for women, although his analysis is limited and he does not analyse the gender order as a social institution (see, for example, Hughes, 1971, pp. 141–50). He notes that working in the public domain women become divided amongst themselves. 'The nurses, as they successfully rise to professional standing, are delegating the more lowly tasks to *aids and maids*' (1971, p. 307, my emphasis). In being admitted to a division of labour derived from and developed in the public domain, women have become involved in the oppressive characteristics of that domain. Hughes points out that the physician can only retain his superior position because he has 'a right hand man' (*sic*), a nurse. He points out further that the nurse, although 'it hurts her' (1971, p. 308), does tasks when they need doing, which are tasks of people below her and also outside the medical hierarchy. We should note, although Hughes does not, that in the ever-increasing division of labour and the associated increasing specialisation, it is the woman in the house who has remained the generalist; it is the women doing people work, the nurse who may be expected to act as the generalist when circumstances demand, notwithstanding her specialist skills. Much of the struggle of nurses for status and work autonomy seem to be connected with their search for specialism.

The Present Status of the Problems about the Division of Labour

By the 1970s more men recognise that problems exist about explaining women's place in the division of labour
Frankenberg (1976) has shown how, because of their pervasiveness, even someone who set out in the 1950s to expose the gender order could be trapped by the values of the male-dominated society. He now argues that although his intention has been to analyse and describe a society where the total dependence of women was made incomplete by the partial inability of

men to earn a living, he made inadequate use of his case data in 1957. While he still thinks he was right that the women dominated the social life of the village, he did not comment on '. . . the lack of women as officials of village societies despite their informal leadership' and 'I might have provided a more convincing analysis of both this and the defeat of the women's parish council candidate' (1976, p. 36).

Abrams and McCulloch were interested, *inter alia*, in the possibility that in communes the social process of mothering might be separated from the exploitation of biological mothers. Although few 'communes were explicitly concerned with "the woman question"' (Abrams and McCulloch, 1976, p. 141), there was the notion that in communes women would live as individuals in their own right and specifically that with the establishment of common property Engels's predictions about the passing of the family and the public care and education of children would come about. In practice Abrams and McCulloch found: 'Of the three links that compose the basic family unit, wife-husband, father-child, mother-child, the first two are often seriously opened up in communes, but the third is hardly touched; motherhood remains an all-demanding and totally female role' (1976, p. 144). Women in the communes they surveyed were not liberated; indeed, Abrams and McCulloch see communes as the reconstitution of familism in which the removal of legally enforceable monogamy and the wage-work/housework division of roles has not created an alternative system 'but . . . the deeper obstacles to equality . . . are made plainer' (1976, p. 145).

This is partly because of the petty-bourgeois nature of the commune movement, but also because the outside world bears upon and constrains the commune in a variety of ways. The latter point they make convincingly but what they assert rather than demonstrate is that the pressure derives from capitalism and the wage-labour economy and that when these are changed the cause of the oppression of women by men will have been removed. It is at this juncture that once again there is a lacuna between the reality of male–female relationships and the theoretical grasp of sociologists. This study demonstrates the influence of the feminist movement and a welcome attempt to relate personal and domestic relationships to the relationships of production and control in the wider society. This is a great advance on the 1960s when it was argued that the family was somehow 'detached' from society, an implausible thesis given the dependence of the public domain on the family, the impact upon it of the happenings in the public domain, the passing to and fro of men between the domains and the increasing tendency for women to pass to and fro also. The notion of 'detachment', of 'lack of fit', was yet one more expression of the male view of the family articulated from the public domain (see, for example, the debate between Parson, Litwak and Seeman and discussed by Parsons and Adams in Anderson, 1971, and the discussion of the notion of lack of 'fit' between family and society in Harris, 1969 and 1977).

A failure of sociological understanding as well as an injustice to women
My argument has been that the general sociological theories which were
enunciated by men focused on the public domain. They constitute a strait-
jacket in which we are still imprisoned and within which attempts to
understand the total society are severely constrained. The domestic labour
debate is a good example: Marxist analysis remains incomplete so long as
reproduction is not included along with production (Beechey, 1979; Kuhn
and Wolpe, 1978), but this is not all. The problems of Marxism in this area
derive from the attempt to apply a theory which started with its focus on
industrial production to the analysis of problems of the domestic arena and
the relation of that arena to the public domain.

The way in which the division of labour has been conceived in all major
theoretical approaches is an injustice to women, but it has wider
consequences. Important aspects of the nature of the relations in the
division of labour have been overlooked because of the concentration on
the public domain and the adoption of the values of that domain. We lack a
theory which can articulate the private and public domains and address
those activities which straddle both domains. This is seen particularly
clearly in the weaknesses of theories about professions and occupations.

*A sociological failure which affects the analysis of the public domain also: the
case of professions and occupations*
Johnson's original analysis, *Professions and Power* (1972), demonstrates
well the particular historical circumstances in which the notion of
professions was able to get a foothold, for example the links between the
emergence of the medical profession and the relationships which the
doctors had established with the rising bourgeoisie. He fails to comment
there on the importance of the services of the new nurses to the success of
the doctors. This has since been demonstrated by others (Austin, 1977;
Carpenter, 1977; Garmornikov, 1978), but the form of Johnson's earlier
analysis made it possible to extend the analysis of the rise of the professions
to include concepts drawn from the gender order and the institution of the
family. His later analysis (Johnson, 1977) based on the work of Carchedi,
focusing as it does narrowly upon production, not only ignores the
relevance of the gender order and the part played by professionalising
occupations in sustaining that order, but allows no obvious route through
which such conceptualisation might be admitted. The problems become
more acute when one focuses specifically on human service or people work.

People work: an analytical problem which concerns both sexes
Freidson (1970) has drawn our attention to the distinction between the
consulting professions and others. An additional distinction should be
noted. Some consulting professions largely do things *for* people although in
so doing they may acquire a good deal of power *over* their clients and
indeed in society more widely, for example, the legal profession. Others in

the course of serving people are involved in doing things *to* them, that is doing people work. The nature of the social relationships involved between a worker and her or his client when undertaking people work should be distinguished from other forms of personal service as Stevenson (1976) does when he differentiates 'human service industries' from the larger group of service industries. The human services involve 'an interaction designed to change the characteristics or condition of one of the people involved in the interaction' (p. 78). 'Human service' captures one facet of these interactions, while Goffman's notion of 'people work' captures another. Human service or people work occurs in many occupations and professions, in various caring, training and servicing activities in both public and private domains. People work is something different from the 'people-processing' which management undertakes and from the tertiary sector more generally. People work involves the very precise and direct manipulation of one person by another.[2]

Insights about people work have come from detailed examination of face-to-face relationships by interactionists. The insights have been limited to interactions in the workplace. Furthermore they have not taken account of the implications for their observations of the material base, its relation to the mode of production, or to the form and activities of the state. Interactionists' observations have not been linked with European or British mainstream sociological theory partly because their authors were not concerned with concepts or analyses of structures (Giddens, 1979, p. 254) and partly because the mode of conceptualisation of classical theories did not readily allow a place for interactionists' findings. But the observation of interactions is important and covers an area of activity in British and European mainstream sociology which deals with alienation of the worker and the potential domination, oppression and misuse of the client.

In the relations between professional and client, as Hughes argued in 1956, the line between service and disservice is a fine one. 'In many of the things which people do for one another, the *for* can be changed to *to* by a slight overdoing or shift of mood' (Hughes, 1971, p. 305). Hughes's focus, like that of later interactionists, was on the analysis of the face-to-face rather than on the material base, the market place, the state, or the way in which the economic or custodial relations between professionals and clients might affect their face-to-face relationship. With this focus he usefully drew attention to certain inherent characteristics of people work overlooked by British and European mainstream sociology. In doing so he tended to attribute the occurrence of oppression in people work to the psychological.

It was left to Goffman (1961) to point out the systematic way in which 'work *for*' might routinely become 'work *to*' because of the institutional setting. Patients in a mental institution are not only the subjects of people work and therefore the work objects of the staff, they are also totally encompassed, the boundaries between work, rest and play having been obliterated. Patients in a general hospital are not so totally dependent over 'an appreciable length of time' (Goffman 1961), but they are utterly dependent on their medical and nursing attendants for the period of their incarceration. Goffman did not take his analysis sufficiently far, however, for he did not locate the asylum sufficiently clearly in the context of the wider society. At a very general level such a link is not hard to make: in societies based upon competition or even upon collective arrangements for production where the ability to produce is what is highly valued, those who are not able and are judged not likely to be able to produce again or ever are liable to be devalued. It seems that this is likely to occur in state socialist as well as capitalist societies.

The Client as a Labourer

Hughes was correct in 1956 to include the patient in the division of labour in health care (1971, p. 306). Goffman's work has shown how even in the most oppressed conditions the patient is an actor and not just a passive recipient of care, but also how her or his actions can be constrained by the components of power and authority in the relations surrounding her or him. The inclusion of the client in the division of labour is crucial for the understanding of all human service work and particularly important for the understanding of people work. This is a dimension to which we have been blinded by our exclusive use of models derived from industrial production. 'The health service is better thought of as a process of continuing interaction between patient and health care professionals and workers than as an industry or predominantly economic activity' (Stacey, 1976, p. 194). Malcolm Johnson misunderstood this, saying: 'Margaret Stacey has expressed doubts about patient consumerism on the grounds that the patient is viewed more as a "work object" than as a "consumer" ' (1977, p. 93). His misunderstanding is a good example of the way in which we are dominated and blinkered by market-place concepts, by the applications of theories developed in the male-dominated public arena to arenas where they are irrelevant or incomplete for both description and analysis. Stevenson refers to the client as 'consumer' (1976, p. 78) but reaches the position that in human services 'production and consumption occur simultaneously' (p. 82). The patient may be a more or less powerful member of the division of labour depending on her or his economic circumstances, social class, education, colour, sex, gender. When profits and fees are introduced into the situation, the relationship, although still predicated on the notion of professional service, is subtly different from those where health care is free at the point of delivery. Jewson (1974 and 1976) has illustrated the way in which historically the power relation in the division of labour between physician and client has shifted in favour of the physician, a shift which can only be understood by reference to the social and economic class structure.

No great attention has been paid in theoretical literature on the professions or in the sociology of medicine to Hughes's insistence that the patient should be included in the division of labour, although interactionists continue to do this in their fieldwork and analysis (for example, Emerson, 1970; Fagerhaugh and Strauss, 1977). Has the lack of attention arisen because to include the patient in the division of labour is revolutionary, challenging the division of labour in the service professions, removing the client from the position of a passive work object to an active participant? (Frankenberg, 1974). The conflicts arise around the issues of the patient as a work object, as a service object and as an active participant in her or his own treatment. The division of labour is not between 'producer' and 'consumer' in this case. The notion of production may be inappropriate for service work. In so far as it is appropriate the client is also a producer.

Lack of Concepts to analyse Human Service and People Work
Thus, there is a problem about what the nature of the relationship is between server and served.

Concepts developed to analyse employer and employee in industry or producer and consumer in the market are both inappropriate for human service as they are for analysis of service in the family. Nor can analytical modes developed for the familial domain readily be applied to the waged sector. Much if not most human service is work *to* people. A question is whether in that relationship the server works in the interests of the served or uses or abuses her or him. 'Service' may be altruistic; that at least is its ethic. It may be based on a reasonable or symmetrical exchange, whether monetary or non-monetary. It may involve either the domination of the served by the server, or, in cases where the client is dominant, the server in servitude. The relationships are different from those of productive industry or commerce. The abuse of power and authority which may occur in the human services where people work is done is different in nature from the abuse which may occur in relations of domination and subordination in productive industry. The kernel of the latter form of abuse is the exploitative nature of the relationship, the extraction of surplus value, although oppression may also be experienced directly as a consequence of the way in which the power and authority of the employer or supervisor are exercised over the employee.

Marxist as well as Interactionist Theories are Inadequate: the Private Domain is not analysed
Stevenson (1976) talks about human service *industries*. While some human services are located in the public domain and may be understood as 'industries', others are located in the family. They include housework, household management and more diffuse activities like 'mothering', which includes work (such as getting the children to bed) but also includes loving and caring and may include hating. An embarrassment about translating some of these activities to the public domain can be seen in the use by nurses of the initials TLC (an apparently technical phrase) for the tender

loving care they feel they should offer the patient. Stevenson's work, in common with most sociological work, is severely limited because he quite excludes unpaid human service and the entire private domain.

In the private domain, while women service men, they also do people work to their children. In this case the children are not consulted, they did not ask to be born. In the public domain, while in many cases in any one consultation the client is voluntary and has put her/himself in the way of being manipulated, this is not always the case. Children are sent to school, to the GP, or to hospital by others. The elderly, the mentally handicapped, indeed the physically handicapped in many cases, and the severely mentally ill may find that someone else has placed them in a dependent 'client' situation. Their social position, officially defined as non-productive or never-to-be-productive people, is somewhat different from that of children who are their parents' heirs and also future citizens. The way in which 'work' is done to the former is likely to differ significantly from that done to the latter. Yet all clients, involuntary and voluntary alike, are not merely passive objects; they are actors in their own right. If they are sufficiently subordinated, all the action that is left to them is not to co-operate or to 'mess up'; on the other hand, they may be wealthy and dominant patrons.

We have trouble dealing with these concepts in the market place because we have not faced up to their importance in the domestic arena and have not adequately related the implications of one arena to the other. Many of the people-work activities were formerly dealt with in the domestic arena and have been transferred into the public arena as the latter has become increasingly invasive and dominant. The precise manipulation of one person by another when the latter is both more skilful and more powerful is common to both private and public domains. When these activities are removed from the private to the public domain they are removed into the waged from the unwaged sector. The rewards are then of a quite different order and the constraints on action and the accountability for actions are predicated on relationships of an altogether different kind from those pertaining in the familial setting. At the same time, some facets of the familial order have been carried over into the public domain. The nurse as servant of the doctor and given the task of daily care of the patient echoes the gender order of the Victorian household (Austin, 1977; Carpenter 1977; Garmarnikov, 1978). Infant school teachers tend to be women, most headteachers are men. The majority of university staffs are men and there are few women professors. Women predominate in all the lower echelons of human service industries. For all these reasons people work cannot be fully understood without taking account of the gender order and of the social and economic division of labour in the family.

Women's activities in socialising children are a form of people work in many ways similar to that which is to be found in the 'caring' services in the public arena. The notion of 'people work' reveals the 'socialisation process' as interactive as well as a matter of social control. The critical difference between the people work of women in the home and people work in the public domain is that the former is unpaid and inextricably tied to woman's estate as wife and mother, while people work in the public sector is contracted by wage, fee, or profit.

The Generational Order

There is also a contradiction in the service which a woman in the home performs: she serves her husband in a subordinate role, but her children in a superordinate role. This is in some ways analogous to the comparison of a physician faced with a wealthy client-patron or a poor patient. The difference is that the woman's two service roles permeate a wide area of her life and that of her children, while the professional encounter is greatly limited in comparison.

The whole question of the position of children in the division of labour is only now beginning to be seen as problematic. Previously it was as uncritically assumed that children were there to be socialised, to be fitted for 'valued social roles'; their place in the social order was as unproblematic as the gender order itself. The question of people work on children has to be made problematic at the level of the division of social labour, for children work and are worked on. As in other forms of people work there may be altruistic service or there may be oppression or abuse. Harris (1977) has discussed how children may be used by their parents as privately produced commodities, realisable in exchange. From a Marxist-feminist perspective Dorothy Smith has argued that in the contemporary division of labour middle-class mothers are recruited by corporate capitalism to play an important role in the maintenance of a social order appropriate for that form of capitalism (Smith, 1973). The oppression of women, the oppression of children and the oppression of children by women 'is a product of the woman's mediation to the child of the externalised order which in fact "oppresses" them both'. In this way 'the mother's service to her children becomes corrupted to a subordination of her children to that order. A mother's *failure* to mediate the external order to her children becomes proof that she does not love them' (p. 29).

What Is Work?

The logic of the analysis in this chapter and of the recognition that terms, concepts and theory all developed in the public domain to deal with the problems of that domain may well be that concepts of 'work' and 'labouring' have in the end to be superseded. To include the notion of the unpaid labourer has been liberating but we probably need to go further. We know that the distinction between work and leisure is one that relates to societies in which the concept of selling one's labour exists; in pre-industrial societies members 'do what is to be done', be it ceremony, hunting, fishing, gathering, tilling, drinking, dancing, fighting, or reproducing. Distinctions between work and leisure of the kind found in Western societies are non-existent. Further, these distinctions are irrelevant for Western housewives, for whom the much-vaunted site of leisure, the home, is their place of work.

Freidson (1978), in a thought-provoking paper, shows a number of problems in defining what is an occupation and draws attention to the many that are left out of the official classification of workers: criminals, unregistered workers (those who are under-age, retired, illegal migrants, unemployed, institutionalised or on welfare benefits); subjective workers in the entertainment trades, including sport and the performing arts, the fine arts and sciences and those who do hobbies and who volunteer whose means of subsistence is derived from other occupations. For them the distinction between work and leisure is blurred. Freidson concludes: 'we must develop conceptions that can analyse the full range [of these occupations] . . . Such methods and concepts must be capable of reaching well beyond the limits of the official economy, into the community, the household and their various systems of exchange' (pp. 11–12). But he overlooks the problem of the two Adams, the distinction between the institutions of the family and those of industry, state and the market place. He includes the housewife as 'the most conspicuous and important' of the full-time informal occupations. He does not mention the subjective rewards which may accrue to the housewife-mother discussed by Caulfield (1977), or the negative emotions associated with the denigrated housework. Subjective rewards he reserves for the 'subjective labour force'. Yet they may also be experienced by those in human services in both public and private domains. Nor does he understand, as Delphy and Leonard (1980) understand, that the entire institutional basis of the division of labour in the family is quite different from that of the market place and requires separate analysis.

Clearly, revisiting the division of labour in the terms which I have set out in this chapter leads to a rethinking of what constitutes work, especially in the human services, and what the rewards and sanctions, incentives and disincentives are and upon what they are based. These phenomena go well beyond those to be found in the market place. Some of the rewards and disincentives are nowadays associated with many kinds of waged work in healing, caring, teaching, guiding and counselling occupations.

New Conceptualisation Needed

There seem to be two sets of problems to be resolved: one is to comprehend the meaning and nature of human service or people work and its implications for the social order in both public and private domains; the second is to understand the way in which the relationships between those domains has changed empirically and is still changing, in particular the way in which the division of labour in the family has been translated to and reinforced in the division of labour in the public domain. To achieve either of these aims it is important to get out of the strait-jacket of theories whose origins and concepts derive exclusively from the public domain. As Delphy and Leonard (1980) correctly argue, this cannot be done until the division of labour in the domestic domain is conceptualised in its own right and carefully studied. The domestic labour debate, which has sought to relate the paid work of the market place to the unpaid work of the housewife, has been limited because its starting point has been a set of concepts located in the public arena. Rosalind Delmar is correct to draw attention to its similarity to the old debate about 'women's two roles' (Delmar, 1980). This debate derives from the public domain focus. The division of labour in the private domain will never be fully understood with those concepts.

There is not space here to explore the divisions of labour in and between the public and private domains further. All that can be done is to suggest the outlines of the ways in which we might begin to envisage the social order, its creation and re-creation, if we are to get out of the conceptual strait-jacket invented for us by our founding fathers, still perpetuated when the BSA was founded and sadly even today by some highly respected sociologists. In order to do this we must admit the importance of feeling-states over a wider range than the recognition of consciousness of kind which we are familiar with in class formation. We have to follow Wright Mills's (1959) dictum of linking the personal and the political. It has been a major contribution of the recent women's movement to put feelings, experiences and consciousness on the agenda for political action; to insist that politics cannot be understood without taking account of the politics of the family, of the experiences of women in their relationships with men. The implications in the political arena have perhaps been made most clearly by Rowbotham (1973 and 1979). Such feminists have insisted that what men have seen as trivial, irrelevant, or tiresomely emotional is critically important for the understanding of the social and political processes of contemporary society. A similar point has to be made with regard to sociological theory. A dimension has been missing from our understanding of occupations in the class structure and in the social structure because male-dominated mainstream sociological theory has ignored an analogous category of essential characteristics in the social division of labour.

We shall never be able to understand the social processes going on around us so long as we tacitly or overtly deny the part played by the givers and receivers of 'care' and 'service', the victims of socialisation processes, the unpaid labourers in the processes of production and reproduction. Morgan (1975) has reminded us that sociologists had not predicted, and were rather taken aback by, the force of the women's liberation movement. That would not have happened if sociologists had not been totally abstracted and distracted by their concerns in the public domain.

This chapter has sought to show not only the classical theories originating in the public domain omitted certain crucial aspects of the division of labour but also that the contributions of the interactionist school of thought address issues overlooked by all the classical European schools.

At the same time interactionist approaches are limited because of their analytic neglect of the gender order and of the economic basis of the relationships they study. The feminist critique has alerted us to the importance of the gender order, but less perhaps to the generational order. Both must be comprehended in any plausible theory of the division of labour.

The legacies of the two Adams linger, both blaming the women victims of the orders they describe. As for women, the wider sharing of the meanings and experiences of their situation which has become available as feminist consciousness has risen in the years since the BSA was founded (but for which the BSA can take any credit only since 1974) has brought sisterly comfort to many women, along with a deeper understanding of the long and difficult struggles ahead in reconceptualisation and in everyday life.

Notes: Chapter 11

The first version of this chapter was read to the staff graduate seminar of the Sociology Department of the University of Warwick, to members of which I am indebted for their corrections, criticisms and comment. My thinking owes much also to collaboration with Marion Price; to the many discussions with members of the workshop on the sociology of health and illness at Warwick and of the workshop on the division of labour in child health care; and to the ideas in papers of postgraduate students and research associates. In common with other academic feminists I also owe a debt, diffuse but very real, to the many debates, discussions and publications of women in the feminist movement outside academic walls. None of these people is, however, responsible for anything I have said here: that responsibility is entirely mine. I also received useful comments on the draft as read at the British Sociological Association from those who attended the session and later from the following people to whom I am also most grateful: Michelle Barratt, Mary Ann Elston, Ronnie Frankenberg, Pauline Hunt, Ann Oakley, Mandy Snell, Elizabeth Wilson, Rue Bucher, Eliot Freidson, Hilary Graham, Mary McIntosh, Hilary Rose and Ivan Waddington.

1   He refers to two early studies of the nature of housework (Lindquist, 1931, and Wilson, 1929) but which clearly were not allowed the publicity accorded to Hannah Gavron (1966) or Ann Oakley (1974a and 1974b).

2   Facets of people work are discussed by McKinlay in *Processing People* (1975). While he discusses the contribution of Hughes and Goffman in relation to organisations he devotes most time to the extreme case of the mortification process. He does not extend his discussion to other facets of people work or examine its relation to the division of labour more generally.

Bibliography

Abbot, J. (1969), *Employment of Sociology and Anthropology Graduates 1966–67* (London: British Sociological Association).

Abell, P. (1977), 'The many faces of power and liberty: revealed preference, autonomy and teleological explanation', *Sociology*, vol. 11, pp. 3–24.

Abrams, M. (1979), 'Social surveys, social theory and social policy, *Quantitative Sociology Newsletters*, no. 1 (Spring), pp. 15–24.

Abrams, P. (1968), *The Origins of British Sociology: 1834–1914, An Essay with Selected Papers* (Chicago: University of Chicago Press).

Abrams, P. (forthcoming), *The Uses of British Sociology*.

Abrams, P., and McCulloch, A., with Abrams, S. and Gore, P. (1976), *Communes, Sociology and Society* (Cambridge: Cambridge University Press).

Althusser, L. (1968), *For Marx* (Harmondsworth: Penguin).

Althusser, L. (1972), 'Marxism is not a historicism', in Althusser, L., and Balibar, E., *Reading Capital* (London: New Left Books).

Althusser, L. (1976), *Essays in Self Criticism* (London: New Left Books).

Altvater E. (1973a), 'Some problems of state interventionism I', *Kapitalistate*, vol. 1, pp. 96–116.

Altvater E. (1973b), 'Some problems of state interventionism II', *Kapitalistate*, vol. II, pp. 76–83.

American Anthropological Association (1980), 'Association comments on DHEW regulations', *Anthropology Newsletter*, vol. 21, no. 2, pp. 1, 11.

Anderson, M. (ed.) (1971), *Sociology of the Family: Selected Readings* (Harmondsworth: Penguin).

Anderson, P. (1976), *Considerations on Western Marxism* (London: New Left Books).

Anderson, P. (1980), *Debates in English Marxism* (London: New Left Books).

Anonymous (1975), 'Professional ethics', *Network*, no. 1, pp. 3–4.

Aron, R. (1950), Social structure and the ruling class I and II, *British Journal of Sociology*, vol. 1, nos 1 and 2, pp. 1–16, 126–43.

Austin, R. (1977), 'Sex and gender in the future of nursing', *Nursing Times* (August), pp. 113–19.

Bachrach, P., and Baratz, M. S. (1970), *Power and Poverty* (New York: Oxford University Press).

Banks, J. A. (1954a), 'The employment of sociologists: graduates, 1952 and 1953', *British Journal of Sociology*, vol. 5, pp. 161–2.

Banks, J. A. (1954b), *Prosperity and Parenthood* (London: Routledge & Kegan Paul).

Banks, J. A. (1958), 'Employment of sociology and anthropology graduates: final report', *British Journal of Sociology*, vol. 9, pp. 271–83.

Banks, J. A. (1967), 'The British Sociological Association – the first fifteen years', *Sociology*, vol. 1, pp. 1–9.

Banks, J. A. (1975), 'From scholarly body to professional association', *Network*, no. 1, pp. 2–3.

Banks, J. A., and Banks, O. (1956), 'Employment of sociology and anthropology graduates, 1952 and 1954', *British Journal of Sociology*, vol. 7, pp. 46–51.

Barker, D. L., and Allen, S. (eds) (1976), *Sexual Divisions and Society* (London: Tavistock).

Barnes, H. E., and Becker, H. P. (1938), *Social Thought from Lore to Science* (Boston, Mass.: D. C. Heath).

Barnes, J. A. (1979), *Who Should Know What?* (Harmondsworth: Penguin).

Barrett, M., *et al.* (eds) (1979), *Ideology and Cultural Production* (London: Croom Helm).

Becker, H. (1963), *Outsiders* (New York: The Free Press).

Becker, H. (1966), introduction to Shaw, Clifford, *The Jack-Roller* (Chicago: University of Chicago Press).

Becker, H. (1970), *Sociological Work* (Chicago: Aldine).

Beechey, V. (1977), 'Female wage labour in capitalist production', *Capital and Class*, no. 3, pp. 45–66.

Beechey, V. (1979), 'On patriarchy', *Feminist Review*, no. 3, pp. 66–82.

Bell, C., and Newby, H. (1977), introduction to Bell, C., and Newby, H. (eds), *Doing Sociological Research* (London: Allen & Unwin).

Bendix, R. (1966), *Max Weber: An Intellectual Portrait* (London: Methuen).

Berger, P., and Luckmann, T. (1966), *The Social Construction of Reality* (New York: Doubleday).

Bernsdorf, W., and Knospe, H. (eds) (1980), *Internationales Soziologenlexikon, Band 1: Beiträge über bis Ende 1969 verstorbene Soziologen* (Stuttgart: Ferdinand Enke Verlag), p. 52.

Bernstein, B. (1971), 'On the classification and framing of educational knowledge', in Young, M. F. D. (ed.), *Knowledge and Control* (London: Collier Macmillan).

Bernstein, B. (1974), *Class, Codes and Control* (London: Routledge & Kegan Paul).

Berry, D. (1974), *Central Ideas in Sociology* (London: Constable).

Blackburn, R. (1967), 'The unequal society', in Blackburn, Robin, and Cockburn, A. (eds), *The Incompatibles: Trade Union Militancy and the Consensus* (Harmondsworth: Penguin), pp. 15–55.

Blackburn, R. (ed.) (1972), *Ideology in Social Science* (London: Fontana).

Blume, S. (1974), *Towards a Political Sociology of Science* (New York: The Free Press).

Boccara, P., *et al.* (1971), *Traité d'Economie Marxiste: le capitalisme monopoliste de l'Etat* (Paris: Editions Sociales).

Booth, C. (1887), 'The inhabitants of Tower Hamlets', *Journal of the Royal Statistical Society*, vol. 50, pt. 2, pp. 326–91.

Bott, E. (1957), *Family and Social Network* (London: Tavistock).

Bottomore, T. (1975), *Marxist Sociology* (London: Macmillan).

Bottomore, T. B., and Nisbet, R. A. (eds) (1979), *A History of Sociological Analysis* (London: Heinemann).

Bottomore, T., and Rubel, M. (eds) (1963), *Karl Marx: Selected Writings in*

Sociology and Social Philosophy (Harmondsworth: Penguin).

Braverman, H. (1974), *Labor and Monopoly Capital* (New York: Monthly Review Press).

British Sociological Association (1953), Minutes of the Eighth Meeting (16 June) of the Sub-Committee on Recruitment, etc., minute 3(iii).

British Sociological Association (1967), *Professional Ethics* (London: BSA).

British Sociological Association (1970), *Report of the Annual General Meeting* (London: BSA).

British Sociological Association (1970), 'Statement of ethical principles and their application to sociological practice', *Sociology*, vol. 4, pp. 114–17.

British Sociological Association (n.d.), *Sociology without Sexism: A Source Book* (London: BSA).

Brown, G., and Harris, T. (1978), *The Social Origins of Depression* (London: Tavistock).

Bryant, C. G. A. (1975), 'Positivism reconsidered', *Sociological Review*, n.s., vol. 23, no. 2, pp. 397–412.

Bryant, C. G. A. (1980), 'Towards an analysis of positivism in British sociology', Transactions of the BSA Conference, 1980.

Buci-Glucksman, C. (1980), *Gramsci and the State* (London: Lawrence & Wishart).

Burns, T., and Stalker, G. M. (1961), *The Management of Innovation* (London: Tavistock).

Butler, D., and Kitzinger, U. (1976), *The 1975 Referendum* (London: Macmillan).

Butler, D., and Stokes, D. (1974), *Political Change in Britain: The Evolution of Electoral Choice*, 2nd edn (London: Macmillan).

Cain, M. (1972), 'Police professionalism: its meaning and consequences', *Anglo American Law Review*, vol. 1, no. 2, pp. 217–31.

Cain, M. (1977), 'An ironical departure: the dilemma of contemporary policing', in *Yearbook of Social Policy in Britain, 1976* (London: Routledge & Kegan Paul).

Cain, M. (1979), 'The general practice lawyer and the client: towards a radical conception', *International Journal of the Sociology of Law*, vol. 7, no. 3, pp. 331–54.

Cain, M., and Finch, J. (1980), 'Towards a rehabilitation of data', Transactions of the BSA Conference, 1980.

Carpenter, M. (1977), 'The new managerialism and professionalism in nursing', in Stacey, M., *et al.* (eds), *Health and the Division of Labour* (London: Croom Helm).

Carr-Saunders, Sir A. M., Jones, D. C., and Moser, C. A. (1958), *A Survey of Social Conditions in England and Wales, As Illustrated by Statistics*, 3rd edn (Oxford: Clarendon Press; 2nd edn by Sir A. M. Carr-Saunders and D. C. Jones, 1937).

Caulfield, M. D. (1977), 'Universal sex oppression? A critique from Marxist anthropology', in Nelson, C., and Olesen, V. (eds), *Catalyst*, nos 10–11 (Summer), pp. 60–77.

Cicourel, A. V. (1964), *Method and Measurement in Sociology* (London: Collier Macmillan).

Clarke, M. (1976), 'First-year sociology courses – a report of a survey', *Sociology*, vol. 10, no. 1, pp. 83–99.

Cohen, G. A. (1979), *Karl Marx's Theory of History* (Oxford: Clarendon Press).

Cohen, P. A. (1980), 'Is positivism dead?', *Sociological Review*, n.s., vol. 28, no. 1, pp. 141–76.

Cohn-Bendit, G., and Cohn-Bendit, D. (1969), *Obsolete Communism, the Left-Wing Alternative* (Harmondsworth: Penguin).

Collison, P. (1963), *The Cuttleslowe Walls* (London: Faber).

Converse, P. E. (1964), 'The nature of belief systems in mass publics', in Apter, D. E. (ed.), *Ideology and Discontent* (New York: The Free Press), pp. 206–61.

Cotgrove, S. (1967), *The Science of Society* (London: Allen & Unwin).

Coward, R., and Ellis, J. (1977), *Language and Materialism* (London: Routledge & Kegan Paul).

Cuff, E., and Payne, G. (1979), *Perspectives in Sociology* (London: Allen & Unwin).

Dawe, A. (1973), 'The role of experience in the construction of social theory: an essay in reflexive sociology', *Sociological Review*, n.s., vol. 21, pp. 25–55.

Dawe, A. (1979), 'Theories of social action', in Bottomore, T., and Nisbet, R. (eds), *A History of Sociological Analysis* (London: Heinemann), pp. 362–417.

Delmar, R. (1980), 'The family and feminist theory', paper read to the staff graduate seminar, University of Warwick, Sociology Department.

Delphy, C., and Leonard, D. (1980), 'The family as an economic system', paper presented to the Conferences on the Institutionalization of Sex Differences, University of Kent, mimeo.

Denzin, N. (1970), *The Research Act* (Chicago: Aldine).

Dore, R. (1973), *British Factory – Japanese Factory* (London: Allen & Unwin).

Durkheim, E. (1952), *Suicide*, trans. J. Spaulding and G. Simpson (London: Routledge & Kegan Paul).

Durkheim, E. (1964), *Division of Labour in Society*, trans. G. Simpson (Glencoe Ill.: The Free Press; London: Collier Macmillan).

Durkheim, E. (1964), *The Rules of Sociological Method*, 8th edn (London: Collier Macmillan).

Duster, T., Matza, D., and Wellman, D. (1979), 'Field work and the protection of human subjects', *American Sociologist*, vol. 14, pp. 136–42.

Edmondson, E. (1979), 'Rhetoric and sociological explanation', DPhil thesis, Oxford University.

Eisenstein, Z. (ed.) (1979), *Capitalism, Patriarchy and the Case for Socialist Feminism* (London and New York: Monthly Review Press).

Emerson, J. P. (1970), 'Behaviour in private places: sustaining definitions of reality in gynaecological examinations', in Dreitzel, H. P. (ed.), *Recent Sociology*, Vol. 2.

Empson, W. (1949), *Seven Types of Ambiguity* (London: Chatto).

Fagerhaugh, S. Y., and Strauss, A. (1977), *The Politics of Pain Management* (Menlo Park, Ca: Addison-Wesley).

Farquharson, A. (1955), 'Dissolution of the Institute of Sociology', *Sociological Review*, n.s., vol. 3, pp. 165–73.

Feyerabend, P. (1975), *Against Method* (London: New Left Books).

Filmer, P., *et al.* (1972), *New Directions in Sociological Theory* (London: Collier Macmillan).

Fincham, J. (1975), 'The development of sociology first degree courses at English universities, 1907–1972', PhD thesis, City University, Department of Social Science and Humanities.

Finn, D., Grant, N., and Johnson, R. (1979), 'Social democracy, education and the crisis', stencilled occasional paper, Centre for Contemporary Cultural Studies, Birmingham.

Fine, B., *et al.* (eds) (1979), *Capitalism and the Rule of Law* (London: Hutchinson).

Firestone, S. (1971), *The Dialectics of Sex* (London: Cape).

Flatow, S. von, and Huisken, F. (1973), 'Zum Problem der Ableitung des bürgerlichen Staates', *Probleme des Klassenkampfs*, 7.

Fletcher, R. (1971), *The Making of Sociology* (London: Michael Joseph).

Folsom, J. K. (1948), *The Family in Democratic Society* (London: Routledge & Kegan Paul).

Ford, J. (1975), *Paradigms and Fairy Tales* (London: Routledge & Kegan Paul).

Foucault, M. (1970), *The Order of Things* (London: Tavistock).

Foucault, M. (1972), *The Archaeology of Knowledge* (London: Tavistock).

Foucault, M. (1973), *The Birth of the Clinic* (London: Tavistock).

Foucault, M. (1977), 'Intellectuals and power', in *Language, Counter-Memory, Practice* (Oxford: Blackwell).

Frank, A. (1969), *Latin America: Underdevelopment or Revolution* (New York: Monthly Review Press).

Frankenberg, R. (1957), *Village on the Border* (London: Cohen & West).

Frankenberg, R. (1974), 'Functionalism and after? Theory and developments in social science applied to the health field', *International Journal of Health Services*, vol. 4, p. 411.

Frankenberg, R. (1976), 'In the production of their lives, men? ... Sex and gender in British community studies', in Barker, D. L., and Allen, S. (eds) (1976), *Sexual Divisions and Society* (London: Tavistock).

Freidson, E. (1970), *Professional Dominance: The Social Structure of Medical Care* (New York: Atherton).

Freidson, E. (1978), 'The official construction of occupation: an essay on the practical epistemology of work', paper given at the Ninth World Congress of Sociology, Uppsala, Sweden (August); University of New York, mimeo.

Gallie, D. (1978), *In Search of the New Working Class* (Cambridge: Cambridge University Press).

Garfinkel, H. (1967), *Studies in Ethnomethodology* (Englewood Cliffs, NJ: Prentice-Hall).

Garmarnikov, E. (1978), 'Sexual division of labour: the case of nursing', in Kuhn, A., and Wolpe, A. M. (eds), *Feminism and Materialism: Women and Modes of Production* (London: Routledge & Kegan Paul).

Gavron, H. (1966), *The Captive Wife* (Harmondsworth: Penguin).

Gergen, K. J. (1973), 'Social psychology as history', *Journal of Personality and Social Psychology*, vol. 26, pp. 309–20.

Giddens, A. (1976), *New Rules of Sociological Method: A Positive Critique of Interpretative Sociologies* (London: Hutchinson).

Giddens, A. (1977), *Studies in Social and Political Theory* (London: Hutchinson).

Giddens, A. (1978–9), 'The prospects for social theory today', *Berkeley Journal of Sociology*, vol. 22, pp. 201–23.

Giddens, A. (1979), *Central Problems in Social Theory* (London: Macmillan).

Giedymin, J. (1975), 'Antipositivism in contemporary philosophy of social science and humanities', *British Journal for the Philosophy of Science*, vol. 26, pp. 275–301.

Gillespie, D. L. (1972), 'Who has power? The marital struggle', in Dreitzel, H. P. (ed.), *Family, Marriage and the Struggle of the Sexes* (New York: Macmillan).

Giner, S. (1972), *Sociology* (London: Martin Robertson).

Ginsberg, M. (1934), *Sociology* (London: Thornton Butterworth).

Ginsberg, M. (1956), *Essays in Sociology and Social Philosophy*, 2 vols (London: Heinemann).

Glasgow Media Group (1978), *Bad News* (London: Routledge & Kegan Paul).

Goffman, E. (1961), *Asylums* (New York: Anchor Books).

Goldthorpe, J. H. (1966), 'Attitudes and behaviour of car assembly workers: a deviant case and a theoretical critique', *British Journal of Sociology*, vol. 17, no. 3, pp. 227–44.

Goldthorpe, J. H. (1973), 'Review article: a revolution in sociology?', *Sociology*, vol. 7, no. 3, pp. 449–62.

Goldthorpe, J. H. (1980), *Social Mobility and Class Structure* (London: Oxford University Press).

Goldthorpe, J. H., and Hope, K. (1974), *The Social Grading of Occupations: A New Approach and Scale* (London: Oxford University Press).

Goldthorpe, J. H., Lockwood, D., Beckhofer, F., and Platt, J. (1968–9), *The Affluent Worker*, 3 vols (Cambridge: Cambridge University Press).

Goode, W. (1963), *World Revolution and Family Patterns* (New York: The Free Press).

Gould, S. J. (1977), *The Attack on Higher Education: Marxist and Radical Penetration* (London: Institute for the Study of Conflict).

Gouldner, A. (1971), *The Coming Crisis of Western Sociology* (London: Heinemann; 2nd edn, 1977).

Gouldner, A. (1975), *For Sociology* (Harmondsworth: Penguin).

Graham, H. (1979), 'Prevention and health: every mother's business: a comment on child health policies in the 70s', in Harris, C. (ed.), *The Family*, Sociological Review Monograph (Keele: University of Keele).

Gramsci, A. (1971), *Selections from the Prison Notebooks* (London: Lawrence & Wishart).

Green, M. (1971), *The Von Richtofen Sisters* (London: Weidenfeld & Nicolson).

Gusfield, J. (1976), 'The literary rhetoric of science', *American Sociological Review*, vol. 41, no. 1, pp. 16–34.

Habermas, J. (1973), *Legitimation Crisis* (London: Heinemann).

Halfpenny, P. (1979), 'Deep relativism and the teaching of ethnographic data analysis on postgraduate courses in sociology', paper given at SSRC/BSA Conference on Graduate Research Methodology Teaching.

Hall, J., and Jones, Caradog (1950), 'Social grading of occupations', *British Journal of Sociology*, vol. 1, no. 1, pp. 31–55.

Hall, S. (1980), 'Cultural studies: two paradigms', *Media, Culture and Society*, no. 2, pp. 57–72.

Halsey, A. H. (1959), review of *The Sociological Imagination*, *Universities and Left Review*, no. 7 (Autumn), pp. 71–2.

Halsey, A. H. (ed.) (1972), *Trends in British Society since 1900: A Guide to the Changing Social Structure of Britain* (London: Macmillan).

Halsey, A. H. (1979), 'Are the British universities capable of change?', *New Universities Quarterly*, vol. 33, no. 4 (Autumn), pp. 402–16.

Halsey, A. H., Heath, A. F., and Ridge, J. M. (1980), *Origins and Destinations* (Oxford: Oxford University Press).

Halsey, A. H., and Trow, M. A. (1971), *The British Academics* (London: Faber).

Hamilton, R. F. (1972), *Class and Politics in the United States* (New York: Wiley).

Harris, C. C. (1969), *The Family* (London: Allen & Unwin).

Harris, C. C. (1977), Changing conceptions of the relation between family and social form in Western society', in Scase, R. (ed.), *Industrial Society: Class, Cleavage and Control* (London: Allen & Unwin).

Harris, M. (1968), *The Rise of Anthropological Theory* (New York: Crowell).

Hawthorn, G. (1975), 'Why I resigned', *Network*, no. 1, p. 5.

Hawthorn, G. (1976), *Enlightenment and Despair* (Cambridge: Cambridge University Press).

Heidegger, M. (1971), *On the Way to Language* (New York: Harper & Row).

Heise, D. R. (1975), *Causal Analysis* (New York: Wiley).

Hindess, B. (1973), *The Use of Official Statistics in Sociology: A Critique of Positivism and Ethnomethodology* (London: Macmillan).

Hindess, B., and Hirst, P. (1975), *Pre-Capitalist Modes of Production* (London: Routledge & Kegan Paul).

Hirsch, J. (1978), 'The state apparatus and social reproduction: elements of a theory of the bourgeois state', in Holloway and Picciotto, op. cit., pp. 57–107.

Hirschi, T., and Selvin, H. C. (1966), 'False criteria of causality in delinquency research', *Social Problems*, vol. 13, no. 3, pp. 254–68.

Hirschi, T., and Selvin, H. C. (1967), *Delinquency Research: An Appraisal of Analytic Methods* (London: Collier Macmillan), pp. 114–41.

Hirst, P. (1979), *On Law and Ideology* (London: Macmillan).

Hobhouse, L. T. (1924), *Social Development: Its Nature and Conditions* (London: Allen & Unwin).

Hobhouse, L. T., Wheeler, G. C., and Ginsberg, M. (1915), *The Material Culture and Social Institutions of the Simpler Peoples: An Essay in Correlation* (London: Chapman & Hall).

Holloway, J., and Picciotto, S. (eds) (1978), *State and Capital* (London: Edward Arnold).

Hope, K. (ed.) (1972), *The Analysis of Social Mobility: Method and Approaches* (Oxford: Clarendon Press).

Hughes, E. C. (1958), *Men and Their Work* (New York: The Free Press).

Hughes, E. C. (1971), *The Sociological Eye: Selected Papers* (Chicago: Aldine; New York: Atherton).

Hughes, J. A. (1976), *Sociological Analysis* (London: Nelson).

Husbands, C. T. (1976), 'Ideological bias in the marking of examinations: a method of testing for its presence and its implications', *Research in Education*, no. 15, pp. 17–38.

Husbands, C. T. (1979), 'The "threat" hypothesis and racist voting in England and the United States', in Miles, R., and Phizacklea, A. (eds), *Racism and Political Action in Britain* (London: Routledge & Kegan Paul), pp. 147–83.

Illich, I. (1977), *Disabling Professions* (London: Marion Boyars).

Jacha, K., Cox, C., and Marks, J. (1975), *The Rape of Reason: The Corruption of the Polytechnic of North London* (London: Churchill).

Jessop, B. (1978), 'Corporatism, fascism and social democracy', ECPR Workshop on Corporatism in Liberal Democracies, Grenoble.

Jessop, B. (1980), 'The transformation of the state in post-war Britain', in Scase, R. (ed.), *The State in Western Europe* (London: Croom Helm).

Jewson, N. D. (1974), 'Medical knowledge and the patronage system in 18th century England, *Sociology*, vol. 8, no. 3, p. 869.

198   *Practice and Progress: British Sociology 1950–1980*

Jewson, N. D. (1976), 'The disappearance of the sick man from the medical cosmology', *Sociology*, vol. 10, no. 2, p. 225.

Johnson, T. (1972), *Professions and Power* (London: Macmillan).

Johnson, T. (1977), 'The professions in the class structure', in Scase, R. (ed.), *Industrial Society: Class, Cleavage and Control* (London: Allen & Unwin).

Johnson, M. L. (1977), 'Patients: receivers or participants', in Barnard, K., and Lee, K. (eds), *Conflicts in the NHS* (London: Croom Helm; New York: Prodist).

Kaplan, A. (1974), *The Conduct of Inquiry* (San Francisco: Chandler).

Keat, R. (1979), 'Positivism and social statistics in social science', in Irvine, J., Miles, I., and Evans, J. (eds), *Demystifying Social Statistics* (London: Pluto Press), pp. 75–86.

Keat, R. (1980), 'The critique of positivism', Transactions of the BSA Conference, 1980.

Klaw, S. (1970), 'The Faustian bargain', in Brown, Martin (ed.), *The Social Responsibility of the Scientist* (New York: The Free Press), pp. 3–15.

Klein, V. (1946), *The Feminine Character* (London: Routledge & Kegan Paul).

Korsch, K. (1970), *Marxism and Philosophy* (London: New Left Books).

Kuhn, A., and Wolpe, A. M. (eds) (1978), *Feminism and Materialism: Women and Modes of Production* (London: Routledge & Kegan Paul).

Kuhn, T. S. (1962), *The Structure of Scientific Revolutions* (Chicago: University of Chicago Press; 2nd edn, 1970).

Lacey, C. (1970), *Hightown Grammar* (Manchester: Manchester University Press).

Laclau, E. (1979), *Politics and Ideology in Marxist Theory* (London: Verso).

Laing, R. D., and Esterson, A. (1964), *Sanity, Madness and the Family: Families of Schizophrenics* (London: Tavistock).

Lakatos, I. (1970), 'Falsification and the methodology of scientific research programmes', in Lakatos and Musgrave, op. cit., pp. 91–196.

Lakatos, I., and Musgrave, A. (eds) (1970), *Criticism and the Growth of Knowledge* (Cambridge: Cambridge University Press).

Lecourt, D. (1975), *Marxism and Epistemology* (London: New Left Books).

Lindquist, R. (1931), *The Family in the Present Social Order* (Chapel Hill, NC: University of North Carolina), ch. 3.

Littlejohn, G., Smart, B., Wakeford, J., and Yuval-Davis, N. (1978), *Power and the State* (London: Croom Helm).

Lockwood, D. (1958), *The Blackcoated Worker* (London: Allen & Unwin).

Lowie, R. (1950), *Social Organization* (London: Routledge & Kegan Paul).

Luxemburg, R. (1970), 'Die "deutsche Wissenschaft" hinter den Arbeitern' (1899/1900), in *Gesammelte Werke*, Vol. 1 (Berlin: Dietz), pp. 767–90.

Madge, J. H. (1953), *The Tools of Social Science* (London: Longman).

McIntosh, M. (1979), 'Women, citizenship and the state', Sociologish Institut Katholicka Universiteit Nÿmegen, Congress on the Intervention State and Inequality; University of Essex, mimeo.

MacIver, R. (1937), *Society: A Textbook of Sociology* (New York: Farrar & Rinehart).

MacIver, R. M., and Page, C. H. (1950), *Society: An Introductory Analysis* (London: Macmillan).

McKinlay, J. B. (1975), 'Clients and organizations', in McKinlay, J. B. (ed.), *Processing People: Cases in Organizational Behaviour* (London and New York: Holt, Rinehart & Winston).

McNamara, J. A., and Wemple, S. (1974), 'The power of women through the family in medieval Europe: 500–1100', in Hartman, M., and Banner, L. W. (eds), *Clio's Consciousness Raised* (New York: Harper, Torchback).

Mann, P. H. (1968), *Methods of Sociological Enquiry* (Oxford: Blackwell).

Marcuse, H. (1964), *One Dimensional Man: Studies in the Ideology of Advanced Industrial Society* (London: Routledge & Kegan Paul).

Marsh, C. (1979a), 'Problems with surveys: method or epistemology?', *Sociology*, vol. 13, no. 2, pp. 292–305.

Marsh, C. (1979b), 'Opinion polls – social science or political manoeuvre?', in Irvine, J., Miles, I., and Evans, J. (eds), *Demystifying Social Statistics* (London: Pluto Press), pp. 268–88.

Marshall, T. H. (1950), *Citizenship and Social Class* (Cambridge: Cambridge University Press).

Marshall, T. H. (1953), 'Impressions of the conference', *British Journal of Sociology*, vol. 4, pp. 201–9.

Marshall, T. H. (1963), *Sociology at the Cross Roads* (London: Heinemann).

Marx, K. (1954–9), *Capital*, ed. F. Engels (Moscow: Foreign Languages Publishing House).

Masterman, M. (1970), 'The nature of a paradigm', in Lakatos and Musgrave, op. cit., pp. 59–90.

Mathieu, N. C. (1977), *Ignored by Some, Derided by Others, the Social Sex Category in Sociology* (London: Women's Research and Resources Centre).

Mead, M. (1935), *Sex and Temperament in Three Primitive Societies* (New York: Wm Morrow).

Mead, M. (1950), *Male and Female: A Study of the Sexes in a Changing World* (London: Gollancz).

Mennell, S. (1974), *Sociological Theory* (London: Nelson).

Menzies, K. (1979), 'Implications of the gap between theory and research', paper given at Canadian Sociological Association Annual Meeting, 1979.

Merton, R. K. (1967), 'On the history and systematics of sociological theory', in *On Theoretical Sociology* (New York: The Free Press).

Miliband, R. (1970), 'The capitalist state: a reply to Nicos Poulantzas', *New Left Review*, no. 59, pp. 53–60.

Miliband, R. (173), 'Poulantzas and the capitalist state', *New Left Review*, no. 82, pp. 83–92.

Mills, C. Wright (1959), *The Sociological Imagination* (New York: Oxford University Press).

Mitchell, J. (1971), *Women's Estate* (Harmondsworth: Penguin).

Mogey, J. F. (1956), *Family and Neighbourhood* (London: Oxford University Press).

Moore, B. (1967), *Social Origins of Dictatorship and Democracy* (London: Allen Lane).

Morgan, D. H. J. (1975), *Social Theory and the Family* (London: Routledge & Kegan Paul).

Moser, C. A., and Kalton, G. (1971), *Survey Methods in Social Investigation*, 2nd edn (London: Heinemann).

Mouzelis, N. (1978), *Modern Greece* (London: Macmillan).

Müller, N., and Neussüss, C. (1970), 'The illusions of state socialism and the contradictions between wage-labour and capital', *Telos*, vol. 25, pp. 13–90.

Nelson, C. (1973), 'Women and power in nomadic societies of the Middle East', in Nelson, C. (ed.), *The Desert and the Sown: Nomads in the Wilder Society*, Research Series No. 21 (Berkeley: University of California, Institute of International Studies).

Nelson, C. (1974), 'Private and public politics: women in the Middle Eastern world', *American Ethnologist*, vol. 1, no. 3, pp. 551–65.

Nettl, J. P. (1966), *Rosa Luxemburg*, Vol. 1 (London: Oxford University Press).

Newby, H. (1977), *The Deferential Worker* (Harmondsworth: Penguin).

Nichols, T. (1979), 'Social class: official, sociological and Marxist', in Irvine, J., Miles, I., and Evans, J. (eds), *Demystifying Social Statistics* (London: Pluto Press), pp. 152–71.

Nichols, T., and Beynon, H. (1977), *Living with Capitalism* (London: Routledge & Kegan Paul).

Nielson, H. J. (1979), 'The parochial voter: alienation and level of government in Denmark, 1978', working paper, Institute of Political Studies, University of Copenhagen.

Oakley, A. (1974a), *Housewife* (London: Allen Lane).

Oakley, A. (1974b), *The Sociology of Housework* (London: Martin Robertson).

O'Connor, J. (1973), *The Fiscal Crisis of the State* (New York: St Martin's Press).

Offe, C. (1972), 'Political authority and class structures: an analysis of late capitalist societies', *International Journal of Sociology*, vol. 2, pp. 73–108.

Offe, C. (1975), 'Further comments on Müller and Neusüss', *Telos*, vol. 25, pp. 99–111.

Oxaal, I. (ed.) (1975), *Beyond the Sociology of Development* (London: Routledge & Kegan Paul).

Panitch, L. (1978), 'Recent theorization of corporatism: reflections on a growth industry', paper given at the Ninth World Congress of Sociology, Uppsala, Sweden (August).

Parkes, C. M. (1972), *Bereavement: Studies of Grief in Adult Life* (London: Tavistock).

Parkin, F. (1979a), *Marxism and Class Theory: A Bourgeois Critique* (London: Tavistock).

Parkin, F. (1979b), 'Social stratification', in Bottomore and Nisbet, op. cit., pp. 599–632.

Parsons, T. (1967), *Sociological Theory and Modern Society* (New York: The Free Press).

Pashukanis, E. (1978), *Law and Marxism: A General Theory* (London: Ink Links).

Pashukanis, E. (1980), 'The general theory of law and Marxism', in Berine, P., and Sharlet, R. (eds), *Pashukanis: Selected Writings on Law and Marxism* (London: Academic Press).

Payne, S. L. (1951), *The Art of Asking Questions* (Princeton, NJ: Princeton University Press).

Peel, J. (1968), 'Details of courses mainly concerned with sociological theories and methods in 29 British universities', compiled for conference of BSA Sociology Teachers' Section.

Perrucci, R. (1980), 'Sociology and the introductory textbook', *The American Sociologist*, vol. 15, no. 1, pp. 39–49.

Phillips, D. L. (1973), *Abandoning Method* (San Francisco: Jossey-Bass).

Platt, J. (1976), *Realities of Social Research* (London: Chatto & Windus for Sussex University Press).

Popper, K. (1959), *The Logic of Scientific Discovery* (London: Hutchinson; 2nd edn, 1968).

Popper, K. (1970), 'Normal science and its dangers', in Lakatos and Musgrave, op. cit., pp. 51-8.

Poulantzas, N. (1969), 'The problem of the capitalist state', *New Left Review*, no. 58, pp. 67-78.

Poulantzas, N. (1973), 'On social classes', *New Left Review* no. 78, pp. 27-54.

Poulantzas, N. (1975), *Classes in Contemporary Capitalism* (London: New Left Books).

Poulantzas, N. (1976), 'The capitalist state: a reply to Miliband and Laclau', *New Left Review*, no. 95, pp. 68-83.

Power, E. (1919), *Medieval Women*, ed. M. M. Postan (Cambridge: Cambridge University Press, 1975).

Reinhold, R. (1980), 'Guidelines on studies of humans stir protest: revised rules will be issued this summer', *New York Times*, 22 April, pp. C1 and C6.

Reiter, R. R. (ed.) (1975), *Toward an Anthropology of Women* (New York and London: Monthly Review Press).

Rex, J. (1961), *Key Problems in Sociological Theory* (London: Routledge & Kegan Paul).

Rex, J., and Moore, R. (1967), *Race, Community and Conflict* (London: Oxford University Press).

Reynolds, L., and Reynolds, J. (eds) (1970), *The Sociology of Sociology* (New York: McKay).

Rice, A. K. (1963), *The Enterprise and its Environment* (London: Tavistock).

Ricoeur, P. (1978), *On Metaphor* (London: Routledge & Kegan Paul).

Roche, M. (1973), *Phenomenology, Language and the Social Sciences* (London: Routledge & Kegan Paul).

Rowbotham, S. (1973), *Woman's Consciousness, Man's World* (Harmondsworth: Penguin).

Rowbotham, S. (1979), 'The women's movement and organising for socialism', in Rowbotham, S., Segal, L., and Wainwright, H., *Beyond the Fragments: Feminism and the Making of Socialism* (London: Merlin).

Runciman, W. G. (1966), *Relative Deprivation and Social Justice* (London: Routledge & Kegan Paul).

Sandywell, B., *et al.* (1976), *Problems of Reflexivity and Dialectics in Sociological Inquiry* (London: Routledge & Kegan Paul).

Schmitter, P. (1974), 'Still the century of corporatism?', *Review of Politics*, vol. 36, pp. 85-131.

Schuman, H., and Presser, S. (1977), 'Question wording as an independent variable in survey analysis', *Sociological Methods and Research*, vol. 6, no. 2, pp. 151-70.

Schuman, H., and Presser, S. (1980), 'Public opinion and public ignorance: the fine line between attitudes and nonattitudes', *American Journal of Sociology*, vol. 85, no. 5, pp. 1214-25.

Scott, J. P. (1976), 'Sociological theory in Britain: a critical comment on D. Morgan's "British social theory" ', *Sociology*, vol. 10, no. 1, pp. 117-20.

Screen (London: Society for Education in Film and Television).

Sharp, R., and Green, H. (1975), *Education and Social Control* (London: Routledge & Kegan Paul).

Shaw, M. (1972), 'The coming crisis of radical sociology', in Blackburn, R. B. (ed.), *Ideology in Social Science* (London: Fontana).

Shaw, M. (1974), *Marxism versus Sociology* (London: Pluto Press).

Skinner, Q. (1969), 'Meaning and understanding in the history of ideas', *History and Theory*, vol. 8, pp. 3–53.

Skinner, Q. (1974), 'Some problems in the analysis of political thought and action', *Political Theory*, vol. 2, no. 3, pp. 277–302.

Sklair, L. (1977), 'Ideology and the sociological utopias', *Sociological Review*, vol. 25, no. 1, pp. 51–72.

Slater, P. (1977), *Origin and Significance of the Frankfurt School* (London: Routledge & Kegan Paul).

Social Science Research Council (1979), *Completion Rates in Sociology and Social Administration* (London: SSRC).

Social Science Research Council (1979), *SSRC Annual Report 1978–9* (London: HMSO).

Social Sciences Citation Index (1969–79) (Philadelphia, Pa: Institute for Scientific Information).

Smith, C. (1975), 'The employment of sociologists in research occupations in Britain since 1973', *Sociology*, vol. 9, no. 2, pp. 309–16.

Smith, D. (1974), 'Woman, the family and corporate capitalism', in Stephensen, M. L. (ed.), *Women in Canada* (Toronto: New Press).

Smith, D. (1974), 'Women's perspective as a radical critique of sociology', *Sociological Inquiry*, vol. 44, no. 1, pp. 7–13.

Smith, D. (1979), 'A sociology for women', in Sherman, J. and Beck, E. (eds), *The Prism of Sex. Essays in the Sociology of Knowledge* (Madison, Wis.: University of Wisconsin Press).

Spring Rice, M. (1939), *Working Class Wives: Their Health and Conditions* (Harmondsworth: Penguin).

Sprott, W. J. H. (1949), *Sociology* (London: Hutchinson).

Sprott, W. J. H. (1954), *Science and Social Action* (London: Watts).

Stacey, M. (1960), *Tradition and Change: A Study of Banbury* (London: Oxford University Press).

Stacey, M. (1968), 'Professional ethics', *Sociology*, vol. 2, p. 353.

Stacey, M. (1969), *Methods of Social Research* (Oxford: Pergamon).

Stacey, M. (1976), 'The health service consumer: a sociological misconception', in Stacey, M. (ed.), *The Sociology of the NHS*, Sociological Review Monograph No. 22 (Keele: University of Keele).

Stacey, M., and Price, M. (1970), 'Women and power', *Feminist Review*, no. 5, pp. 33–52.

Stacey, M., and Price, M. (forthcoming), *Women, Politics and Power* (London: Tavistock).

Stevenson, G. (1976), 'Social relations of production and consumption in the human service occupations', *Monthly Review*, vol. 28, no. 3, pp. 78–87.

Stockman, N. (1977), 'What *is* positivism, anyway?', duplicated, Department of Sociology, University of Aberdeen.

Symposium on 'Aspects of Sociology' (1970), *Encounter*, vol. 34, no. 3 (March), pp. 57–95.

Tapper, N. (1980), 'A professional association?', *Royal Anthropological Institute News*, no. 36, pp. 6–7.

Therborn, G. (1976), *Science, Class and Society* (London: New Left Books).

Thomas, K. (1971), *Religion and the Decline of Magic* (London: Weidenfeld & Nicholson).

Thompson, E. P. (1978), *The Poverty of Theory* (London: Merlin Press).

Thompson, E. P. (1980), *Writing by Candlelight* (London: Merlin Press).

Thompson, K., and Tunstall, J. (1971), *Sociological Perspectives* (Harmondsworth: Penguin).

Times, The (1980), 'Plans to re-examine specification for social sciences PhD', 16 May, p. 3.

Townsend, P. (1979), *Poverty in the United Kingdom* (Harmondsworth: Penguin).

Tribe, K. (1978), *Land, Labour and Economic Discourse* (London: Routledge & Kegan Paul).

Trist, E. C. (1963), *Organizational Choice* (London: Tavistock).

Tropp, A. (1956), 'The present state and development of professional sociology', *British Sociological Association Bulletin*, no. 1, pp. 1–7.

Turner, B. (1974), *Weber and Islam: A Critical Study* (London: Routledge & Kegan Paul).

Turner, B. (1977), 'The structuralist critique of Weber's sociology', *British Journal of Sociology*, vol. 28, pp. 1–16.

Urry, J. (1973), 'Thomas S. Kuhn as sociologist of knowledge', *British Journal of Sociology*, vol. 24, pp. 462–73.

Urry, J. (1980a), *The Anatomy of Capitalist Societies: The Economy, Civil Society and the State* (London: Macmillan).

Urry, J. (1980b), 'Sociology: a brief survey of recent developments', in Dufour, B. (ed.), *New Perspectives in the Humanities and Social Sciences* (London: Temple Smith).

Von Wright, G. H. (1971), *Explanation and Understanding* (London: Routledge & Kegan Paul).

Wakeford, J. (comp. and ed.) (1979), 'Research methods syllabuses in sociology departments in the UK', British Sociological Association Conference on Methodology (January).

Webb, E. J., Campbell, D. T., Schwartz, R. D., and Sechrest, L. (1966), *Unobtrusive Measures: Nonreactive Research in the Social Sciences* (Chicago: Rand McNally).

Weber, Marianne (1976), *Max Weber: A Biography*, trans. H. Zohn (New York: Wiley).

Weber, M. (1930), *The Protestant Ethic and the Spirit of Capitalism*, trans. T. Parsons (London: Allen & Unwin).

Weber, M. (1958), *The Religion of India* (New York: The Free Press; London: Collier Macmillan).

Weber, M. (1968), *Economy and Society*, ed. G. Roth and C. Wittich (New York: Bedminster).

Weigert, A. J. (1970), 'The immoral rhetoric of scientific sociology', *The American Sociologist*, vol. 5, no. 2, pp. 111–19.

Westergaard, J., and Resler, H. (1976), *Class in a Capitalist Society: A Study of Contemporary Britain* (Harmondsworth: Penguin).

Wicker, A. W. (1969), 'Attitudes vs. actions', *Journal of Social Issues*, vol. 25, no. 4, pp. 41–78.

Widgery, D. (1976), *The Left In Britain* (Harmondsworth: Penguin).

Willer, D. (1967), *Scientific Sociology: Theory and Method* (Englewood Cliffs, NJ: Prentice-Hall).

Willer, D., and Willer, J. (1973), *Systematic Empiricism: Critique of a Pseudoscience* (Englewood Cliffs, NJ: Prentice-Hall), pp. 96–105.

Willis, P. (1977), *Learning to Labour* (Farnborough: Saxon House).

Wilson, E. (1980), *Only Halfway to Paradise: Women in Postwar Britain 1945–1968* (London: Tavistock).

Wilson, M. (1929), 'Use of time by Oregon farm home-makers', Oregon Agricultural Experiment Station, Bulletin 256.

Winch, P. (1958), *The Idea of a Social Science* (London: Routledge & Kegan Paul).

Winckler, J. (1977), 'The corporatist strategy: theory and administration', in Scase, R. (ed.), *Industrial Society: Class, Cleavage and Control* (London: Allen & Unwin), pp. 43–58.

Wirth, M. (1977), 'Towards a critique of the theory of state monopoly capitalism', *Economy and Society*, vol. 6, pp. 284–313.

Woodward, J. (1965), *Industrial Organization: Theory and Practice* (London: Oxford University Press).

Wootton, A. (1978), *Dilemmas of Discourse* (London: Allen & Unwin).

Wootton, B. (1950), *Testament for Social Science* (London: Allen & Unwin).

Working Papers in Cultural Studies, No. 9 (1976), University of Birmingham, Centre for Contemporary Cultural Studies (Spring).

Worsley, P. (1974), 'The state of theory and the status of theory', *Sociology*, vol. 8, no. 1, pp. 1–17.

Wright, E. O. (1976), 'Class boundaries in advanced capitalist societies', *New Left Review*, no. 98, pp. 3–41.

Wright, E. O., and Perrone, L. (1977), 'Marxist class categories and income inequality', *American Sociological Review*, vol. 42, no. 1, pp. 32–55.

Young, M. F. D. (ed.) (1971), *Knowledge and Control* (London: Collier Macmillan).

Index

For Product Safety Concerns and Information please contact our EU
representative GPSR@taylorandfrancis.com
Taylor & Francis Verlag GmbH, Kaufingerstraße 24, 80331 München, Germany

www.ingramcontent.com/pod-product-compliance
Lightning Source LLC
Chambersburg PA
CBHW070732270326
41926CB00070B/2841